Chicago
FOR
DUMMIES®
1ST EDITION

by Laura Johnston

Hungry Minds™

Best-Selling Books • Digital Downloads • e-Books • Answer Networks
e-Newsletters • Branded Web Sites • e-Learning

New York, NY ◆ Cleveland, OH ◆ Indianapolis, IN

Chicago For Dummies, 1st Edition

Published by
Hungry Minds, Inc.
909 Third Avenue
New York, NY 10022
www.hungryminds.com
www.dummies.com

Library of Congress Control Number: 2001091995

ISBN: 0-7645-5387-9

ISSN: 1534-9160

Printed in the United States of America

10 9 8 7 6 5 4 3 2 1

1B/QT/QY/QR/IN

Distributed in the United States by Hungry Minds, Inc.

Distributed by CDG Books Canada Inc. for Canada; by Transworld Publishers Limited in the United Kingdom; by IDG Norge Books for Norway; by IDG Sweden Books for Sweden; by IDG Books Australia Publishing Corporation Pty. Ltd. for Australia and New Zealand; by TransQuest Publishers Pte Ltd. for Singapore, Malaysia, Thailand, Indonesia, and Hong Kong; by Gotop Information Inc. for Taiwan; by ICG Muse, Inc. for Japan; by Intersoft for South Africa; by Eyrolles for France; by International Thomson Publishing for Germany, Austria and Switzerland; by Distribuidora Cuspide for Argentina; by LR International for Brazil; by Galileo Libros for Chile; by Ediciones ZETA S.C.R. Ltda. for Peru; by WS Computer Publishing Corporation, Inc., for the Philippines; by Contemporanea de Ediciones for Venezuela; by Express Computer Distributors for the Caribbean and West Indies; by Micronesia Media Distributor, Inc. for Micronesia; by Chips Computadoras S.A. de C.V. for Mexico; by Editorial Norma de Panama S.A. for Panama; by American Bookshops for Finland.

For general information on Hungry Minds' products and services please contact our Customer Care department; within the U.S. at 800-762-2974, outside the U.S. at 317-572-3993 or fax 317-572-4002.

For sales inquiries and resellers information, including discounts, premium and bulk quantity sales and foreign language translations please contact our Customer Care department at 800-434-3422, fax 317-572-4002 or write to Hungry Minds, Inc., Attn: Customer Care department, 10475 Crosspoint Boulevard, Indianapolis, IN 46256.

For information on licensing foreign or domestic rights, please contact our Sub-Rights Customer Care department at 212-884-5000.

For information on using Hungry Minds' products and services in the classroom or for ordering examination copies, please contact our Educational Sales department at 800-434-2086 or fax 317-572-4005.

For press review copies, author interviews, or other publicity information, please contact our Public Relations department at 317-572-3168 or fax 317-572-4168.

For authorization to photocopy items for corporate, personal, or educational use, please contact Copyright Clearance Center, 222 Rosewood Drive, Danvers, MA 01923, or fax 978-750-4470.

Hungry Minds is a trademark of Hungry Minds, Inc.

About the Author

Laura Johnston, a native Midwesterner, moved to Chicago six years ago from New York City. As a freelance writer, she traveled to places as far-flung as the Middle Eastern country of Oman and wrote about extreme adventures, such as long-distance dog sled racing in Yukon Territory, Canada, and Alaska. She has contributed to seven *For Dummies* books, including *Blues For Dummies*, with Chicago blues legend Lonnie Brooks and Wayne Baker Brooks. Laura is a managing partner of Identity 3.0, LLC, a branding firm specializing in company identification, and lives in downtown Chicago.

Dedication

This book is dedicated to my parents, Keith and Barbara Johnston.

Author's Acknowledgments

I would like to acknowledge the inspiration for this book. My grandparents, Ray and Monie Johnston, met in the late 1920s on the commuter train between Chicago and Aurora and spent more than 60 years together. Their stories about Chicago make me feel connected to the city today.

Thanks to writer Mike Michaelson, who provided the framework for this book. Thanks to Hungry Minds and its dedicated and talented staff: Lisa Torrance, for her sure-handed guidance; Matthew X. Kiernan, Linda Brandon, and Esmeralda St. Clair, for their insightful editing; and Kevin Thornton, for taking a chance on me. Thanks to John Kilcullen, for the one great idea that launched 1,000-plus books.

My thanks also go to: Sarah Quail, whose friendship connected me to this project; my business partners and friends, Nina Duseja and Susan Kirchner, for generously allowing me time to write; Brad and Chady Johnston, whose company kept me sane after long days of writing; and Andy Tiebert, for making life in Chicago a brilliant adventure.

Publisher's Acknowledgments

We're proud of this book; please send us your comments through our Hungry Minds Online Registration Form located at www.dummies.com.

Some of the people who helped bring this book to market include the following:

Editorial

Editors: Linda Brandon, Matthew X. Kiernan

Copy Editor: Esmeralda St. Clair

Cartographer: Roberta Stockwell

Editorial Manager: Christine Beck

Editorial Assistant: Jennifer Young

Senior Photo Editor: Richard Fox

Assistant Photo Editor: Michael Ross

Cover Photos: Front and Back Cover Photos: © Kelly/Mooney Photography

Production

Project Coordinator: Regina Snyder

Layout and Graphics: Amy Adrian, Brian Drumm, Joyce Haughey, Jill Piscitelli, Julie Trippetti

Proofreaders: Susan Moritz, Marianne Santy, Charles Spencer, TECHBOOKS Production Services

Indexer: TECHBOOKS Production Services

Special Help
Lisa Torrance

General and Administrative

Hungry Minds, Inc.: John Kilcullen, CEO; Bill Barry, President and COO; John Ball, Executive VP, Operations & Administration; John Harris, CFO

Hungry Minds Consumer Reference Group

Business: Kathleen Nebenhaus, Vice President and Publisher; Kevin Thornton, Acquisitions Manager

Cooking/Gardening: Jennifer Feldman, Associate Vice President and Publisher; Anne Ficklen, Executive Editor; Kristi Hart, Managing Editor

Education/Reference: Diane Graves Steele, Vice President and Publisher

Lifestyles: Kathleen Nebenhaus, Vice President and Publisher; Tracy Boggier, Managing Editor

Pets: Dominique De Vito, Associate Vice President and Publisher; Tracy Boggier, Managing Editor

Travel: Michael Spring, Vice President and Publisher; Brice Gosnell, Publishing Director; Suzanne Jannetta, Editorial Director

Hungry Minds Consumer Editorial Services: Kathleen Nebenhaus, Vice President and Publisher; Kristin A. Cocks, Editorial Director; Cindy Kitchel, Editorial Director

Hungry Minds Consumer Production: Debbie Stailey, Production Director

◆

The publisher would like to give special thanks to Patrick J. McGovern, without whom this book would not have been possible.

◆

Contents at a Glance

Introduction..1

Part I: Getting Started 7

Chapter 1: Discovering the Best of Chicago 9
Chapter 2: Deciding When to Go 15
Chapter 3: Planning Your Budget 25
Chapter 4: Planning for Special Travel Needs 35

Part II: Ironing Out the Details 45

Chapter 5: Getting to Chicago 47
Chapter 6: Deciding Where to Stay 57
Chapter 7: Off the Rack: Booking Your Room 65
Chapter 8: Chicago's Best Hotels 69
Chapter 9: Tying Up the Loose Ends 93

Part III: Settling into Chicago 103

Chapter 10: Orienting Yourself in Chicago 105
Chapter 11: Getting Around Chicago 115
Chapter 12: Money Matters 119

Part IV: Dining in Chicago 121

Chapter 13: The Lowdown on the Chicago Dining Scene 123
Chapter 14: Chicago's Best Restaurants 131
Chapter 15: On the Lighter Side: Top Picks for Snacks
and Meals on the Go 157

Part V: Exploring Chicago 161

Chapter 16: Chicago's Best Sights 163
Chapter 17: More Cool Things to See and Do 179
Chapter 18: And on Your Left, Lake Michigan:
Seeing Chicago by Guided Tour 193
Chapter 19: A Shopper's Guide to Chicago 199
Chapter 20: Four Great Chicago Itineraries 213
Chapter 21: Exploring Beyond Chicago: Five Great Trips 221

Part VI: Living It Up After the Sun Goes Down:
Chicago Nightlife 231

Chapter 22: The Play's the Thing: The Chicago Theater Scene 233
Chapter 23: The Performing Arts 241
Chapter 24: Hitting the Clubs and Bars 247

Part VII: The Part of Tens 261
Chapter 25: Top Ten Chicago Experiences 263
Chapter 26: Top Ten Things to Do in Bad Weather 267
Chapter 27: Top Ten Things to Do with Kids 271

Appendix: Quick Concierge 275

Worksheets 283

Index 291

Book Registration Information ....Back of Book

Cartoons at a Glance

By Rich Tennant

"I think we should arrange to be there for 'Hot Dog-Italian Beef-Pizza-Week,' and then shoot over to the 'Antacid Festival.'"

page 7

"That's the third time tonight that's happened. They start out playing the blues, but by the end, everyone's playing a polka. I blame the new bass player from Milwaukee."

page 231

"Welcome to our nonstop flight to Chicago. Will you be sitting in first class or a bit nearer the stockyards?"

page 45

I enjoyed yelling out improvisational situations at Second City last night too. But this is the Chicago Ballet...

page 261

"The closest hotel room I could get you to the Magnificent Mile for that amount of money is in Cleveland."

page 103

"I'd give you a hot dog with everything, but I'm out of Fruit Loops."

page 121

"We do offer an authentic William 'The Refrigerator' Perry football jersey for sale, we just don't have a wall large enough to display it on."

page 161

Cartoon Information:
Fax: 978-546-7747
E-Mail: richtennant@the5thwave.com
World Wide Web: www.the5thwave.com

Maps at a Glance

Central Chicago Accommodations 72
Near North and River North Accommodations 77
Dining in the Loop and Near North 134
Dining in Lincoln Park and Wrigleyville.....................................138
Dining and Nightlife in Bucktown/Wicker Park..........................145
Central Chicago Attractions 166
Magnificent Mile Shopping 201
State Street/Loop Shopping...208
Oak Park Attractions 222
Hyde Park Attractions...228
Loop After Dark..249
Lincoln Park and Wrigleyville After Dark..................................252

Table of Contents

Introduction *1*
    About This Book 1
    Conventions Used in This Book 2
    Foolish Assumptions 3
    How This Book Is Organized 3
        Part I: Getting Started 3
        Part II: Ironing Out the Details 4
        Part III: Settling into Chicago 4
        Part IV: Dining in Chicago 4
        Part V: Exploring Chicago 4
        Part VI: Living It Up After the Sun Goes Down:
          Chicago Nightlife 4
        Part VII: The Part of Tens 5
    Icons Used in This Book 5
    Where to Go from Here 6

Part 1: Getting Started *7*
    Chapter 1: Discovering the Best of Chicago **9**
    Celebrating a Renaissance 9
    Finding the Very Best to See and Do in Chicago 11
        Cheering on the Cubbies 11
        Getting the blues — a good thing 11
        Discovering the Third Coast 12
        Soaking up some culture 12
        Seeing "Sue" and other museum stars 12
        Admiring the architecture 13
    Eating Your Way Through Town 13
    Can We Talk? 14

    Chapter 2: Deciding When to Go **15**
    The Secret of the Seasons 15
        Springtime in Chicago 16
        Summer heats up the scene 16
        Falling for fall 17
        Winter in the Midwest 17
        Being temperature wise 18
    Hot Dates: Chicago Calendar of Events 19
        January 19
        February 20
        March 20
        April 20
        May 20
        June 21
        July 22

August 22
September 23
October 23
November 23
December 24

Chapter 3: Planning Your Budget 25

Estimating the Cost of Your Trip 25
Lodging 26
Transportation 26
Restaurants 27
Attractions 27
Shopping 27
Entertainment 28
Keeping a Lid on Hidden Expenses 29
Taxes and fees 29
Gratuities 29
Incidentals 29
Handling Money 30
Choosing traveler's checks or the green stuff 30
Using plastic 31
Budgeting Tips to Offset Money Madness 31

Chapter 4: Planning for Special Travel Needs 35

We Are Family: Traveling with Your Kids 35
Choosing kid-friendly sleeps and eats 36
Getting kids involved in trip planning 37
Hiring a baby sitter 37
Flying with kids and staying sane 38
Surviving the great American road trip with kids ... 39
Traveling Tips for Seniors 40
Advice for Travelers with Disabilities 41
Out and About: Tips for Gay and Lesbian Travelers ... 42

Part II: Ironing Out the Details 45

Chapter 5: Getting to Chicago 47

Using a Travel Agent: Your Friend or Foe? 48
Joining an Escorted Tour or Traveling on Your Own ... 49
Tallying the Pros and Cons of Package Tours 50
Winning the Airfare Wars 51
Surfing the Web to fly the skies 52
Deciding which airport to fly into 52
Booking well to make your flight more pleasant 53
Getting Here by Car 54
Getting Here by Train 55

Chapter 6: Deciding Where to Stay 57

Discovering the Value of Your Dollar 58
Location, Location, Location! 58
Magnificent Mile 59
Gold Coast 60

The Loop 60
Streeterville 61
Finding the Type of Place That Suits Your Style 62
Bed and breakfasts 62
Hotels for families with kids 63
Hotels for travelers with disabilities 63

Chapter 7: Off the Rack: Booking Your Room **65**
Wrestling Rack Rates 65
Beating hotels at their own game 66
It all adds up: Taxes and other charges 67
Booking a Room at the Last Minute 68

Chapter 8: Chicago's Best Hotels **69**
Chicago Hotels A to Z 70
Runner-up Accommodations 88
Hotel Index by Neighborhood 90
Hotel Index by Price 91

Chapter 9: Tying Up the Loose Ends **93**
Deciding About Travel Insurance 93
Getting Sick Away from Home 94
Renting a Car: Pros and Cons 95
Getting the best rate 96
Snaring a deal on the Web 96
Identifying additional charges 96
Sitting Pretty: Getting Tickets 97
Staying Informed: The Latest News 98
The Right Stuff: Packing Wisely 100
Sun, rain, wind: Packing for a Chicago day 100
Choosing your suitcase 101

Part III: Settling into Chicago *103*

Chapter 10: Orienting Yourself in Chicago **105**
Arriving in Chicago 105
By plane to O'Hare Airport 106
By plane to Midway Airport 108
By Train 109
Understanding the Lay of the Land 109
Chicago by Neighborhood 110
Street Smarts: Where to Get Information After You Arrive 112

Chapter 11: Getting Around Chicago **115**
Riding the Rails and the Roads 115
Bussing it 115
Riding high and going underground 116
Backseat Riding: Taking a Cab 118
Hoofing It 118

Chapter 12: Money Matters **119**
Dollars and Cents: Where to Get Cash 119
What to Do If Your Money Gets Stolen 119

Part IV: Dining in Chicago 121

Chapter 13: The Lowdown on the Chicago Dining Scene 123

Scoping the Major Dining Destinations 124
Sampling Chicago's Local Favorites 124
Around the World, Restaurant-Style 125
Italian, Chicago-style 125
It's all Greek to me 126
Best of the wurst 126
Dim sum and then some 127
Samplings from around the world 127
Dressing Up and Dressing Down 128
Reserving a Table 129

Chapter 14: Chicago's Best Restaurants 131

My Favorite Chicago Restaurants 132
Index of Restaurants by Neighborhood 152
Index of Restaurants by Cuisine 153
Index of Restaurants by Price 154

Chapter 15: On the Lighter Side: Top Picks for Snacks and Meals on the Go 157

Snacking with the Pros 157
Carnivore favorites 157
Refreshing Italian ice 158
World-famous Chicago hot dogs 158
Sandwiches on the go 158
Grabbing a Burger 159
Breaking for Coffee 159

Part V: Exploring Chicago 161

Chapter 16: Chicago's Best Sights 163

The Top Sights 164
Index of Top Attractions by Neighborhood 177
Index of Top Attractions by Type 177

Chapter 17: More Cool Things to See and Do 179

Especially for Architecture Lovers 179
Fourth Presbyterian Church 179
Marquette Building 180
Water Tower 180
Wicker Park 180
Especially for Movie Lovers 181
Chicago Cultural Center 181
Oriental Institute Museum 181
Second-run movie theaters 182
Especially for Romantics 182
Dining at the Chicago Historical Society 182
Jazz at the Art Institute of Chicago 182

Especially for Fishermen 183
   Battling the elusive salmon 183
   Catching the lazy lake perch 183
Especially for Sports Fans 183
   Comiskey Park 184
   Soldier Field 184
   United Center 184
Especially for Serious Museum Buffs 184
   Chicago Historical Society 184
   DuSable Museum of African-American History 185
   Museum of Broadcast Communications 185
   Museum of Contemporary Art 186
   Oriental Institute Museum 186
   Terra Museum of American Art 187
Especially for Book Lovers 187
   Harold Washington Library Center 187
   Newberry Library 188
Especially for Kids 188
   Peggy Notebaert Nature Museum 188
   Ride the ducks 189
   Speeding on a Seadog 189
   Sleeping among the dinosaurs 189
   Brookfield Zoo 189
Especially for Teens 190
   Bike Chicago 190
   Climbing "Mount Chicago" 190
   Illinois Center Golf 191
   Morton Arboretum 191
   Skate on State 191

**Chapter 18: And on Your Left, Lake Michigan:
Seeing Chicago by Guided Tour** **193**
Sampling the City with Orientation Tours 193
Water, Water Everywhere: Boat Tours 194
Bricks and Mortar, Steel and Glass: Architectural Tours 196
Cultivating International Appreciation:
   Neighborhood Tours 196
Gangsters and Ghosts: Specialty Tours 197

Chapter 19: A Shopper's Guide to Chicago **199**
Buying from the Big Department Stores 199
Shopping: Prime Hunting Grounds 200
   Magnificent Mile and environs 202
   Magnificent Mile Malls 204
   Oak Street 207
   State Street and the Loop 209
   Lincoln Park 210
   Bucktown/Wicker Park 210
   Old Town 211
   River North 211

Southport Avenue 212
West Lakeview 212

Chapter 20: Four Great Chicago Itineraries 213

Chicago in Three Days 213
Day One 215
Day Two 215
Day Three 216
Chicago in Five Days 216
Day Four 216
Day Five 217
Chicago for Shopaholics 218
Chicago for Kids 219

Chapter 21: Exploring Beyond Chicago: Five Great Trips ..221

Getting to Know Oak Park's Native Sons 221
Getting to Oak Park 221
Touring Oak Park 223
Dining in Oak Park 224
Shopping in the Historic Village of Long Grove 224
Getting to Long Grove 224
What to do in Long Grove 224
Dining in Long Grove 225
Exploring Evanston's Suburban, Urban Charm 225
Getting to Evanston 225
What to see and do in Evanston 225
Dining in Evanston 226
Ambling Up the North Shore 226
Getting to the North Shore 226
Dining in Wilmette 227
Hanging Out in Hyde Park 227
Getting to Hyde Park 227
Exploring Hyde Park 228
Dining in Hyde Park 229

**Part VI: Living It Up After the Sun Goes Down:
Chicago Nightlife 231**

**Chapter 22: The Play's the Thing: The Chicago
Theater Scene 233**

Finding Out What's Happening 234
Getting Tickets 234
Getting the best seat available 235
Getting the lowest prices 235
Understanding Chicago Theater 101 236
The Loop: An awakening theatrical giant 236
Lincoln Park: The cutting edge 236
Other notables 237
Taking Note of Theater Etiquette 238
Deciding what to wear 238
Tipping tips 238

Arriving late 239
Enjoying the theater with kids 239
Dining: Before or After? 239
Eating before the show 239
Waiting until after the show 240
Get Me to the Theater on Time 240

Chapter 23: The Performing Arts 241

Deciding When to See a Show 241
Finding out what's on 241
Going with the flow: Cultural seasons 242
Picking Your Pleasure 242
Striking up the . . . orchestra 243
Music on the half-shell 243
Taking in the tenors, sopranos, and more 244
Being one with the dance 244
Tactics for Obtaining Tough Tickets 245
Getting to the Show on Time 245

Chapter 24: Hitting the Clubs and Bars 247

Hanging Out at Chicago's Best Bars 248
Searching Out Your Kind of Music 254
Catching the blues 254
Jazzing up the night 254
Rocking to the latest in live music 255
Staying Up Late: The Club Scene 257
Laughing Until Your Stomach Hurts 258
Discovering the Gay and Lesbian Scene 259

Part VII: The Part of Tens..............................261

Chapter 25: Top Ten Chicago Experiences 263

Strolling the Lakefront 263
Sightseeing on the Chicago River and Lake Michigan 263
Shopping on Michigan Avenue 264
Visiting Marshall Field's around the Holidays 264
Cheering the Cubbies 264
Getting the Blues 265
Hearing Music Under the Stars 265
Taking in a Show 265
Riding the El 265
Discovering Wonders at Chicago's Museums 266

Chapter 26: Top Ten Things to Do in Bad Weather 267

Taking Tea 267
Hitting a Michigan Avenue Mall 267
Immersing Yourself in the Art Institute 268
Luxuriating at a Spa 268
Reading at a Cafe 268
Working Out in a Health Club 268
Seeing the Stars at the Planetarium 268
Catching Up on a Movie 269

Watching the Weather from the Oceanarium 269
Going Out for Dinner 269

Chapter 27: Top Ten Things to Do with Kids........................271

Exploring North Bridge Activities 271
Delighting in Animals 271
Nurturing Future Baseball Fans 271
Getting Interactive at a Museum 272
Cruising Michigan Avenue 272
Riding the Roller Coaster 272
Getting Your Hands Dirty 272
Oohing and Aahing at the Dinos 273
Watching the Presses Roll 273
Indulging in a Sundae 273

Appendix: Quick Concierge...**275**

Toll-Free Numbers and Web Sites 278
Getting More Information 280
Visiting tourist offices 280
Surfing the Web 280
Hitting the books 281

Worksheets **283**

Index...**291**

Book Registration Information ....*Back of Book*

Introduction

● ●

*L*et's get one thing straight right up front: Chicago is the best-kept big-city secret in the United States. A bold statement, you say? Fitting, though, for this straight-shooting metropolis on the prairie.

Chicago is loud and smart, crude and glamorous, brash and refined. In some ways it's casually elegant, and in others, unabashedly goofy. You see the contrasts in the glamour of Michigan Avenue's elegant hotels and the boisterousness of the fans screaming for "Da Bears" at Soldier Field. Flashy sports cars idle curbside at Rush Street's hot spots, while farther west, art-school hipsters look for the offbeat in Wicker Park. Then again, you can find Midwesterners in their Lands' End pullovers and khakis just trying to make sense of it all.

Of America's three largest cities in terms of population — New York, Los Angeles, and Chicago — Chicago is the most American. This city constantly reinvents itself, and has pulled itself up by its bootstraps in the last two decades to become a vibrant, cosmopolitan place. It has been said that Chicago is the most livable city in the United States. It's also one of the most visitable. Firmly rooted on Midwestern soil, not buffeted by winds of dot-com change, Chicago is very much its own kind of town. I think it'll be your kind of town, too. In this book, I give you the resources to make your Chicago experience a singular one.

About This Book

My favorite way to travel is with a person who has lived in that place. That's my intention for you with this book. Sure, I hit the must-see tourist destinations, and I highlight the sights that actually merit their popularity. But more often, I point you to off-the-beaten-path places that Chicagoans frequent. The beauty of this approach is that in Chicago, unlike our first-and-second coastal cities, you can actually gain admission to these places. Chicago is much less elitist, much less concerned with the ultimate in trendy, than those cities. The City of Big Shoulders also has open arms.

This book is a guidebook and also a reference book. You can read it cover to cover, or you can jump in anywhere to find the information you want about a specific task, such as finding a hotel, or an aspect of your trip, such as dining. Whether you are sitting in your living room trying to make a reservation or standing on the corner of State and Madison wondering where to eat, *Chicago For Dummies,* is set up so that you can get the facts, descriptions, and recommendations you want, quickly. The book is written so that you can open the book up to any chapter and dig in to get the information that you need without any hassles.

Please be advised that travel information is subject to change at any time — this is especially true of prices. I therefore suggest that you write or call ahead for confirmation when making your travel plans. The author, editors, and publisher cannot be held responsible for the experiences of readers while traveling. Your safety is important to us, however, so we encourage you to stay alert and be aware of your surroundings. Keep a close eye on cameras, purses, and wallets, all favorite targets of thieves and pickpockets.

Conventions Used in This Book

In this book I include lists of hotels, restaurants, and attractions. As I describe each, I often include abbreviations for commonly accepted credit cards. Take a look at the following list for an explanation of each:

AE – American Express

CB – Carte Blanche

DC – Diners Club

DISC – Discover

JCB – Japan Credit Bank

MC – MasterCard

V – Visa

I divide the hotels into two categories — my personal favorites and those that don't quite make my preferred list but still get my hearty seal of approval. Don't be shy about considering the "runner-up" hotels if you can't get a room at one of my favorites or if your preferences differ from mine. The amenities that the runners-up offer and the services that each provides make all these accommodations good choices to consider as you determine where to rest your head at night.

I also include some general pricing information to help you decide where to unpack your bags or dine on the local cuisine. I use a system of dollar signs to show a range of costs for one night in a hotel or a meal at a restaurant (included in the cost of each meal is an appetizer, main course, dessert, and coffee). Check out the following table to decipher the dollar signs:

Cost	Hotel	Restaurant
$	$75–$125	Under $25
$$	$125–$200	$25–35
$$$	$200–$300	$35–$45
$$$$	$300–$400	$45–$60
$$$$$	$400 and up	Over $60

Foolish Assumptions

As I wrote this book, I made some assumptions about you and what your needs may be as a traveler. Here's what I assumed about you:

- ✔ You may be an inexperienced traveler looking for guidance when determining whether to take a trip to Chicago and how to plan for it.

- ✔ You may be an experienced traveler who hasn't had much time to explore Chicago and wants expert advice when you finally do get a chance to enjoy that particular locale.

- ✔ You're not looking for a book that provides all the information available about Chicago or that lists every hotel, restaurant, or attraction available to you. Instead, you're looking for a book that focuses on the places that give you the best or most unique experience in Chicago.

If you fit any of the criteria, then *Chicago For Dummies* gives you the information you're looking for!

How This Book Is Organized

This book is divided into seven parts, covering the major aspects of your trip. Each of these is broken down into its component parts, so that you can go right to the specific subtopic you want (you don't have to read about all the nightlife if you're just looking for a blues club, for example). Following are brief summaries of each of the parts.

Part 1: Getting Started

Here's where I sketch out your trip so it starts to take form: when to go, how to get here, and how much it's all going to cost. I let you in on the best hotels, restaurants, and attractions. You get the low-down on the annual calendar of events, from summer street festivals to holiday traditions, and an idea of Chicago's changeable weather patterns. And, we talk money: how much to bring to Chicago and where to spend it.

Part II: Ironing Out the Details

Now, I begin to add some detail and color to the picture. How do you make travel arrangements — through the Web, a travel agent, or on your own? Should you take a guided or escorted tour, or go alone? How should you choose the neighborhood that you'll call home base? What's the best way to book a hotel? And, what should you pack to fulfill that Boy Scout motto, "Be prepared"? I review Chicago's best hotels and debate their pros and cons.

Part III: Settling into Chicago

Getting around in a new place is always a challenge. From the time you step out of your plane, train, or automobile, I guide you into and around the city. I cover the public transit system and show you how to get around using your own two feet. I also discuss that key element of getting along in a big city — money — and where to get it.

Part IV: Dining in Chicago

Food is taken very seriously in Chicago. I show you the big picture — ethnic foods, Chicago specialties — and then point you in some interesting directions. I give you reviews of Chicago's best restaurants by location, price, and cuisine and also describe the best places for snacks. You never know when you're going to run out of gas with all that touring you're doing!

Part V: Exploring Chicago

What are the best things to see and do in Chicago? The answer is different for everyone. Here, I describe the top attractions and map out some sample itineraries. Whether you are a museum lover or hater, a serious shopper or just window shopping, traveling with kids in tow or not, you find ways to fill your days here.

Part VI: Living It Up After the Sun Goes Down: Chicago Nightlife

Chicago after dark offers opera to blues, plays to nightclubs, and lounging to dancing. I help you figure out how much everything costs and ways to get discount tickets. You find out where Chicagoans go to have a drink and wind down — or rev up — after dark.

Part VII: The Part of Tens

My favorite part — the top ten of everything that matters when you visit Chicago, from my top-ten favorite Chicago experiences, to how best to spend a rainy or snowy day, to the best ways to entertain kids in the city.

You can also find two other elements near the back of this book. I include an appendix — your Quick Concierge — containing plenty of handy information that you may need when traveling in Chicago, such as phone numbers and addresses of emergency personnel or area hospitals and pharmacies, contact information for babysitters, lists of local newspapers and magazines, protocol for sending mail or finding taxis, and more. Check out the appendix when searching for answers to all the little questions that may come up as you travel.

A bunch of worksheets is also included to make your travel planning easier. Among other things, you can determine your travel budget, create specific itineraries, and keep a log of your favorite restaurants so that you can hit them again the next time you're in town. The worksheets are located in the back of the book and are printed on yellow paper.

Icons Used in This Book

These icons appear in the margins throughout this book:

Find out useful advice on things to do and ways to schedule your time when you see the Tip icon.

Watch for the Heads Up icon to identify annoying or potentially dangerous situations, such as tourist traps, unsafe neighborhoods, budgetary rip-offs, and other circumstances to beware of.

Look to the Kid Friendly icon for attractions, hotels, restaurants, and activities that are particularly hospitable to children or people traveling with kids.

Keep an eye out for the Bargain Alert icon as you seek out money-saving tips and/or great deals.

You get insider information on where locals eat, shop, and spend time in Chicago.

 Colorful quotes and famous sayings to shed light on the things you're seeing and doing in Chicago.

Where to Go from Here

The typical visitor will discover that Chicago today is a living, vibrant, wonderfully diverse city, and one that offers something for everyone, whatever your tastes, inclinations, or budget may be. This book helps you make decisions about how you can tailor Chicago to be your kind of town.

Part I
Getting Started

The 5th Wave   By Rich Tennant

"I think we should arrange to be there for 'Hot Dog-Italian Beef-Pizza-Week,' and then shoot over to the 'Antacid Festival.'"

In this part . . .

This part guides you through the important steps in preparing your trip to Chicago. The city's highlights, the not-to-be-missed attractions and activities, are outlined in Chapter 1. Chapter 2 helps you decide when to go based on weather considerations and event schedules. And in Chapter 3, you can find money tips and budgeting advice. Guidance is offered in Chapter 4 for those with special needs, such as families with kids, gay travelers, or travelers with disabilities.

Chapter 1

Discovering the Best of Chicago

In This Chapter

▶ Benefiting from the building boom

▶ Kicking back: Baseball and the blues

▶ Getting highbrow: Performing arts, museums, and architecture

▶ Eating and talking around town

Hog Butcher for the World,
Tool Maker, Stacker of Wheat,
Player with Railroads and the Nation's Freight Handler;
Stormy, husky, brawling,
City of the Big Shoulders.

—Carl Sandburg, *Chicago*

In this chapter, you get a sampling of the qualities that make Chicago the most American of American cities. Today, you'd hardly recognize Chicago by Sandburg's description. No longer home to stockyards, the city is a cosmopolitan, vibrant place. But Chicago still retains its unique identity: big and brawling, inventive, and wonderfully diverse. Chicago is the least pretentious and most livable metropolis in the United States — and maybe the most visitable, too.

Celebrating a Renaissance

Chicago is basking in a cultural and building renaissance. The city has always been associated with rebuilding itself, and now is no exception. The city is in the midst of its biggest building boom since the 1920s, lagging behind only Atlanta and Phoenix in the number of construction permits issued in 1998 and 1999. Visitors and residents alike benefit from this building fever. All over the city, shopping and theater districts have been expanded or restored, and new hotels and attractions are opening their doors to visitors. Downtown Chicago's **State Street,** that great street, long gasping for life, has come back with a vengeance as a retail and residential center (see Chapter 19 for shopping details). Major retailers such as Borders Books & Music, Old Navy, and Toys "R" Us have staked out sites on State Street. Several new hotels, including a spectacular renovation of the former Reliance Insurance building into the Hotel Burnham, have given the State Street area a sparkle that it hasn't had for years (see Chapter 8 for hotel information).

On and near State Street's northern end, culture is coming alive in the North Loop theater district. **The Goodman Theater** has an impressive new home, and several theaters have had facelifts, including the **Oriental** and **Palace Theaters.** (See Chapter 22 for the theater scene.)

In the North Michigan Avenue area, the **Park Hyatt,** a showpiece of the hotel chain, opened in the fall of 2000 to rave reviews. A **Peninsula Hotel** is under construction a couple blocks away. And although not new, two other Michigan Avenue properties continue to wow visitors: The **Ritz-Carlton** (A Four Seasons Hotel) was ranked number-one in North America in 2000 by *Condé Nast Traveler* readers, followed in the number-two place by the **Four Seasons Hotel** (see Chapter 8).

Shopping on Michigan Avenue is world-famous. Hey, it's not quite Rodeo Drive, but I bet your dollar goes farther here. The avenue increased its shopping cachet with the opening in 2000 of **The Shops at North Bridge,** a three-story mall complex featuring Nordstrom department store (see Chapter 19).

Just east of Michigan Avenue, the neighborhood of Streeterville saw the recent addition of the **Museum of Contemporary Art,** which brings amazing programming to the cultural scene (see Chapter 17). Two hotels and two movie theaters are under construction in the area. Directly east of here, a lively, renovated **Navy Pier** has become the city's number-one tourist destination since its reopening in 1995. The view of the city, as you walk out on Navy Pier, then turn, and watch the city glimmer in the twilight, is among the best city views in the world (see Chapter 16). Construction has not been limited to buildings. Mayor Richard M. Daley, in his third term as mayor, is working feverishly to beautify metropolitan Chicago. City workers are planting flowerbeds, effacing graffiti, and reshaping schools. Green space is being created, too. The 16-acre, $230-million **Millennium Park,** with a Frank O. Gehry-designed band shell and pedestrian bridge, is being created just north of the Art Institute on South Michigan Avenue.

Airwaves in the Windy City

While you're here, don't forget to tune in. Chicago's National Public Radio Station WBEZ-FM (91.5 FM) is home to Ira Glass's *This American Life* program every Saturday afternoon at 1 p.m. On your Chicago TV screen, WGN-TV (Channel 9), part of the Tribune Company media empire, can fill you in on Chicago's sports teams' progress — or lack thereof.

Finding the Very Best to See and Do in Chicago

Chicago does some things better than any other city: You just have to know what they are and how to find them. Read on for some of the activities that make Chicago a special place to visit.

Cheering on the Cubbies

Baseball at **Wrigley Field** is a quintessential Chicago experience (see Chapter 16). The ivy-covered field is the coziest little park in baseball.

Even though the Cubs lost 97 games in the 2000 season, tickets can still be hard to come by on a perfect summer day. Wrigley Field gives you room to breathe, and watching a game under the Midwestern skies, which are vast with low-lying puffy clouds, is a terrific way to spend a day in Chicago.

Getting the blues — a good thing

Chicago is the blues capital of the world. And if you get to know this style of music, you may gain a greater appreciation for other popular forms, such as jazz and rock 'n' roll. There is nothing quite as sweet as hanging out at **Buddy Guy's Legends** on a Thursday night and discovering that the man seated next to you is B.B. King's drummer, visiting Chicago on a rare night off. Even if you don't love the blues, do yourself a favor and check it out when you're here. (See Chapter 24 for more blues clubs.)

Discovering the Third Coast

While residents of the first two coasts (East and West, that is) may consider it a surprise, Chicagoans consider themselves residents of the *Third Coast* — Lake Michigan's shore, that is. Thanks to the foresight of city founders who, in 1836, wrote that the lakefront was a public ground "to remain forever open, clear, and free" from construction, the shore has no warehouses or shipping docks. Instead, you find 30 miles of sand beaches, green lawns, beds of flowers, and bicycle paths. More than half of the 2,800 acres of lakefront were created by filling in the lake and building a string of splendid lakeshore parks (Lincoln, Grant, Burnham, Jackson, Rainbow, and Calumet). While you're here, join Chicagoans at the lake to walk, run, or just relax.

Soaking up some culture

Chicago's **Lyric Opera** continually sells out 100% of the time, but don't fear. Subscription holders routinely hand in unused tickets before the performance, so you can still get some great seats. Directed by well-known conductor Daniel Barenboim, the **Chicago Symphony Orchestra** is world-class. And the city recently adopted the **Joffrey Ballet,** which now performs in venues around the city. (See Chapter 23 for more on the performing arts.) The local theater companies include the **Goodman** and **Steppenwolf Theaters.** Steppenwolf, located in Lincoln Park, focuses on original, edgy drama. The Goodman has a less cutting-edge repertoire and includes some musicals each season. (See Chapter 22 for more on theaters.)

If you skip Chicago's theater scene, you just may miss out on the next Broadway smash hit. Two of the most widely applauded Broadway productions of the past few years started at the Goodman Theater: Arthur Miller's *Death of a Salesman,* starring Brian Denehy, and Eugene O'Neill's *Moon for the Misbegotten,* with Cherry Jones and Gabriel Byrne.

Nobody does comedy better than **Second City** (see Chapter 24), a training ground for comedians, such as John Belushi, Dan Ackroyd, Bill Murray, and Chris Farley. Other theater highlights include the refurbishing of the Oriental and Palace Theaters and the opening of the **Old Town School of Folk Music theater and education center,** 4454 N. Lincoln Avenue between Wilson and Montrose Avenues; ☎ 773-768-2000; Internet: www.oldtownschool.org, presenting traditional and contemporary folk music from around the world, and the **Chicago Shakespeare Theater** (see Chapter 22) on Navy Pier.

Seeing "Sue" and other museum stars

Yes, the biggest T-Rex fossil ever unearthed is now residing at Chicago's **Field Museum of Natural History** (see Chapter 16). As long as you're going to see "Sue" (if you're on a first-name basis with the famous T-Rex), you should know that an entire "campus" of museums is nearby, including **Adler Planetarium & Astronomy Museum** and the **John G. Shedd Aquarium.** And they've both revamped and improved their facilities. The Shedd, the nation's oldest and largest indoor aquarium, is housed in a 1929 beaux-arts structure. A modern addition, the Oceanarium, was finished in 1990. The Shedd is currently being restored and reconfigured, and two new partially underground wings are being added in an $85-million project that will last several years. The Adler is also doing a top-to-bottom renovation of its original 1930 Art Deco building, which has 12 sides adorned with astrological signs and is topped by a dome. The facility has been improved with a new $20-million wing that curves around the building and contains a new virtual-reality theater. Farther south, the incomparable **Museum of Science and Industry** wows kids and adults with a real-life submarine, airplane, ant colony, and more.

Downtown, the **Museum of Contemporary Art** was opened in the mid-1990s and features spectacular cultural programming. The **Art Institute** is Chicago's ground zero for masterpieces of art. And, a brand new natural science museum in Lincoln Park — the **Peggy Notebaert Nature Museum** — is an environmental museum for the 21st century.

Admiring the architecture

One advantage to having your city burn to the ground: You can rebuild it with style. Thanks to the Great Fire of 1871, Chicago's architects were able to start over and "make no small plans," as city planner and visionary Daniel Burnham said. Chicago is the birthplace of modern architecture, and of the skyscraper. Chicago is home to 45 Mies Van Der Rohe buildings, 75 Frank Lloyd Wright buildings, plus dozens by the first Chicago school and the second Chicago school. Enough said? The Chicago Architecture Foundation helps visitors discover the city's architectural gems (see Chapter 16).

Eating Your Way Through Town

If you have to eat while you're here, you're in luck. Food doesn't get much better than the Mexican cuisine at **Frontera Grill** or **Salpicon,** the ribs at **Twin Anchors,** burgers at **Iron Mike's Grille,** sushi at **Kamehachi,** or Italian at **Tuscany on Taylor** in Little Italy. And if that's not enough, how about cocktails at **Cru,** steak and mammoth baked potatoes slathered in butter at **Gibson's,** or deep-dish pizza at **Gino's East.** (See Chapter 14 for all the restaurants.) Oh, I can't forget to mention Italian beef sandwiches and garlicky Chicago hot dogs. And don't forget to finish off your meal with a Frango chocolate mint from **Marshall Field's** department store (see Chapter 19 for more on shopping). Feeling hungry yet?

Can We Talk?

Chicago has fostered a number of talk shows, including Jenny Jones, Jerry Springer, and, of course, Oprah Winfrey. If you want to check out a talk show and laugh, cry, or boo and hiss with the best of them, Chicago is the place to do it (see Chapter 16 for more on attending a show). After all, Chicagoans have been talking and dispensing advice for decades. (The newspaper advice columnist and Chicagoan, Ann Landers, has been dishing out advice to the lovelorn, frustrated, and just plain confused for more years than I can count.)

Chapter 2

Deciding When to Go

. . . .

In This Chapter

▶ Weighing the pros and cons of winter, spring, summer, and fall

▶ Spelling out the facts and fallacies about Chicago weather

▶ Checking out a month-by-month listing of events

. . . .

*W*hen should you go to Chicago? That depends. What kind of weather do you like? Chicago has it all — sometimes within a day! No doubt you have heard the wisecracks about Chicago's weather, such as the city having only two seasons — winter and August. And that tongue-firmly-in-cheek piece of advice: "If you don't like the weather, stick around for five minutes."

As with many sayings, both have an element of truth. Chicago weather does hit the extremes. And it's oh-so-changeable. I've left my apartment on a sunny, summer day in jeans and a T-shirt only to witness the temperature drop 15 degrees in 15 minutes. In this chapter, I tell you what you need to know about the city's ever-changing seasons and the many festivals, so that you can determine your ideal time to go.

The Secret of the Seasons

Most Chicago visitors find that the ideal times to visit are late spring through early fall. In the **spring,** you soak up blossoms, blooms, and equable temperatures. Spring in Chicago may be short, but it's invigorating and widely welcomed. Some Chicagoans, eager for warm weather, lie out on roof-deck lounge chairs in 55-degree, April weather. **Fall,** with its golds, reds, and browns, provides crisp, clear days with idyllic balmy interludes. Pleasant weather sometimes lingers into late November.

Chicago has a reputation for being extremely cold in the **winter.** In truth, it's not much colder than any other northern city. Daunting days of sub-zero temperatures and minus-40-degree wind chills do occur. Salt trucks rumble incessantly over Chicago's frozen streets, and potholes almost large enough to swallow cars bring rush-hour traffic to a halt. **Summer** isn't exactly a piece of cake, either: During the dog days, you may have whole strings of days when temperatures stay in the 90s and high humidity drains your energy.

But those are the extremes. Lake Michigan has a moderating effect on Chicago weather, air-conditioning the city in summer and warming the cold in the winter. (Of course, in the Windy City, the lake also has a negative effect — that same breeze that cuts the humidity in the summer can bite straight through the thickest down jacket in the winter.) For information on how to pack for these extremes, see Chapter 9.

What follows is a rundown of the pros and cons of each season.

Springtime in Chicago

Many of Chicago's 30 million visitors annually choose spring for their travels. Here are the best reasons to go to Chicago in the springtime:

- ✔ It's warming up! It's staying light longer in the day! All Chicago is waking up after a long winter's nap.

- ✔ Chicago plants thousands of tulips and daffodils, which pop up optimistically during the season and brighten the streetscape.

But keep in mind the following springtime pitfalls:

- ✔ Just because it's warming up doesn't mean that the weather is necessarily nice. Strong winds can blow, and buckets of rain can fall during long strings of gray days.

- ✔ You're a bit in limbo as far as events go. Festivals don't start until June, and you've missed the holiday season and the decorations.

Summer heats up the scene

Ahhh, summer. Lazy days and quiet nights . . . Well, not in Chicago! Summer is festival time. Knowing what lies ahead, Chicagoans jam-pack summers full of outdoor activity — so much that the choice of activities on weekends can be overwhelming. Here are some points to consider:

- ✔ It may be hot and humid, but you can usually count on a cool lake breeze. If you're venturing to the suburbs, however, the temperatures can be ten degrees higher.

- ✔ Everyone is outside, soaking up the good weather while it lasts. People stay out late, eating and drinking at sidewalk cafes.

- ✔ It's perfect weather for taking boat cruises, strolling along Navy Pier, and enjoying other activities on the lakefront.

But, again, keep in mind the following:

- Festivals can be hot and cramped. (Then again, that's the point, right?)

- Because of the heat, everyone is at the lake, making the area a congested free-for-all: Rollerbladers skating into bikers biking into runners running into Fido who just broke off his leash!

- School is out, and the kid-oriented attractions are swarming. Be prepared to leave extra time for parking and standing in line at attractions such as the John G. Shedd Aquarium, Sears Tower Skydeck, and Museum of Science and Industry.

Falling for fall

In my opinion, fall is a beautiful time of year — no matter where you are. Here are some autumn bonuses for the Chicago scene:

- You get the best weather in the fall; still warm enough, but not so hot and humid that you're going to have a meltdown. You have the best shot at an uninterrupted string of beautiful days.

- The cultural scene is back in swing, with openings for the opera and symphony seasons.

Some things to look out for, however:

- Convention season is in full swing. Getting a hotel room or restaurant table can be a challenge. And if you do, you may find yourself surrounded by dozens of computer geeks . . . or dentists . . . or restaurant owners. Then again, you may enjoy that!

- Beware of unpredictable September or October Indian summer heat waves. (Don't forget the shorts and sunscreen — just in case!)

Winter in the Midwest

Winter brings visions of softly falling snowflakes, but the reality is, those lovely snowflakes result in slick roads and salt trucks. Consider the following when planning a winter vacation in Chicago:

- After Christmas, a peaceful hush settles over the city. You can have Michigan Avenue to yourself on the weekdays. After-holiday sales keep the stores busy on the weekends, but otherwise, you can pretend that the city is all yours.

- During the holidays, the city looks beautiful. All Michigan Avenue is lit up. Chicago goes all-out with Christmas decorations.

✔ Mayor Daley has made an effort to make Chicago attractive to tourists in the winter with events like WinterBreak Chicago, which fills the month of February with a series of blues concerts and more.

✔ Hotel prices sink during the slowest weeks of the winter, making it much easier to get a good room at a great rate.

Winter does have its downside, however. Consider the following:

✔ December is a bad month for crowds. Michigan Avenue is packed, literally — so much so that it's hard to make your way down the street.

✔ Between conventions, family vacations, and savvy travelers, winter is rapidly becoming a more popular time to go. Tourists are catching on to the fact that winter travel is cheaper in Chicago, but so far, the cold months are still less crowded than most others.

✔ Did I mention that it can get really cold in the winter?

✔ Because business is slow, hotels, restaurants, and stores take the opportunity to renovate, meaning that various areas that serve the public may be closed for maintenance purposes.

✔ Winter is the other time of year (along with springtime) when shows may close for a week; remember, performers need vacations, too.

Being temperature wise

Table 2-1 gives you the lowdown on the average temperatures in Chicago. Remember, though, that these are only averages. You may want to pack an outfit or two for cooler or warmer weather, depending on when you plan to travel.

Table 2-1 Chicago's Average Temperatures and Precipitation											
	Jan	Feb	Mar	Apr	May	June	July	Aug	Sept	Oct	Nov	Dec
High (°F)	20	34	44	59	70	79	85	82	76	64	48	35
Low (°F)	14	18	28	39	48	58	63	62	54	42	31	20
Rainfall (in.)	1.6	1.3	2.6	3.7	3.2	4.0	3.6	3.5	3.4	2.3	2.0	2.1

Hot Dates: Chicago Calendar of Events

Chicago abounds with ethnic parades and other lively events — most of them free. In fact, you can choose from among a wide array of events, no matter what the month. The annual events, food, music, art, and flower fairs have established niches in the city's yearly schedule, along with the national parades and street celebrations staged by many of Chicago's numerous ethnic groups. Pick your time, choose your interest, and enjoy.

The best way to stay on top of the city's current crop of special events is to ask the **Chicago Office of Tourism** (☎ 312-744-2400) or the Illinois Bureau of Tourism (☎ 800-2CONNECT) to mail you a copy of *Chicago Calendar of Events,* an excellent quarterly publication that surveys special events, including museum exhibitions, concert and theatrical performances, parades, and street festivals. Also ask to be sent the latest material produced by the **Mayor's Office of Special Events** (☎ 312-744-3315) or the **Special Events Hot Line** (☎ 312-744-3370), which keeps current with citywide and neighborhood festivals.

Remember that new events may be added every year and that some events may be discontinued or rescheduled. Call ahead to the sponsoring organization, the Chicago Office of Tourism, or the Mayor's Office of Special Events to verify dates, times, and locations.

January

Opening Day seems far away, but those "wait-until-next-year" Cubbie fans never stop dreaming. The **Chicago Cubs Convention,** held at the Chicago Hilton and Towers, hosts players signing autographs and collectors buying, selling, and swapping memorabilia. Call ☎ 773-404-CUBS for more information on this mid-January event.

The **Chicago Boat, Sports, and RV Show** (☎ 312-946-6262) is for those who dream of spring. Held at McCormick Place the last week in January.

Again, spring fever comes early at a time of year when a little color and fragrance are more than welcome. Go to the **Lincoln Park Conservatory** (☎ 312-742-7737) and **Garfield Park Conservatory** (☎ 312-746-5100) for the **Azalea and Camellia Flower Shows** where spring-blooming plants, such as azaleas, tulips, and hyacinths, are featured during this end-of-January-through-February event.

February

A twisting dragon joins a fierce-looking lion dancer in the **Chinese New Year Parade** that winds its colorful way from Wentworth Avenue at 24th Place to Princeton Avenue and Cermak Road in Chinatown. Call ☎ 312-326-5320 for more information on this parade, which takes place on the Sunday following the Chinese New Year (between January 21 and February 19, depending on the lunar calendar).

In the dead of winter, come fantasize about convertibles and get your hands on the shiniest, newest automobiles for the coming year at the **Chicago Auto Show.** Presented since 1901, this show at McCormick Place attracts close to a million car owners and wannabe owners. Call ☎ 630-495-2282 for more information on this mid-February event.

Watch more than 10,000 American Kennel Club dogs strut their stuff at the **International Cluster of Dog Shows** held at McCormick Place South. Call ☎ 773-237-5100 for more information on this event, which takes place the third week in February.

March

A Chicago tradition since the 1840s, the annual **St. Patrick's Day Parade** along Dearborn Street from Wacker Drive to Van Buren Street brings out a celebrity grand marshal, local pols, and union bosses. The Chicago River is dyed green for the big day on the Saturday closest to March 17.

The **Spring Flower Shows** held at Lincoln Park Conservatory (☎ 312-742-7737) and Garfield Park Conservatory (☎ 312-746-5100) feature lilies, daffodils, tulips, pansies, and other flowering perennials. The Spring Flower Shows usually open the week before Easter.

April

Neither rain nor sleet nor snow nor hail (all very real possibilities in early spring) keeps eternally hopeful Cubs fans away from Wrigley Field or Sox fans away from Comiskey Park on **Opening Day,** generally during the first week of April. Call ☎ 773-404-CUBS, or for the White Sox ☎ 312-674-1000.

May

The **Cinco de Mayo Festival** held at McCormick Place offers a weekend celebration of Mexican food, music, games, and family-oriented activities. (Remember, Chicago's Pilsen neighborhood is the country's second-largest Mexican-American community.) Held the weekend prior to May 5. Call ☎ 312-791-7000 for information.

One of the country's largest contemporary art fairs, the **Art 2001 Chicago** held at Navy Pier Festival Hall hosts more than 200 art galleries and 2,000 artists during Mother's Day weekend. Call ☎ **312-587-3300** for more information.

"Sweet Home Chicago" is "sweet home" to the **Chicago Blues Festival,** a huge blues event in Grant Park. At festival time, a bus shuttles aficionados between the city's numerous blues clubs. Call ☎ **312-744-3315** for more information on this end-of-May/early June event.

June

A week or so after the blues musicians leave Grant Park, music fans head to the same venue to listen to top gospel performers at the **Chicago Gospel Festival.** Call ☎ **312-744-3315** to attend this event in early June.

Entertainment, readings, food, and books galore abound at **Printers Row Book Fair,** one of the nation's largest free outdoor book fairs. Located on Dearborn Street between Polk and Congress. Call ☎ **312-987-9896** for more information on this event, which occurs the first weekend in June.

Sample Carson's ribs, Eli's cheesecake, and Uno's pizza at **Taste of Chicago.** This huge festival at Grant Park has close to 100 food booths to feed 3 million hungry visitors. Call ☎ **312-744-3370** for more information on this late June and early July event.

Ravinia Festival in Highland Park is the open-air summer home of the Chicago Symphony Orchestra and many visiting performers from Tony Bennett to Lyle Lovett. Call ☎ **847-266-5100** to make ticket reservations for June through September.

Fine art from more than 200 painters, sculptors, and jewelry designers, plus an art auction, garden walk, food and drink, and children's art activities can all be found at the **Old Town Art Fair,** located in the Old Town neighborhood at Lincoln Park West and Wisconsin Street (☎ **312-337-1938**; Internet: www.oldtownartfair.org). Attend during the second full weekend in June.

The **Grant Park Music Festival** hosts free outdoor musical concerts. Bring your blanket, picnic basket, and maybe even a frisbee. Call ☎ **312-742-4763** to enjoy this event, which occurs the last week in June through August.

Park yourself on Broadway to see the creative floats and colorful marching units in the **Gay and Lesbian Pride Parade.** The route is Halsted Street from Belmont Avenue to Broadway, south to Diversey Parkway, and east to Lincoln Park. Call ☎ **773-348-8243** for more information. Plan to attend on the last Sunday in June at 2 p.m.

July

Fireworks (launched from barges in Monroe Harbor), concerts, and spirited marches mark the **Independence Day Celebration** in Grant Park. Concurrent with Taste of Chicago, the crowds are enormous: Take public transportation. Call ☎ **312-744-3315** for more information on this July 3 event.

The 33-year-old **Sheffield Garden Walk** allows you to snoop around the private gardens of Lincoln Park homeowners at Sheffield and Webster Avenues. Food and drink vendors, live bands, and more make this a hopping event for Lincoln Park singles. Call ☎ **773-929-WALK** for more information and plan on attending in mid-July.

You won't believe the crowds — or the name bands — that the city's oldest church (700 West Adams at Des Plaines Avenue) turns out for the annual **Old St. Patrick's World's Largest Block Party** blowout. Okay, the admission price is steep — $35 — but we're talking six bands over two nights on two stages, plus all the beer you can drink (and people do drink all they can). Call ☎ **312-648-1021** for more on this mid-July event.

The **Venetian Night Boat Parade** of beautifully decorated and illuminated boats takes place to elaborate fireworks and music by the Grant Park Symphony Orchestra, performing works by Italian composers. It's held along the water at Monroe Harbor. Call ☎ **312-744-3315** for more information on the parade, which occurs at the end of July.

August

The Chicago Air & Water Show showcases action on, in, and over Lake Michigan, with stunt pilots and skydivers, wing walkers and precision flyers, plus water-skiing, windsurfing, and air-sea rescue. You'll have a hard time ignoring the show (unless you're oblivious to sonic booms, C-130 cargo planes, stealth bombers, and F-16 fighters roaring over your head). Hugely popular are the U.S. Air Force Thunderbirds, who usually make an appearance. If you bring a portable radio, you can plant yourself on any beach up and down the lakefront and avoid the crowds at North Avenue Beach. Call ☎ **312-744-3315** for more information on this mid-August show.

End-of-festival-season is marked by the **Chicago Jazz Festival,** which always has some national names. Like all other Chicago festivals, it's free. Jam sessions at local jazz clubs stretch into the wee hours. Call ☎ **312-744-3315** for more information on this festival, which is held in Grant Park on Labor Day weekend.

September

Around the Coyote hosts one of the nation's largest concentrations of artists. Tour hundreds of artists' studios and see music performances, and fashion shows in the Wicker Park and Bucktown neighborhoods. Call ☎ 773-342-6777 to tour and plan on the second weekend in September.

Just a few years old, **World Music Festival Chicago** — the City's Department of Cultural Affairs major undertaking — brings in top performers from Zimbabwe to Sri Lanka and Hungary and points in between. Call early for schedules and tickets (☎ 312-744-6630); many performances sold out last year. Shows are a mix of free and ticketed performances (most are $10 and less). The Museum of Contemporary Art, the Chicago Cultural Center, the Old Town School of Folk Music, and the Hot House host many events at the festival, held in September.

October

One of Chicago's largest parades — **Columbus Day Parade** — lasts two hours, includes more than 200 bands and floats, and features a celebrity grand marshal (President George H. W. Bush and Mrs. Bush have served, as did the late Joe DiMaggio). The route is Dearborn Street from Wacker Drive to Van Buren Street. Call ☎ 312-828-0010 and set aside the closest Monday to October 12.

The **Chicago International Film Festival,** the oldest competitive film festival in the country, has screenings for more than two weeks at theaters across the city. Call ☎ 312-425-9400 for more information on the middle-to-late-October film festival.

The world-class **Chicago Marathon** begins and ends in Grant Park and usually attracts many elite runners who hope to attempt world-record times because the course is flat, and therefore fast. Call ☎ 312-527-2200 for information and set aside the last Sunday in October.

November

The **Christmas Around the World/Holidays of Light Festival** showcases trees decorated in the holiday traditions of more than 90 nations and ethnic groups at the Museum of Science and Industry. Enjoy native songs, dances, and caroling. Call ☎ 773-684-1414 for more festival information. It takes place in late November through early January.

Disney sponsors the **Magnificent Mile Lights Festival,** a colorful parade of characters that makes its way south on Michigan Avenue from Oak Street to the Chicago River. As the parade passes, lights are illuminated block by block. Carolers, elves, and minstrels appear with Santa along the avenue all day and into the evening. Call ☎ **312-642-3570,** and plan to attend the festival on the Saturday before Thanksgiving.

December

The free tickets to Chicago's annual interactive choral event are much in demand. Held at Orchestra Hall, **Do-It-Yourself Messiah** is conducted by the choral director of the Chicago Symphony Orchestra.

A Christmas Carol, an annual favorite for more than two decades, will be performed from Thanksgiving to the end of December in the Goodman Theater's new home in the North Loop theater district. Call ☎ **312-443-3800** early for tickets because the show sells out.

Colorful illuminated displays enliven the zoo at the **Zoo Lights Festival** held at the Lincoln Park Zoo (2200 N. Cannon Drive; ☎ **312-742-2000;** Internet: www.lpzoo.com). The festival begins around Thanksgiving and runs until New Year's. On a Saturday in early December (in 2001, the date is December 2), you can participate in Caroling to the Animals, a daylong tradition. Chicago stages a massive midnight fireworks display at Navy Pier for **New Year's Eve,** where you also find a big party with dancing into the wee hours. Call ☎ **312-742-2001** for more information and get ready for December 31.

Chapter 3

Planning Your Budget

. . . .

In This Chapter

▶ Figuring out how much money is enough

▶ Handling money on your trip

▶ Budgeting like a pro: Where to splurge, where to save

. . . .

*C*hicago has a way of eating up your money: dinner at **Harry Caray's** (see Chapter 14), cabs, admission fees, tips for the bellhop and maid, the bottle of Advil bought at **Navy Pier** (see Chapter 16), coffee at **Corner Bakery** (see Chapter 20) — and all that wonderful shopping. Making matters worse, ATMs are on practically every corner. With cash and credit so accessible, spending can get out of hand fast.

Before you go, it's a good idea to come up with a realistic idea of how much you can spend. You don't want to worry constantly about spending money, but you don't want to faint when you get your credit card bills, either. The idea is to have fun and enjoy yourself without agonizing over every dollar you spend. For peace of mind and for the sake of your bank account, know when you can afford to splurge and when to economize. This chapter gives you some ideas of how to allocate your funds. After all, you don't want to find yourself still paying for this trip when you set off on your next adventure!

Estimating the Cost of Your Trip

Budgeting a trip to Chicago — or to anywhere else for that matter — is a matter of give and take. First decide where you'd like to stay and what you'd like to do, then look at your budget to see if you can swing it. Unless your bank account is bottomless, you'll need to make some trade-offs. Are you prepared to sacrifice some hotel comforts to pay for tickets to a hit musical? Can you eat hot dogs for lunch in exchange for splurging on a couple of dinners at restaurants owned by superstar chefs? Are you just as happy taking home photos as expensive souvenirs? Then maybe you can have cocktails downtown on North Michigan Avenue in **The Signature Room at the 95th** at the top of the **John Hancock Center Observatory** (see Chapter 16). It's all a matter of your priorities.

Lodging

Lodging is pretty easy to figure out. The cost is set after you book your accommodations and is less flexible than other areas of your budget, such as attractions. You have to have a place to stay. So, as in other real estate matters, it's location, location, and location that determine the cost of your lodgings. The more central you are to Chicago's Magnificent Mile, the more expensive the hotel. If you're prepared to stay a little bit away from downtown, you can save on lodging. But if being in the middle of the action is valuable to you, then you can find other areas of your budget for economizing. For me, location is most important. I will take a smaller room in a hotel that's centrally located over a larger room in a hotel that's far from the main attractions. I like to walk everywhere and would rather spend a bit more on the room and less on cab fare. But that's just me. You need to decide if the time spent traveling on public transportation or the expense of taking cabs is worth the money you save by staying in a hotel that's located away from the center of the city. (For more on hotels, see Chapter 8.)

According to the Hotel/Motel Association of Illinois, the average hotel room rate is $125 for downtown Chicago and $100 for the metropolitan area. When you figure in room tax, you're going to be spending at the very least $100 for a room — although you can shave off a few dollars by staying at the downtown Motel 6 or on the Near North side, for example. If you're able to spend $150, you can figure in a few extra comforts and conveniences. Push this up to $200 a night and you can get a comfortable and well-located hotel room. (See Chapter 8 for the low-down on the Chicago hotel scene.)

Transportation

You don't need a car in Chicago. Hey, I *live* here, and I don't own a car. Why, with the high costs of owning an automobile — insurance, registration, gas, parking, and wear and tear (on vehicle and nerves) — would I own a car? You can get about easily, and usually safely, on Chicago's relatively efficient public transportation system and on foot. A bus or subway ride costs only $1.50, and a transfer that provides two additional rides (if taken within a two-hour window) is only an additional 30 cents. Cabs are plentiful and relatively inexpensive. The average cab ride in the downtown area averages $5 to $7. All of which means that you won't need a rental car. So, assuming you spend $20 a day on cabs and public transportation, you save a sizable chunk of the $40 to $50 that you may otherwise spend on car rental, plus valet parking at your hotel, which runs about $25 a day. That amounts to at least $45 a day to apply to other expenses.

 Watch the meter. Taxis cost $1.90 as soon as the driver starts the meter. Add 40 cents for each ⅙ of a mile, and 50 cents for each additional passenger aged 12 to 65.

Restaurants

Because Chicago has so many restaurants, inexpensive and moderately priced eateries are easy to find. Many have the equivalent of blue-plate specials. In fact, even when you splurge at a top-tier restaurant, it's a good idea to consider a multicourse tasting menu. In most cases it's a much better deal than ordering á la carte, and usually is designed to showcase some of the chef's best efforts.

You can save on breakfast if you choose a hotel whose room rates include continental breakfast or, in some cases, a full buffet. Otherwise, look for a coffee shop where you can get a roll or bagel, juice, and beverage for about $3. With careful choices (especially if you opt for soup and salad), it is possible to bring in lunch for $7 to $10. A decent dinner in a nonfranchise restaurant can be found for $20 or less.

Hit **Lou Mitchell's** in the Loop for breakfast (see Chapter 14), and you won't need lunch. Not only is the place a Chicago classic where you can watch the locals, but you'll be well fed for little money. You get free donut holes while you wait in line, and for about $7 you can get a gigantic omelet that will keep you going 'til dinner. (P.S. You also get a bonus: soft serve ice cream in a tiny paper cup when you finish!)

Attractions

Admission fees for museums, observation decks, and other attractions can add up quickly. To figure out how much to budget, refer to the chapters on sightseeing, compile a list of must-see attractions, and total the price of admissions. You can trim this budget and still see a great deal of Chicago — and have a good time — if you can schedule museum visits for the one day a week that most offer free admission. If you're going to hit most of the big museums, then buy a **CityPass,** which can save you about 50%. You can buy the passes online at www. citypass.com or at the Art Institute of Chicago, Sears Tower Skydeck, John G. Shedd Aquarium, Field Museum, Adler Planetarium & Astronomy Museum, or Museum of Science and Industry. Also consider building some of Chicago's many free attractions, such as the **Cultural Center and Mercantile Exchange,** into your sightseeing itinerary.

Shopping

This, of course, is a highly flexible category. Budgeting often involves at least one four-letter word: *sale.* Check the daily newspapers (especially the Sunday editions) for news of sales. To be sure of hitting the city's most spectacular sales, plan to visit in January. And when it comes to Chicago souvenirs, why not be creative? Instead of bringing home over-priced Chicago Cubs jerseys from the souvenir store, you can buy something unique, such as a package of money from your free tour of the **Federal Reserve Bank of Chicago.** The bills are shredded, of course, but it makes a fun gift.

Entertainment

Entertainment is a tough category in which to economize. If you enjoy a cocktail, figure at least $7 to $8 a pop at a downtown bar. If you're headed for a jazz or blues club, allow for a cover charge plus drinks (perhaps with a minimum drink requirement). Some lively neighborhood bars serve reasonably priced drinks. And some entertainment won't cost you a dime, such as noontime **"Under the Picasso" concerts** at Daley Plaza, and free movies at the **Chicago Cultural Center,** located on South Michigan Avenue just north of the Art Institute, and **Oriental Institute Museum** in suburban Hyde Park. In the summer, most music festivals in Grant Park are free and the people-watching alone can keep you entertained all night long. Generally, you can see a show in Chicago for much less than you'd pay on Broadway, and tickets are cheaper still if you take advantage of discounts that are up to 50% the day of the show at **Hot Tix** booths. Locations include: 163 E. Pearson Street (the Chicago Waterworks Visitor Center) on Michigan Avenue; 78 W. Randolph Street in the Loop; and in Tower Records at 214 S. Wabash Avenue (see Chapter 22).

Table 3-1 gives you a glimpse at what things may cost while you're in Chicago.

Table 3-1	What Things Cost
Cab from O'Hare Airport to downtown hotel	$30
Cab from Midway Airport to downtown hotel	$24
Shuttle from O'Hare to downtown hotel	$15.50
Shuttle from Midway to downtown hotel	$11.50
Subway or bus ride	$1.50
Transfer (good for two additional rides)	$0.30
Ticket to John Hancock Center Observatory	$7
Ticket to Sears Tower Skydeck	$6.75
Sightseeing boat tour (2 hours)	$11
Hot dog at Gold Coast Dogs	$2
Dinner for one at Boston Blackie's	$10
Dinner for one at Café Luciano	$20
Steak dinner at The Saloon	$35
Admission to the Art Institute of Chicago	$8
Movie ticket	$8.50–$9.50

Keeping a Lid on Hidden Expenses

Funny how the second you walk out of your hotel room, your wallet can suddenly spring a leak. Big cities have a way of taking a few dollars here, a few dollars there, and before you know it, you're a three-times-a-day regular at the cash machine. Here are some of my tips for keeping (some) cash in your wallet.

Taxes and fees

These expenses aren't usually paid in cash, so you may not take note of them, as you should. When you arrange any commercial transaction — hotel rooms, car rentals, dining — be sure to ask for the total cost as well as the great-sounding price the business quotes you. Read on to see how taxes and fees can expand the price:

- Chicago sales tax is 8.75%. Restaurants in the central part of the city add another 1% tax to your bill.

- Hotel room tax is 3%.

- Many restaurants add a 15 to 18% gratuity to the bill if your party is larger than five people.

Gratuities

The average tip for most service providers, such as waiters and cab drivers, is 15%, rising to 20% for particularly good service. In restaurants, simply doubling the tax results in a 17.5% tip. A 10 to 15% tip is sufficient if you just have a drink at a bar. Bellhops get $1 or $2 a bag, hotel housekeepers should receive at least $1 per person per day, and valet parking and coat-check attendants expect $1 to $2 for their services.

Incidentals

You may not notice the little costs each time they occur, but if you're stopping for coffee twice a day, buying bottled water, or purchasing a second map because you left the first one in your hotel room, you could easily be spending $20 to $30 extra per day without noticing it. Buy water at a drugstore and bring a bottle with you. Make your morning cup of coffee in the hotel room and stop once as a treat. Make some trail mix from nuts and raisins and put it in individual baggies. Be careful not to waste too much on incidentals, and you'll be happier in the end.

Handling Money

With the proliferation of ATMs, it's never a problem to get cash when you're away from home — even from your credit card. But if you're visiting the ATM every day, you might start racking up significant fees. In that case, consider traveler's checks. Here's the lowdown on the pros and cons of each.

Choosing traveler's checks or the green stuff

Traveler's checks are something of an anachronism from the days before the ATM (automated teller machine) made cash accessible at any time. The only sound alternative to traveling with dangerously large amounts of cash, traveler's checks were as reliable as currency. Unlike personal checks or cash, traveler's checks could be replaced if lost or stolen.

These days, traveler's checks seem less necessary because most cities (including Chicago) have 24-hour ATMs that allow travelers to withdraw small amounts of cash as needed, and avoid the risk of carrying a fortune around in an unfamiliar environment. Generally, carrying the smallest amount of cash possible — enough to pay for cabs, tips, and other incidentals — is wise.

Two major ATM networks are **Cirrus** (☎ 800-424-7787 or 800-4CIRRUS) and **Plus** (☎ 800-843-7587). Check the back of your card for the name of your bank's network. Often, you'll find it is linked to at least two or three networks.

Of course, as with anything else, you pay for the convenience of instant cash. Many banks impose a fee ($1, $1.50, or even $2) every time a card is used at an ATM in a different city or bank. If you're withdrawing money every day, you may be better off with traveler's checks — provided that you don't mind showing identification every time you want to cash a check.

You can get traveler's checks at almost any bank. **American Express** offers denominations of $10, $20, $50, $100, $500, and $1,000. You pay a service charge of 1 to 4%. You can also get American Express traveler's checks over the phone by calling ☎ 800-221-7282; by using this number, Amex gold and platinum cardholders are exempt from the 1% fee. AAA members can obtain checks without a fee at most AAA offices.

Visa offers traveler's checks at Citibank locations nationwide, as well as several other banks. The service charge is 1.5 to 2%; checks come in denominations of $20, $50, $100, $500, and $1,000. **MasterCard** also offers traveler's checks. Call ☎ 800-223-9920 for a location near you.

Be vigilant when using ATMs. Whenever possible, choose machines in well-lighted locations where plenty of people are about. And stay alert while processing your request for cash. Robberies (and worse) can and do occur around ATMs.

Using plastic

Invaluable when traveling, credit cards are a safe way to carry money and provide a convenient record of all your expenses. You can also withdraw cash advances from your credit cards at any bank (though you'll start paying hefty interest on the advance the moment you receive the cash, and you won't receive frequent-flier miles on an airline credit card). At most banks, you don't even need to go to a teller; you can get a cash advance at the ATM if you know your personal identification number (PIN). If you forgot your PIN or didn't even know you had one, call the phone number on the back of your credit card and ask the bank to send it to you. It usually takes five to seven business days, though some banks provide the number over the phone if you tell them your mother's maiden name or pass some other security clearance.

Budgeting Tips to Offset Money Madness

Let's say you tallied up your expected expenses, tried to make some trade-offs, and the grand total still seems too high. Now is the time to think about some serious ways to economize, such as

- ✔ **Going in the off-season:** If you can travel during nonpeak months, airline tickets are much cheaper. And during the low season (the depth of winter) you can find hotel prices that are as much as half what they are during peak months.

- ✔ **Traveling on off days of the week:** If you can travel on a Tuesday, Wednesday, or Thursday, you may find cheaper airfares. When you inquire about airfares, ask if you can obtain a lower rate by flying on a different day. Also remember that staying over a Saturday night can cut your airfare by more than half.

- ✔ **Reserving your flight well in advance:** Advance Purchase Excursion (APEX) fares can be a great deal.

- ✔ **Trying a package tour:** For many destinations, one call to a travel agent can net you airfare, hotel, ground transportation, and even some sightseeing, all for much less than if you tried to put the trip together yourself. See the section on package tours in Chapter 5 for specific suggestions.

✔ **Buying a Chicago CityPass:** CityPass includes admission to Adler Planetarium & Astronomy Museum, Art Institute of Chicago, Field Museum, Museum of Science and Industry, John G. Shedd Aquarium, and Sears Tower Skydeck. The adult rate is $30.50, the senior rate (65+) is $25, and the youth rate (3 to 11 years) is $22.75. The value of the passes is $61, so you're saving loads. After you present your CityPass at the first attraction, booklets are valid for nine days. For more on CityPass, see "Estimating the Cost of Your Trip" in this chapter.

✔ **Packing light:** That way, you can carry your own bags and take a bus rather than a cab from the airport.

✔ **Reserving a hotel room with a kitchen:** It may not feel like as much of a vacation if you still have to do your own cooking and dishes, but you save a lot of money by not eating in restaurants three times a day. Even if you only make breakfast and an occasional bag lunch in the kitchen, you still save in the long run. And you won't be shocked by a hefty room-service bill.

✔ **Always asking for discount rates:** Membership in AAA, frequent-flier plans, trade unions, AARP, or other groups may qualify you for discounted rates on car rentals, plane tickets, hotel rooms, even meals. Ask about everything; you may be pleasantly surprised.

✔ **Asking if your kids can stay in your room for no charge:** A room with two double beds usually doesn't cost more than a room with one queen-size bed. And many hotels won't charge you the additional person rate if the additional person is pint-size and related to you. Even if you have to pay $15 or $20 for a rollaway bed, you save hundreds by not taking two rooms.

✔ **Trying expensive restaurants at lunch instead of dinner:** Lunch tabs are usually a fraction of what dinner would cost at most top restaurants, and the menu often boasts many of the same specialties.

✔ **Not renting a car:** Unless you do much traveling to the suburbs and beyond, a car can be a liability in Chicago — an unnecessary cost — especially when you add the high cost of parking. Buses, trains, and cabs can save you big bucks.

✔ **Studying the public transit system and street pattern:** You can find plenty of advice in this book about riding the CTA. Know in advance where taking a bus or train is advisable, and remember that the 30-cent transfer is a great deal. Chicago is a good walking city, and many of the attractions that you want to see can be explored on foot. Be sure to pick up a free public-transit map at any CTA station, download maps from the CTA Web site at www.transitchicago.com, or call (888) YOUR-CTA.

✔ **Taking advantage of the CTA Visitor Pass:** Passes are a good investment for visitors who plan to spend much time sightseeing around the city. Passes can quickly pay for themselves — a one-day pass is $5, a two-day pass is $9, a three-day pass is $12, and a five-day pass is $18.You receive unlimited rides on all CTA buses or trains. To purchase, call (888) YOUR-CTA or buy online at the CTA Store at www.transitchicago.com. Allow ten business days to receive your passes. You can also purchase passes at select museums, tourist attractions, the airports, and Visitor Information Centers. Call (888) YOUR-CTA for locations.

✔ **Skipping the souvenirs:** Your photographs and your memories should be the best mementos of your trip. Keep a journal. Buy a Polaroid I-Zone and decorate the journal with sticker photos. If you're worried about money, you can do without the T-shirts, refrigerator magnets, key chains, salt-and-pepper shakers, and other trinkets.

✔ **Avoiding the hotel minibar:** If you have midnight cravings, stock up on beverages and snacks at a supermarket. Even premium prices at a grocery store are cheaper than the minibar.

✔ **Not paying for amenities that you won't use:** If you don't expect to have time for a swim in the pool or a workout in the health club, choose a hotel that doesn't have (and charge for) those facilities.

✔ **Taking advantage of freebies:** On certain days, some major museums waive admission. Chicago also has many fine free museums, such as the **Museum of Broadcast Communications** and the **Oriental Institute Museum.**

✔ **Not drinking in hotel bars:** The only exceptions are bars such as the Palm Court at the **Drake Hotel** and the Salon in the **Hotel Inter-Continental,** where the price of a drink includes excellent jazz.

✔ **Keeping an eye on the time:** Breakfast specials may end at 10 a.m., the early-bird dinner menu at 6:30 p.m. — just when you realize that you're hungry.

Chapter 4

Planning for Special Travel Needs

• •

In This Chapter

▶ Honing in on special tips for families

▶ Traveling as a senior

▶ Finding the best places for travelers with disabilities

▶ Getting information for gay and lesbian travelers

• •

True, Chicago is a big city — but don't be intimidated. If you have special needs, you may find Chicago is much easier to maneuver in than many other cities its size. Chicago isn't as congested as New York or as sprawling as Los Angeles. The hustle and bustle on the sidewalks isn't so frantic that you have to be on constant alert lest the crowd runs over you. The pace is slightly slower here. The good news for families, seniors, disabled travelers, and gay and lesbian travelers is that Chicago has activities and specialized services for just about anyone.

We Are Family: Traveling with Your Kids

Chicago is friendly to the under-13 set. Stroll along the stretch of North Michigan Avenue known as the Magnificent Mile (between the Chicago River and Oak Street), and you'll be dodging families with kids in tow. Kids love to visit **Niketown** and ogle the Michael Jordan memorabilia. And children enjoy a visit to the three-level **FAO Schwarz** toy store, with its giant waving teddy bear in an upstairs window. **American Girl** is a mecca to moms and daughters laden with the signature, dark-red shopping bags, and many girls bring their American Girl dolls, dressed in their day-in-the-city finest, to buy new outfits for them at the store. (See Chapter 19 for more on Michigan Avenue shopping.) You can also see wide-eyed youngsters peering out of the horse-drawn carriages that clip-clop along Mag Mile and tony Oak Street.

Before leaving on the trip, try to adjust to a new time zone in advance. Put kids to bed half an hour earlier each night for a couple of nights, for example, if Chicago is west, and you'll gain time. Or, if you're traveling east, put them to bed half an hour later. After you arrive, tour the area around your hotel so that you know where to go if you need medical attention, and where to buy necessities, such as diapers, formula, and medicines.

When you're looking for a little open space, try **Navy Pier** (see Chapter 16 for more on this, Chicago's most popular attraction), with its giant Ferris wheel, magic shop, ice rink, speedboat rides, and wonderful children's museum. **Lincoln Park** (see Chapter 16) has a zoo, farm, paddleboats, and kite-flying area. The list is virtually endless.

Kids can take a cruise on a river and lake designed especially for them. During a one-hour excursion, the **Wacky Pirate Cruise** (☎ 312-902-1500) mixes buccaneer antics with low-impact learning about history and ecology. Cruises operate Thursday through Sunday from the Mercury dock at Michigan Avenue and Wacker Drive. The fare is $11 for adults, $6 for children. Well-staged European-style marionette shows take place at a converted grocery store. **Puppet Parlor's** repertoire includes 50 different productions, incorporating such classics as *Hansel and Gretel* and *The Wizard of Oz*. It's at 1922 W. Montrose Avenue (☎ 773-774-2919). No. 78 Buses stop close to the door.

Choosing kid-friendly sleeps and eats

Your choice of hotel probably isn't only a matter of budget. Choosing a hotel may also depend on the ages of the children who accompany you, and — face it — how well they generally behave. Nothing is more embarrassing to parents, or annoying to other guests, than noisy children running amok through a quiet hotel. Find out if the hotel has a pool (many downtown Chicago hotels don't have one); ask if a video arcade is nearby (River North, for example, is near ESPN Zone, an attraction devoted to sports entertainment and dining, along with dozens of games — see Chapter 27). Some hotels may even offer play areas and programs. Make sure to ask about these services when you call for a reservation.

After you are in a hotel room, childproof it. Bring a nightlight, remove small objects from children's reach, watch cords, remove breakable items, and be careful around pools.

Chicago is well endowed with kid-friendly restaurants. There are the obvious choices, such as the **Hard Rock Café** (see Chapter 20), **Rainforest Café**, 605 N. Clark Street at Ohio Street, ☎ 312-787-1501, and **Ed**

Debevic's, 640 N. Wells Street at Ontario Street, ☎ **312-664-1707.** Then there is **Harry Caray's** restaurant (see Chapter 14) and its showcases packed with memorabilia. Youngsters also have fun in the wacky New Orleans–style environment of **Heaven on Seven** (see Chapter 14). At the original on Wabash Avenue, kids can skip the exotic gumbo and jambalaya and order a hamburger and chocolate pudding from a plain, old luncheon-counter menu. Kids may also get a kick out of **Billy Goat Tavern** (see Chapter 15), the real-life inspiration for the famous *Saturday Night Live* skit that features John Belushi and "cheeburger, cheeburger, chip, chip, Pepsi."

Parents and children should go over safety issues before leaving. Make sure to create a plan so children know what to do if they get lost. Put your child's name and some kind of identification inside a pocket or on the inside of a jacket.

Getting kids involved in trip planning

One of the best ways to get kids excited about an upcoming trip is to include them in the trip planning activities. By doing so, not only will you be getting their input on what sights to see and do, but you'll also be heading off any "I-didn't-know-we-were-going-to-do-that" arguments.

Share material from this book with your kids — go through the attractions listed in Chapters 16 and 17. Tell your kids that they can go deep into a coal mine or climb into a captured World War II U-boat at the **Museum of Science and Industry.** Ask them if they'd like to ride a high-speed elevator to the top of one of the world's tallest buildings or go to a McDonald's that's also a rock 'n' roll museum (see Chapter 20). Children who are involved in planning the trip have a vested interest in getting maximum enjoyment from it.

Hiring a baby sitter

Adults who want to schedule some adults-only R&R shouldn't leave finding a babysitter to chance. Make prior arrangements — giving you time to check references — and add to your travel budget the amount that you'll need to cover babysitting. Expect to pay around $13 an hour, with a four-hour minimum. Most agencies require at least 48 hours' notice. For recommendations, check with the concierge or front desk at your hotel. Many hotels maintain lists of reputable babysitting agencies. Otherwise, call the American Registry for Nurses & Sitters, Inc. (☎ **800-240-1820** or 773-248-8100). Many hotels use this state-licensed agency, whose caregivers are subjected to background checks, asked to furnish multiple references, and trained in infant and child CPR.

Flying with kids and staying sane

How do you avoid becoming the person everyone hopes won't sit next to them on the airplane to Chicago? Here are some tips for traveling with little ones:

✔ Call ahead to order special kids' meals and confirm seating arrangements. Some airlines offer bassinets for babies traveling in the bulkhead row — parents may prefer the bulkhead row, with the extra room for changing and letting toddlers sit on the floor. Other parents prefer regular seating for the extra under-chair baggage storage.

✔ When you're packing, try not to overpack, but definitely do *not* underpack on necessities. If you know the number of diapers your child wears, add an extra three. Bring a changing pad in case the tiny restroom has no pull-out changing table. One coloring book — not five — is sufficient. Two toy cars — not the entire collection of 30 — is all you want to carry. Pick one stuffed animal and one blanket. Remember, you're not relocating your entire nursery.

✔ Use a stroller in the airport for nonwalking or barely walking children and check it at the gate. The stroller will be waiting for you right outside of the plane when you deplane.

For every age, special techniques can help you get there with fewer hassles, less crying, and less stress for mom and dad.

✔ **Newborn:** Children under the age of 3 months are the easiest for parents to travel by air with. But keep in mind: Stick to your regular feeding schedule and fill your diaper bag with necessities. Bottle feeding babies at an airplane's take-off and departure help them relieve the pressure in their ears.

✔ **3 to 6 months:** A great time to travel! Remember, feeding schedules and sleep schedules should be kept consistent to avoid baby "meltdowns." Bring a diaper bag with all the necessities and toys that are bright, squeaky, or chewy. Pack crackers and bottles.

✔ **6 to 12 months:** A harder time to travel because babies are starting to crawl and do not like to stay seated for long stretches of time. (Many parents wind up carrying and walking children back and forth down the narrow aisle of a plane!) Bring a diaper bag, new toys, and books. Adhere to feeding and sleep schedules.

✔ **12 to 18 months:** Hard for travel also because of the transition from baby to toddler. Try to tire toddlers out by walking (or even running!) through the airport. Walk back and forth on moving sidewalks and look for the airport childrens play area. (At O'Hare, head for Kids on the Fly, an exhibit in Terminal 2 set up by the Chicago Children's Museum. Kids can run, jump, and tumble on airplane-themed slides and obstacles.) Pack books, balls for the airport (deflatable if possible), goldfish crackers or other small snacks, sippy cups or bottles, a favorite blanket or stuffed animal, diapers, wipes, and a change of clothes.

✔ **18 to 24 months:** Children are starting to test their limits. They may find the most inopportune times to sit down and refuse to get up, such as during the announcement of final boarding. Be patient.

✔ **24 months to preschool age:** Travel gets easier as you can start to reason with the child. Children this age like activities and are interested in new surroundings. To avoid accidents, make frequent trips to the restroom. Pack extra clothes, new toys and books, a favorite blankie or stuffed animal, snacks, and sippy cups.

✔ **Older kids:** Have children pack their own carry-ons with special items that can hold their interest. Pack a goodie bag with a walkman and tapes of music or stories, game-boys, books, paper and pencils/crayons, sticker books, small plastic toys, bubbles for the airport, and a magnetic drawing board and games.

Surviving the great American road trip with kids

Traveling by car presents a whole different set of challenges: Those long stretches of open road; the kids asking, "Are we there yet?" for the 10,000th time. Here are tips for keeping kids entertained — and adults sane — on the Great American Road Trip.

✔ Pack a cooler with extra drinks, snacks, fruits, and veggies.

✔ Get out every few hours for air, bathroom breaks, and diaper changes.

✔ Try to stick to a regular feeding schedule and sleep schedule.

✔ Look at your map for interesting things to visit on the way to your destination.

✔ Have a really long arm to reach all the toys and bottles that have fallen out of your children's hands for the tenth time in the last 5 minutes and have rolled under your seat. A flashlight can help locate those items that roll under the seat.

✔ Use window shades for the sun.

✔ Bring audio tapes of stories or children's songs. You may even put a small television/VCR in the back between the two front seats so the kids can watch videos. Because a video lasts 30 minutes to an hour, it's a great help for long stretches with nothing to do.

✔ Carry a first-aid kit, box of wipes for clean-ups, roll of paper towels, extra blankets, plastic bags for motion sickness, change of clothes, and cellphone in case of road emergencies.

Traveling Tips for Seniors

Chicago provides many resources for seniors, including discounted admission for museums and other attractions, and for citywide programs. For museum and attraction discounts, call the individual locations, which are listed in Chapter 16 and Chapter 17. For information on discounts on citywide programs, call the Chicago Park District at ☎ 312-742-PLAY.

Seniors can get a reduced fare of 75 cents per ride and 15 cents for transfers on the Chicago Transit Authority, which runs both the El (elevated) trains, city buses, Metra trains, and PACE buses. Unfortunately, this is probably not a realistic option for a short-term visitor, as it takes at least a week to receive your discounted pass. You must apply in person at the Regional Transit Authority offices at 181 W. Madison (☎ 312-917-0734). Bring a driver's license or passport. Explain that you are from out of town so you receive the pass within a week (otherwise, processing takes three weeks). Also, seniors should be aware that many of the El stations are difficult to navigate because of stairs — or out-of-order escalators. Call the CTA at ☎ 312-836-7000 for a list of El stations that have elevators. If mobility is an issue, you may be better off riding the CTA buses. Be sure to ask about discounts whenever you book a hotel or flight, or purchase a ticket to an event or attraction.

Turning 50 entitles you to join the **AARP** (American Association of Retired Persons), 601 E. Street NW, Washington, DC 20049 (☎ 800-424-3410; Internet: www.aarp.org), which offers discounts on car rentals, accommodations, airfares, and sightseeing. It's open to anyone 50 or older, retired or not, and makes a good introduction to the world of travel bargains available to seniors.

Mature Outlook, P.O. Box 9390, Des Moines, IA 50306-9519 (☎ 800-336-6330; Fax: 847-286-5024; Internet: www.sears.com), is a similar organization, offering discounts on lodging, dining, and car rentals. The $20 annual membership fee also gets you $100 in Sears coupons and a bimonthly magazine. Membership is open to all Sears customers 18 and over, but the primary focus is on the 50-and-over market.

Most of the major domestic airlines, including American, Continental, TWA, United, and US Airways, offer discount programs for senior travelers — be sure to ask whenever you book a flight.

Mature Traveler Newsletter, which covers senior citizen travel, is a valuable resource. A subscription ($30 a year) is available from GEM Publishing Group, Box 50400, Reno, NV 89513-0400 (☎ 800-460-6676). GEM also publishes **The Mature Traveler's Book of Deals,** a collection of more than 1,000 senior discounts on airlines, lodging, tours, and attractions around the country; it costs $9.95.

Another helpful publication is **101 Tips for the Mature Traveler,** available from Grand Circle Travel, 347 Congress St., Suite 3A, Boston, MA 02210 (☎ **800-221-2610** or 617-350-7500; Fax: 617-350-6206; Internet: www.gct.com).

If you want to travel and have a learning experience simultaneously, you might check out **Elderhostel, Inc.,** 75 Federal St., Boston, MA 02110 (☎ **877-426-8056;** Internet: www.elderhostel.org), which organizes programs for those 60 and older and frequently offers programs in Chicago. For example, Elderhostel might offer a program at the School of the Art Institute, located on South Michigan Avenue. Participants generally live in a college dorm, take courses at the college in the morning, and explore the city in the afternoon.

Hundreds of other travel agencies specialize in vacations for seniors. But beware: Many of them are of the tour bus variety, with free trips thrown in for those who organize groups of 20 or more. Seniors seeking more independent travel should probably consult a regular travel agent.

Advice for Travelers with Disabilities

People with disabilities have more travel choices and resources than ever before. A good place to start is **A World of Options,** a 658-page book of resources for disabled travelers that covers everything from biking trips to scuba outfitters. It costs $45 and is available from **Mobility International USA,** P.O. Box 10767, Eugene, OR 97440 (☎ **541-343-1284,** voice and TTY; Internet: www.miusa.org). For more personal assistance, call the Travel Information Service at ☎ **215-456-9603** or 215-456-9602 (for TTY).

Visitors to Chicago find that most attractions are completely accessible. Public museums such as the **Art Institute, Adler Planetarium & Astronomy Museum,** and the **Field Museum** observe Americans with Disabilities Act (ADA) guidelines, as do the **Sears Tower Skydeck** and **Chicago Board of Trade.** Pedestrians with disabilities find that downtown Chicago is pretty good about curb cuts and other basics. Unfortunately, the Windy City's notoriously unpredictable weather often compels Chicagoans and visitors to catch a ride. Despite efforts in recent years to improve its accessibility, the public transportation system lags behind those of other urban centers in meeting ADA standards. Although the Regional Transit Authority — which runs Chicago's CTA, PACE (the suburban bus line; ☎ **847-364-PACE;** Internet: www.pacebus.com), and Metra (the commuter rail line to the suburbs; ☎ **312-322-6777;** Internet: www.metrarail.com) — claims to be accessible, a trip can be arduous and frustrating. As any Chicagoan with a disability can tell you, accessible bus service is spotty. Only one in five buses is equipped with a lift, and fewer than half of all train stations have elevators. Riders with disabilities need to plan public-transit trips carefully. Call the CTA (☎ **312-836-7000**) for information about accessible bus routes and train stations.

By calling in advance, people with disabilities can receive an application for a pass that allows holders to ride for half price. Apply early because the CTA asks applicants to allow three weeks for delivery. Call **Paratransit** (☎ 312-432-7025) for a description of special services and taxi access programs available in the city.

Travelers with disabilities may also want to consider joining a tour that caters specifically to them. One of the best operators is **Flying Wheels Travel,** 143 West Bridge, P.O. Box 382, Owatonna, MN 55060 (☎ 800-535-6790; Internet: www.flyingwheels.com). It offers escorted tours and cruises, as well as private tours in minivans with lifts. Another good company is **FEDCAP Rehabilitation Services,** 211 W. 14th Street, New York, NY 10011. Call ☎ 212-727-4200 or Fax 212-721-4374 for information about membership and summer tours.

Many of the major car rental companies offer hand-controlled cars for disabled drivers. **Avis** can provide a vehicle at any of its locations in the United States with 48-hour advance notice; **Hertz** requires 24 to 72 hours' notice at most of its locations. **Wheelchair Getaways** (☎ 800-873-4973; Internet: www.blvd.com/wg.htm) rents specialized vans with wheelchair lifts and other features for the disabled in more than 100 cities across the United States.

Vision-impaired travelers can contact the **American Foundation for the Blind,** 11 Penn Plaza, Suite 300, New York, NY 10001 (☎ 800-232-5463), for information on traveling with seeing-eye dogs.

Here are some useful sources to assist with your travel planning:

- **Mayor's Office for People with Disabilities:** ☎ 312-744-MOPD.
- **Chicago Office of Tourism TTY number:** ☎ 312-744-2947.
- **Access-Able Travel Source,** P.O. Box 1796, Wheat Ridge, CO 80034 (☎ 303-232-2979; Internet: www.access-able.com).
- **Society for the Advancement of Travel for the Handicapped,** 347 Fifth Ave., Suite 610, New York, NY 10016 (☎ 212-447-0027; Fax: 212-725-8253; Internet: www.sath.org).

Out and About: Tips for Gay and Lesbian Travelers

The **Gay and Lesbian Pride Week Planning Committee** (☎ 773-348-8243) is an excellent resource for imparting information about restaurants, bars, and neighborhoods where the gay and lesbian communities gather. Another good source of information is the **Gay & Lesbian Chamber of Commerce** (☎ 888-GL-CHAMBER; Internet:

www.glchamber.org). The **Windy City Times** and other gay publications are available at many shops and bars in neighborhoods with large gay and lesbian populations. The Web site **Outchicago** (www.outchicago.org) is a community-based gay, lesbian, bisexual, and transgender resources page.

Among Chicago's gay-friendly neighborhoods are Lakeview, New Town, and Andersonville. Lakeview's main thoroughfare is Belmont, between Broadway and Sheffield. Lakeview is where you find the city's primary gay and lesbian bookstore, **People Like Us,** 1115 W. Belmont Avenue (☎ **773-248-6363**). Within Lakeview is a smaller neighborhood known as New Town (or, colloquially, Boys' Town). Andersonville centers around the half-dozen or so blocks of North Clark Street immediately north of Foster Avenue.

Part II
Ironing Out the Details

The 5th Wave   By Rich Tennant

"Welcome to our nonstop flight to Chicago. Will you be sitting in first class or a bit nearer the stockyards?"

In this part . . .

*B*y nature, I'm a planner. In fact, for me, planning the trip is half the fun. Ah, the possibilities! If you're a planner too, you'll love this part of the book. I debate the pros and cons of your travel options, including travel agents, package tours, and even airports. You'll be able to contemplate what you want in a hotel, whether or not to rent a car, and how to reserve theater or sightseeing tickets. And — planner's nirvana — I discuss what to pack and how to travel in comfort.

Chapter 5

Getting to Chicago

· ·

In This Chapter

▶ Working with travel agents

▶ Taking a package tour

▶ Getting a great deal on a flight

▶ Discovering other ways to get here from there

· ·

*W*hen you talk about getting to Chicago, most people get here via O'Hare Airport — *the* passageway to Chicago. If most travelers to Chicago are going to share a single experience, that experience is O'Hare International Airport. No longer the world's busiest airport, O'Hare still reigns as a major hub for making connections worldwide (mostly because American and United Airlines use O'Hare as their hub). O'Hare boasts its own police force, ZIP Code, medical center, cemetery, and chapel. Some 72.6 million people passed through O'Hare in 1999. If you come to Chicago, you may well be one of them. (For more on surviving O'Hare, see Chapter 10.)

Don't forget Chicago's smaller airport, Midway, which is bursting at the seams, and the ongoing political debate over where and whether to build a third airport. Air service into the Windy City offers a wide range of choices, from major domestic and international carriers to small, no-frills airlines. Not that many airlines have an overabundance of frills these days!

All roads lead to Chicago: The city is a major hub in the interstate highway system and remains connected to the rest of North America with passenger rail service. In the center of the country, Chicago is an easy destination by train, plane, or automobile.

Using a Travel Agent: Your Friend or Foe?

A good travel agent is like a good auto technician or a good plumber: hard to find, but invaluable after you find the right person. The best way to find a good travel agent is the same way that you find a good plumber — word of mouth.

Any decent travel agent can help you find a bargain airfare, hotel, or rental car. But a *good* travel agent can stop you from ruining your vacation by trying to save a few bucks. The best agents can

- Tell you how much time to budget in a destination;
- Help you find a cheap flight that doesn't require you to change planes in every other city;
- Get you a better hotel room than you can find on your own;
- Arrange for a competitively priced rental car; and
- Recommend restaurants.

Travel agents are worth using when you've never been to Chicago before, and the agent has. Agents are worth using when they've had many clients go to Chicago before and have first-hand feedback on hotels and attractions. And they're useful if you have many complicated details to sort out — visas, connecting flights, multiple hotel bookings, and theater tickets to reserve.

Travel agents work on commission. The good news? You don't pay the commission. Airlines, hotels, and tour companies do. The bad news? Unscrupulous travel agents try to persuade you to book vacations that generate the most money in commissions. In recent years, some airlines and resorts limited or eliminated travel agent commissions. More and more agents began charging a fee for their services. As the practice spreads, the best agents will be even harder to find.

To make sure you get the most out of your travel agent, do a little homework. Pick out some accommodations and attractions you think you'd like. Check airline prices on the Web (see "Winning the Airfare Wars" later in this chapter for more information on how to do that) so you can do a little prodding. Then take your copy of *Chicago For Dummies* and your Web information to the travel agent and ask him to make the arrangements for you. Because travel agents have access to more resources than even the most complete Web travel site, they should be able to get you a better price than you could get by yourself. And they can issue your tickets and vouchers. If they can't get you into the hotel of your choice, they can recommend an alternative, and you can look for an objective review in your guidebook right then and there.

Joining an Escorted Tour or Traveling on Your Own

Do you prefer to let a bus driver worry about traffic while you sit in comfort and listen to a tour guide explain everything you see? Or do you prefer going out and following your nose, even if you don't catch all the highlights? Do you like to have many events planned for each day, or would you rather improvise? The answers to these questions can determine whether you should choose the guided tour or travel à la carte.

Some people love escorted tours and having structure in their vacation. Tours free travelers from spending too much time behind the wheel, take care of all the details, and tell you what to expect at each attraction. You know your costs up front, and surprises are minimal. Escorted tours can take you to the maximum number of sights in the minimum amount of time with the least amount of hassle.

Other people need more freedom and spontaneity. Free spirits usually can't stand guided tours. If you're in this category, then you prefer to discover a destination and don't mind getting caught in a thunderstorm without an umbrella or finding that a recommended restaurant is no longer in business. For free spirits, that's just the adventure of travel.

If you're a structure-loving traveler, your local travel agent can help you hook up with a guided tour of Chicago. An example is a package available from **City Escapes** that is booked exclusively through travel agencies. The package includes a two-night stay at the **Chicago Hilton & Towers** and a three-hour tour of the Loop, lakefront, South Side, Hyde Park, Michigan Avenue and the Gold Coast. Total cost? Only $209 per person (based on double occupancy).

If you choose an escorted tour, ask some questions before you buy:

- ✔ **What is the cancellation policy?** Do you have to put a deposit down? Can the company cancel the trip if it doesn't get enough people? How late can you cancel if you're unable to go? When do you pay? Do you get a refund if you cancel? What if the company cancels?

- ✔ **How jam-packed is the schedule?** Do they try to fit 25 hours into a 24-hour day, or is there ample time for relaxing by the pool or shopping? If you don't enjoy getting up at 7 a.m. every day and not returning to your hotel until 6 or 7 p.m., certain escorted tours may not be for you.

- ✔ **How big is the group?** The smaller the group, the more flexibility and the less time you'll spend waiting for people to get on and off the bus. Tour operators may be evasive about group size — in fact, they may not know the exact size of the group until everybody has made reservations. You should be able to get a rough estimate. Some tours have a minimum group size and may be canceled if they don't attract enough people.

✔ **What's included?** Don't assume anything. You may have to pay to get yourself to and from the airport. Or a box lunch may be included in an excursion, but drinks may cost extra. Or beer may be included but wine may not.

✔ **How much choice do you have?** Can you opt out of certain activities, or does the bus leave once a day, with no exceptions? Are all your meals planned in advance? Can you choose your entree at dinner, or does everybody get chicken cordon bleu?

If you choose an escorted tour, consider buying trip-cancellation insurance, especially if the tour operator asks for payment up front. But don't buy insurance from the tour operator! If the operator doesn't fulfill its obligation to provide you with the vacation you paid for, there's no reason to think it will fulfill its insurance obligations, either. Get travel insurance through an independent agency. See the section on travel insurance in Chapter 9.

Tallying the Pros and Cons of Package Tours

Package tours are a way of buying your airfare and accommodations at the same time — saving you a ton of money. In many cases, a package that includes airfare, hotel, and transportation to and from the airport costs you less than the hotel alone would if you booked it yourself. That's because packages are sold in bulk to tour operators, who resell them to the public.

Packages vary greatly. Some offer a better class of hotels than others. Some offer the same hotels for lower prices. Some offer flights on scheduled airlines and others book charter flights. In some packages, your choices of accommodations and travel days may be limited. Others let you choose between escorted vacations and independent vacations; others allow you to add on just a few excursions or escorted day trips (also at prices lower than if you booked them yourself) without booking an entirely escorted tour.

Each destination usually has one or two packagers that are better than the rest because they buy in even bigger bulk. The time you spend shopping around will be well rewarded.

The best place to start looking is the travel section of your local news-paper. **Liberty Travel** (☎ 888-271-1584; Internet: www.libertytravel.com) is a major tour packager, particularly if you're located in the Northeast, and frequently places full-page ads in Sunday travel sections. Don't expect high-quality service, but considering the bargain prices, it's easy to forgive the lack of frills. Another resource for packages is **American Express Vacations** (☎ 800-241-1700).

Although for many destinations, the airlines are active tour packagers, Chicago has pretty slim pickings. At press time, only **American Airlines Flyaway Vacations** (☎ 800-321-2121) was offering packages. However, with Chicago's increasing popularity, that could change. Try **Delta Dream Vacations** (☎ 800-872-7786) or **United Airlines Vacations** (☎ 800-351-4200) to see if they have added Chicago offerings.

Package prices vary based on availability, dates, and hotel properties. For example, at press time **American Airlines Flyaway Vacations** offered an off-season rate that included round-trip airfare from New York and five nights at Chicago's Hotel Allegro for $882 per person. From Los Angeles, the price was $875 per person. A rental car added $174 to $331.

Winning the Airfare Wars

Airfares demonstrate capitalism at work — in fact, passengers in the same cabin on the same airplane rarely pay the same fare. Rather, they each pay what the market will bear. Business travelers pay for the flexi-bility to buy their tickets at the last minute, change their itinerary, or get home before the weekend. Passengers who can book their tickets far in advance, stay over Saturday night, or are willing to travel on a Tuesday, Wednesday, or Thursday pay the least, usually a fraction of the full fare. On most flights, even the shortest hops, the full fare can reach $1,000 or more, but a 7-day or 14-day advance purchase ticket may only cost $200 or $300. It pays to plan ahead.

Airlines periodically hold sales, particularly on their most popular routes. These fares have advance purchase requirements and date-of-travel restrictions, but you can't beat the price: usually no more than $400 for a cross-country flight. Keep your eyes open for these sales as you're planning your vacation, then pounce. Sales tend to take place in seasons of low-travel volume. You'll almost never see a sale around the peak summer vacation months of July and August, or around Thanks-giving or Christmas, when people need to fly, regardless of the fare.

Consolidators, also known as bucket shops, are good places to check for the lowest fares. Their prices are much better than the fares you could get yourself, and are often even lower than those your travel agent can get. You see their ads in the small boxes at the bottom of the page in your Sunday travel section. Some of the most reliable consolidators include **1-800-FLY-4-LESS** or **1-800-FLY-CHEAP.** Another good choice, **Council Travel** (☎ **800-226-8624**) caters especially to young travelers, but its prices are available to people of all ages.

Surfing the Web to fly the skies

Several Web sites have made a name by providing truly good deals on airfare. Web sites can act as virtual travel agents. A few of the better-respected ones are **Travelocity** (Internet: www.travelocity.com), **Microsoft Expedia** (Internet: www.expedia.com), and **Yahoo!** (Internet: http://travel.yahoo.com/travel). Each has its own quirks, but they all provide variations of the same service. Just enter the dates you want to fly and the cities you want to visit, and the computer looks for the lowest fares. Expedia's site will e-mail you the best airfare deal once a week if you choose. Travelocity uses the SABRE computer reservations system that most travel agents use, and has a "Last Minute Deals" database that advertises really cheap fares for those who can get away at a moment's notice.

Great last-minute deals are also available directly from the airlines themselves through a free e-mail service called **E-savers.** Each week, the airline sends you a list of discounted flights, usually leaving the upcoming Friday or Saturday, and returning the following Monday or Tuesday. You can go to each airline's Web site, which allows you to familiarize yourself with their routes and policies. Or, if you want to be more efficient, **Epicurious Travel** (Internet: http://travel.epicurious.com/travel) e-mails your information directly to each airline after you fill out the individual forms. See the appendix for a complete list of airline Web sites.

Good news: Average airfares are lower into Chicago than into Anaheim, Boston, Dallas, Los Angeles, New York, Orlando, San Francisco, and Washington, D.C. And, average ground transportation costs are lower in Chicago than in Anaheim, New York, San Francisco, and Washington, D.C.

Deciding which airport to fly into

Because Chicago has two airports, O'Hare and Midway, you have more options and chances to lock in a lower fare. Midway is a little closer to downtown Chicago and a slightly cheaper ride by cab or shuttle. Because of varying traffic and road conditions, it's difficult to predict which airport offers a faster ride into the central city and back. Under optimum conditions, the journey between either airport and the city takes around 40 minutes — perhaps even a little less. During rush hour, the same journey can take one to two hours. Both airports are served by CTA trains, which are oblivious to traffic conditions.

Booking well to make your flight more pleasant

Seats in the front row of each airplane cabin, called the bulkhead seats, have the most legroom. However, because there's no seat in front of you, there's no place to put your carry-on luggage, except in the overhead bin. The front row also may not be the best place to see the in-flight movie. Airlines have started putting passengers with young children in the bulkhead row so the kids can sleep on the floor — a terrific option for families.

Emergency-exit row seats also have extra legroom and are assigned at the airport, usually on a first-come, first-served basis. When you check in, ask whether you can be seated in one of these rows. You must be at least 15 years old. In the unlikely event of an emergency, you'll be expected to open the emergency exit door and help direct traffic.

Preparing for a long flight

Want to turn a potentially long flight into a pleasant experience? Those who travel often know, like the Girl Scouts, that it pays to be prepared.

✔ **Wear comfortable clothes.** The days of getting dressed up in a coat and tie to ride an airplane went out with Nehru jackets and poodle skirts. And dress in layers; the supposedly controlled climate in airplane cabins is anything but predictable. You'll be glad to have a sweater or jacket that you can put on or take off as the temperature on board dictates.

✔ **Bring some toiletries aboard on long flights.** Take a travel-size bottle of moisturizer or lotion to refresh your face and hands at the end of the flight. If you're taking an overnight flight (also known as *the red-eye*), don't forget to pack a toothbrush. If you wear contact lenses, take them out before you board, or at least bring eye drops.

✔ **Bring a bottle of water.** The water can serve as an antidote to the Sahara-like cabin conditions.

✔ **Bring entertainment.** If you're flying with kids, don't forget chewing gum (for ear pressure problems), a deck of cards or favorite toys to keep them entertained, extra bottles or pacifiers, and a stocked diaper bag. (See Chapter 4 for special tips for families.)

You may want to ask for a seat toward the front of the plane. The minute the captain turns off the *Fasten Seat Belts* sign after landing, people jump up out of their seats, and then stand around for five or ten minutes while the ground crew puts the gangway in place. The closer to the front of the plane you are, the less hurry-up-and-waiting you'll have to do. Why do you think they put first class in the front?

If you have special dietary needs, be sure to order a special meal. Most airlines offer vegetarian meals, macrobiotic meals, kosher meals, meals for the lactose intolerant, and other special preparations. Ask when you make your reservation if the airline can accommodate your dietary restrictions. Some people without special needs order special meals anyway, because they are made to order, unlike the mass-produced dinners served to the rest of the passengers.

Getting Here by Car

Chicago is easier to get to by road for more people than any other city in the nation. Within a 300-mile radius of the heart of the city (or a comfortable one-day drive) lies one of the most densely populated areas of the country. The Windy City also is a major intersection on the interstate highway system. East-west highways I-80, I-88, I-90, and I-94 run through Chicago. The city is connected to north-south interstate routes I-55, I-57, and I-65.

If you are traveling as part of a group, you may save money by driving — although driving through Chicago may be hard on your nerves. However, do budget the cost of parking, which can run as high as $30 a day in downtown Chicago.

 If you plan to drive to Chicago but don't intend to use your car while in the city, consider perimeter parking lots. For bargain perimeter parking, check with the Chicago Transit Authority (CTA). For only $1.50, **CTA's Park and Ride lots,** located near many train line terminals, allow visitors to stow their cars for up to 24 hours. For long-term parking, CTA's Cumberland lot, ten minutes east of O'Hare, costs $1.75 for every 12 hours. (Call ☎ **800-YOUR-CTA** for locations and restrictions.)

Also consider parking in a lot located within walking distance of the Loop. **Standard Parking** has several lots, including two on Michigan Avenue, at the corners of Van Buren and Wacker. It charges $16 a day. **System Parking,** 631 W. Kinzie at Jefferson, charges $18 a day.

Traffic on our expressways can be brutal. Avoid arriving or departing during the heart of morning and evening rush hours (about 6:45 to 9:30 a.m. and 3:45 to 6:30 p.m.). All the major arteries, including the Dan Ryan, Eisenhower, Kennedy, and Stevenson Expressways, can gridlock. Don't be lured into rush-hour driving by the prospect of *reverse commuting* (coming into town in the afternoon and leaving in the morning). It's a myth. Once upon a time, traffic may have been lighter outbound in the morning and inbound in the evening — but today, that has been negated by the large number of people who live in Chicago and commute to jobs in the suburbs.

Getting Here by Train

Unlike many cities, Chicago has not been abandoned by the railroad. Thanks to Amtrak, trains still pull into and out of Union Station (at Adams and Canal Streets, just west of the Loop across the Chicago River). A number of the trains carry the nostalgic names of legendary trains of the past, such as Broadway Limited, the Capital, the Empire Builder, California Zephyr, and Southwest Chief. For example, the City of New Orleans leaves each evening for an overnight trip to the Big Easy.

For fares, schedules, and reservations, check with a travel agent or call Amtrak (☎ **800-USA-RAIL** or 312-558-1075; Internet: www.amtrak.com).

Chapter 6

Deciding Where to Stay

In This Chapter

▶ Choosing the right neighborhood

▶ Selecting the hotel or bed-and-breakfast that's right for you

▶ Special strategies for families and travelers with disabilities

*Y*ou may be the kind of traveler who considers a hotel room as simply a place to sleep and stow your luggage. In that case, you don't need two pools, a half-dozen restaurants and lounges, a glittering grand ballroom, and a health club. Nor do you need to shell out big bucks for the overhead associated with those nonessential extras.

On the other hand, if you enjoy taking full advantage of a hotel's amenities — afternoon tea with harp music, a day at the spa, arcades packed with shops — you can find hotels with those, too. But you usually pay extra for the privilege. You can even enjoy the best of both worlds by staying at a no-frills property and visiting other hotels to enjoy tea and jazz, and relax with a cocktail by the fountain in a fancy lobby piano bar. In Chicago, you can find rooms at both ends of the price and comfort spectrum, and a great many in between.

Because you need a place in Chicago to hang your hat and rest your head, the most important part of planning a trip is nailing down where you're going to stay. Four crucial factors come into play: price, location, roominess, and amenities.

Start by figuring out your travel budget (for tips, see Chapter 3). Determine how much you have to spend on a hotel. Now, you can decide *where* to spend it.

Discovering the Value of Your Dollar

Hotel reviews in Chapter 8 designate one to four dollar signs, which
represent price categories. All prices are for a double room, excluding
taxes:

✔ **$ ($75 to $125):** To find hotels in this category, you usually need
  to look beyond the city core. Some of our recommendations, for
  example, are in Near North neighborhoods, a $5 to $8 cab ride
  from the Magnificent Mile and a little farther from the Loop. You
  can also take cheap, reliable public transportation. In most cases,
  a hotel in this category won't offer conveniences, such as room
  service and valet parking, or such amenities as robes, hair dryers,
  and imported toiletries. Often, these hotels occupy older buildings, which in some cases have been charmingly restored. You
  usually get a private bathroom, but make sure to ask.

✔ **$$ ($125 to $200):** Moving up one level, overall quality begins to
  improve markedly. The rooms are larger, the decor less Spartan,
  and the degree of comfort higher. The hotel may have a fitness
  center or offer privileges (free or discounted) at a nearby gym.
  Many hotels in this price range offer complimentary breakfast,
  evening cocktails, or both — which can result in added savings.

✔ **$$$ ($200 to $300):** At this price you can expect and should
  receive many extra comforts. Look for attentive service (although
  usually with a hand out) and a full range of amenities — from
  overpriced minibars and French-milled soap to terry robes and
  dual-extension phones. You're likely to find marble (and sometimes a mini TV) in the bathrooms, and workstations with plenty
  of desk space and computer ports. Usually, an in-house business
  center and health facility, a concierge ready to help with dinner
  suggestions and reservations as well as tour and theater tickets,
  and a lounge are all available to you.

✔ **$$$$ ($300 to and up):** The crème de la crème. Accommodations
  feature designer furnishings and fabrics, comfortable seating, and
  work areas. Bathrooms often have dual sinks. You'll find coffeemakers and bottled water in the room and a mint or chocolate
  truffle on the pillow after evening turndown service (a perk that
  has disappeared from all but these top-echelon properties). You
  should feel pampered at one of these hotels. After all, you're
  paying for it.

Location, Location, Location!

Chicago's core is relatively compact. If shopping along North Michigan
Avenue is the primary objective of your visit, then you want to stay at a
hotel along or near the **Magnificent Mile.** Then again, you could stay in

the **north Loop** and walk or take the 151 Bus north along Michigan Avenue. Likewise, if you have business in the financial district along South LaSalle Street, a hotel in the **Gold Coast** won't put you too terribly far away. Public transportation is plentiful; cab rides around the downtown core are relatively swift. Streets don't gridlock as often or intensely as they do in, say, New York or London. However, beware of the bridges: In the summer, traffic can be held up for ten minutes as bridges are raised to allow private yachts egress along the Chicago River.

Nonetheless, finding convenient lodgings in the neighborhood where you spend the bulk of your time is obviously helpful; near your hotel is where you can enjoy taking a stroll the most. Having a couple of first-rate restaurants nearby, or a museum or gallery or two makes sense. To make this easy, in Chapter 8 I recommend hotels and list the neighborhood beneath its name; check these locations against the maps to see where the hotel is in relation to the attractions you want to see.

My listings concentrate on the Magnificent Mile, Gold Coast, Loop, and Streeterville. Other neighborhoods you might consider include

- ✔ **Near North:** This part of town is away from the mainstream, but near interesting neighborhoods and Lincoln Park.

- ✔ **River East:** Fairly close to the Loop and the Magnificent Mile, but River East has a tendency to empty out after dark.

- ✔ **River North:** An immensely popular tourist area, with the inevitable sprinkling of tourist traps, but River North also has some lower-priced hotels.

Magnificent Mile

If your mission is shopping, shops aplenty stretch along North Michigan Avenue from the Michigan Avenue Bridge across the Chicago River and north to Oak Street. This retail bounty includes four high-rise malls, upscale shops along Oak Street just west of Michigan Avenue, and bargain stores (see Chapter 19 for shopping). You can also find many of Chicago's priciest hotels, along with a bargain or two.

In a nutshell:

- ✔ Chicago's premier shopping is right here.

- ✔ Many major bus routes include North Michigan Avenue.

- ✔ Convenient access to the numerous boat trips and bus tours that begin at the Michigan Avenue Bridge are available.

But . . .

✔ You can often find yourself in jostling crowds.

✔ Traffic can get snarled during evening rush hour.

✔ Michigan Avenue can be noisy, with horns, sirens, and crews of street musicians banging on empty containers.

Gold Coast

This high-rent district is immediately north of the Magnificent Mile. You can find yourself within an easy walk of the lakefront and not too far from prime shopping. Hotels here are near the nightlife of Rush and Division Streets.

In a nutshell:

✔ It has easy access to Oak Street Beach, lakefront walking, and biking.

✔ It's an ideal spot for sampling nightlife.

✔ Many quiet residential backwaters with leafy streets and handsome brownstones adorn the district.

But . . .

✔ The Rush-and-Division-Streets area is packed with out-of-towners in search of action.

✔ Noisy bars and clubs can be a turn-off.

✔ Many of the high-profile restaurants have long waits, even with reservations.

The Loop

The traditional heart of Chicago, its downtown, is home to one of Chicago's most famous thoroughfares — "State Street, that great street." State Street has been through some hard times in recent years. Many big department stores closed and shoppers fled to the suburbs or stayed on the Magnificent Mile. Chicago has made a commitment to the Loop and the downtown core is beginning to rebound. New hotels are opening, shops are returning, and a revitalized theater district is drawing evening crowds. Loop hotels, in fierce competition with those north of the river, offer some attractive rates and package deals.

In a nutshell:

> ✔ This are has a good mix of theater, shops, and hotels.
>
> ✔ The Loop offers an unbeatable location for doing business in the LaSalle Street corridor.
>
> ✔ It's location offers easy access to the Art Institute, Cultural Center, Mercantile Exchange, Board of Trade, and the best of Chicago's public art.

But . . .

> ✔ The Loop is still relatively empty after dark — although it is bouncing back from its once-comatose state.
>
> ✔ Despite civic improvements, State Street still looks a bit dowdy in parts.
>
> ✔ Expect to be solicited by panhandlers.

Streeterville

A handy location combined with an influx of residents into converted loft spaces and high-rises makes Streeterville a great place to stay. Streeterville contains many good restaurants and faces Lake Michigan. Despite its proximity to high-end real estate, Streeterville offers a number of modestly priced hotel options.

In a nutshell:

> ✔ An incredibly diverse selection of restaurants to fit a wide range of budgets can be found here.
>
> ✔ It's close to the attractions of enormously popular Navy Pier.
>
> ✔ This area is adjacent to the prime shopping of the Magnificent Mile.

But . . .

> ✔ Many of the streets are narrow and easily blocked.
>
> ✔ Navy Pier can be a zoo, with boisterous crowds and difficult parking that spill into the east side of the neighborhood.
>
> ✔ Though the neighborhood has become gentrified, a few sleazy pockets remain in its southeast corner.

Finding the Type of Place That Suits Your Style

When it comes to accommodations, Chicago *does* have something for everyone in terms of style, size, price, and location. You can suit both your personality and your pocketbook.

If you want luxury, you can find it at properties, such as the **Four Seasons** or the **Fairmont.** If you're interested in combining history and upscale accommodations, look no farther than **The Drake** and the venerable **Hotel Inter-Continental Chicago.**

If you're comfortable with chains — or have a favorite — you can find the **Hilton, Hyatt, Sheraton, Radisson, Embassy Suites,** and others. Even **Motel 6** is represented with a classy hotel by that chain's no-frills standards, close to the heart of the Magnificent Mile. If you prefer a suite and want to pay a little less for it, travel less than five miles north to the **City Suites Hotel.**

For European-style digs, look into accommodations at small boutique hotels, such as the **Whitehall, Raphael,** and **Tremont.** Or try the **Hotel Allegro** and **Hotel Burnham,** stylish hostelries converted from tired old buildings in Chicago's revitalized Loop.

Bed and breakfasts

On the surface, it may seem that Chicago doesn't have the wealth of bed-and-breakfasts that you're likely to find in a resort area. Nonetheless the bed-and-breakfast inn is a viable option for Windy City visitors. Many Chicagoans are delighted to share their homes by providing hosted bed-and-breakfast accommodations in the European style.

You'll also find a wide range of unhosted bed-and-breakfast accommodations. These consist of a suite or an apartment that you have all to yourself — a home away from home. Sometimes the host is there to greet you, and leaves you with a set of keys and breakfast items in the refrigerator.

One of the best ways to locate either kind of bed-and-breakfast accommodation is through a reservation service, such as the **Heritage Bed & Breakfast Registry of Chicago** (☎ **800-431-5546** or 312-857-0800; Internet: www.heritageregistry.com). For example, $115 a night gets you a hosted guest room on the top floor of a 34-story Gold Coast high rise. For $135 a night, you can unpack in a one-bedroom apartment in the Printers Row neighborhood of the south Loop.

Another registry is **Bed & Breakfast/Chicago, Inc.** (☎ **800-375-7084** or 773-248-0005; Internet: www.chicago-bed-breakfast.com), which represents about 70 establishments, all within the city, from the south Loop to the Lakeview neighborhood (with a few farther north). These are a mix of hosted guest rooms in houses and apartments, and unhosted accommodations in self-contained apartments. The registry also owns and operates a bed-and-breakfast in the Lincoln Park area, with five rooms in the main house plus three apartments in a carriage house.

Hotels for families with kids

Families won't want to pick a hotel where peace and quiet are valued commodities, and parents find themselves cringing at every sound a child makes. When you have kids in tow, bigger often is better, in terms of hotel size. You may want to avoid small boutique hotels, where a certain "hush" pervades the atmosphere, and go for the hustle and bustle of a 2,000-room behemoth, such as the Hyatt Regency, where the noise of kids will blend right in. If you opt for an all-suite hotel, you have an extra room with a separate TV. That may help adults and youngsters better coexist in the relative confinement of a hotel. All-suites hotels typically also have kitchens with refrigerators and microwaves (for economizing with a dine-in meal) and a dining area.

Location can also be an important consideration for families traveling with children. Pick a property in River North and you're just steps away from such kid-pleasers as Rock-N-Roll McDonald's, Hard Rock Café, and Rainforest Cafe.

Hotels for travelers with disabilities

Finding wheelchair-accessible accommodations in Chicago can be something of a challenge. Many of the city's storied hotels are old and not designed for guests with disabilities. Many older hotels (such as the **Hotel Inter-Continental Chicago**) have been renovated to include a small number of wheelchair-accessible guest rooms. The problem is that the tiered floors and sweeping staircases that made these hostelries famous aren't tailored to meet the needs of patrons with mobility impairments. The best bets for travelers with disabilities are the newer hotels, such as the **Courtyard by Marriott.** Unfortunately, accessibility and low cost are not typically found together. Most inexpensive digs don't offer wheelchair-accessible rooms at all. Remember to be explicit about your needs when you make your reservation.

Chapter 7

Off the Rack: Booking Your Room

In This Chapter

▶ Beating the rack rates

▶ Landing a room without a reservation

*T*ravelers accustomed to spending big bucks for a hotel room the size of a broom closet are in for a pleasant surprise in Chicago. Certainly, the city has glitzy upscale hotels that ask $300 to $400 a night. But enough variety also exists to satisfy just about every taste and pocketbook. How do you get the most hotel for your money? This chapter lets you in on the city's best secrets.

Wrestling Rack Rates

Rack rate is the maximum amount that a hotel charges for a room. Rack rate is what you are charged if you walk in off the street and ask for a room for the night. You sometimes see the rate printed on the fire/ emergency exit diagrams posted on the back of your door.

Hotels are happy to charge you the rack rate, but you don't have to pay it! Hardly anybody does. Perhaps the best way to avoid paying the rack rate is surprisingly simple: Just ask for a cheaper or discounted rate. You may be pleasantly surprised.

Price depends on many factors, not the least of which is how you make your reservation. A travel agent may be able to negotiate a better deal with certain hotels than you could get by yourself. (That's because the hotel gives the agent a discount in exchange for steering business toward that hotel.) Reserving a room through the hotel's toll-free number may result in a lower rate than if you called the hotel directly. On the other hand, the central reservations number may not know about discounts at specific locations. Local franchises may offer a special group rate for a wedding or family reunion, but may neglect to tell the central booking line. Your best bet is to call both the local number and the central number and see which gives you a better deal.

Beating hotels at their own game

If you're smart, you never have to pay the rack rate. Here are some ways to get better deals — much, much better:

- ✔ **Weekend packages:** A decade ago, Chicago emptied out on weekends and most hotels offered attractive packages as inducements. With Chicago's emergence as a world-class tourist destination, hotels became busier on weekends. Still, business hotels in particular offer discounts to keep volume up. If your first-choice hotel doesn't, try another. Many deals are advertised in the travel section of major newspapers.

- ✔ **Holiday rates:** If you travel during a holiday, ask if the hotel offers a special rate.

- ✔ **Corporate discounts:** Many hotels, especially branches of the large chains, offer corporate rates. Find out whether these rates apply to you.

- ✔ **Senior and AARP rates:** If you're over 64 (or over 49 and an AARP member), you may be eligible for a senior discount.

- ✔ **All-in-one/inclusive packages:** Packages often include lodging, meals, transportation, sightseeing, or some combination. If you were planning to do these things anyway, a package may save you money.

- ✔ **Family rates or packages:** Deals for families vary from hotel to hotel and from weekday to weekend. Ask what's available and be sure to find out *exactly* how many kids at what age can stay free.

Getting the best room

Somebody has to get the best room in the house, and that somebody may as well be you! Here are a couple of tips for landing a room you'll love.

- ✔ **Always ask for a corner room.** They're usually larger, quieter, and closer to the elevator. Corner rooms often have more windows and light than standard rooms and they don't always cost more.

- ✔ **Ask if the hotel is renovating.** If it is, request a room away from the renovation work.

- ✔ **Pick your smoking preference.** Many hotels now offer nonsmoking rooms; if smoke bothers you, by all means ask for one.

- ✔ **Inquire about the location of the hotel's restaurants, bars, and discos.** These places can be a source of irritating noise.

If you aren't happy with your room when you arrive, talk to the front desk staff. If they have another room, they should be happy to accommodate you, within reason.

When is the off-season?

Chicago is becoming a year-round, seven-days-a-week destination. If you are looking for bargains on hotel rooms and budget-stretching lodging packages, there are seasonal bargains. From January through March, you usually find some good buys — providing a mega-convention is not swallowing up huge numbers of hotel rooms. Late fall, when the weather can often be extremely mild and pleasant, is also a time to snare good room rates, particularly on weekends when the business travelers have left.

Check for weekend packages at hotels in the heart of the Loop that probably have the need to fill space vacated by weekday business clients. Also watch for holiday packages that throw in shopping vouchers, as well as "romantic getaway" deals that incorporate perks, such as champagne brunches and carriage rides.

It all adds up: Taxes and other charges

That $99 room you booked will run closer to $115 by the time you add hotel-motel tax, which is 14.9% in Chicago (compared to, say, 10% in Springfield, Illinois). And that's before you even make a phone call! Often a service charge of up to $1 or more is added to your bill, even for local calls and long-distance calls that you charge to your phone card. Then there is the cost of overnight parking, which can run as high as $20 a day at downtown hotels.

If you snack in your room, stock up on munchies and bottled water, juice, and soda at a nearby convenience store or supermarket. If you crack open those tempting goodies in the minibar, you can pay $4.50 for a can of Coke and a similarly inflated amount for a couple of cookies or a package of peanuts.

You can offset added expenses by checking into a hotel that includes extras, such as breakfast and evening cocktails, in its room rates. **Embassy Suites,** for example, includes a hot breakfast buffet and an evening cocktail gathering. Two Kimpton hotels, **Monaco** and **Allegro,** offer guests wine each evening. A trio of Near North hotels (**Surf, City Suites,** and **Park Brompton**) serves breakfast featuring legendary Ann Sather cinnamon rolls.

Booking a Room at the Last Minute

If you show up in Chicago without a reservation, shame on you! But there are still options other than seeking a room at the YMCA or sleeping on a park bench. If a hotel says it is full, try again a little after 6 p.m., when rooms that are reserved, but not secured with a credit card, go back into the pool.

When booking a room at the last minute, you can usually negotiate a better rate if you phone (even from around the corner) rather than showing up at the desk with luggage in hand and a look of desperation in your eyes.

Another option is to check with reservation bureaus, which buy up rooms in bulk and resell them. They usually offer sizeable discounts off rack rates (but remember that the rack rate is the maximum price a hotel charges). Often, these bureaus are able to find space when other hotels in the city are sold out. So you may luck out with one of the following:

- ✔ **Accommodations Express** (☎ 800-950-4685). Eighty percent of Chicago hotels participate in this service; discounts are 10 to 40% off rack rates.

- ✔ **Hotel Reservations Network** (☎ 800-96-HOTEL; Internet: www. hoteldiscount.com). Forty hotels participate; 20 to 50% off rack rates.

- ✔ **Quikbook** (☎ 800-789-9887; Internet: www.quikbook.com). Twenty hotels participate; 10 to 40% off rack rates.

Chapter 8

Chicago's Best Hotels

· ·

In This Chapter

▶ Scoping out the best hotels in the city

▶ Knowing your options if you can't get your main pick

▶ Finding the best accommodations for young children

▶ Indexing hotels by location and price

· ·

Chicago is on a hotel-building binge. Lest you think I exaggerate, ten new properties will open their doors in the downtown area by 2003, with 3,317 new rooms. And that's in addition to the 12 new hotels with 3,660 rooms built since 1998! Existing hotels are polishing themselves up, too, in an effort to keep up with the Joneses (skip ahead to the map showing "Central Chicago Accommodations"). Some 13 hotels will have finished renovations by June 2001. What does this mean to the intrepid traveler — other than construction cranes on the horizon and scaffolding on the streets? In the past, conventioneers told tales of sleeping on cots in hotel hallways because there was literally no room at the inn. Now travelers have more lodging options than ever before (see the "New or improved: Chicago hotels worth noting" sidebar for more details). Increased competition means wriggle room on prices is more likely, too — especially if hoteliers find they have *over*built. (Keep your fingers crossed!)

 When a major convention is in town, look out. Getting a room can be difficult, so book early. To find out if an upcoming convention coincides with the dates you plan to visit Chicago, call the Chicago Convention & Tourism Bureau at ☎ 312-567-8500, or check their Web site at www. chicago.il.org (click on "For Meeting Planners").

To help you choose the right place for you, this chapter begins with an alphabetical list of my favorite hotels with reviews providing all that you need to know to make an informed decision. Later in the chapter, see the list of runner-up hotels, an index of hotels by price and neighborhood, and the "Near North and River North Accommodations" map.

Each listing includes a price rating between one and four dollar signs. The number of dollar signs reflects the average of a hotel's high- and low-end *rack rates* (the maximum rate a hotel charges for a room) for a standard double room for one night, excluding taxes. The more dollar signs under the name, the more you pay. It runs like this:

$ = $75 to $125

$$ = $125 to $200

$$$ = $200 to $300

$$$$ = $300 and up

Where rack rates hovered within about $10 of an even hundred (say, $210), I assigned the lower designation (in this case, $$) because that represents the bulk of the rooms available. But remember that rack rates are negotiable. Prices are subject to availability and vary seasonally (the lower rates tend to be offered January through March). When you call, you should always ask if the hotel has any special offers or discounts.

This icon designates hotels that are especially good for families. The hotel may offer play areas, kids' menus in the restaurants, or swimming pools, and all have an open, nonstuffy atmosphere that makes families feel at ease. (Nothing stresses a parent more than Junior knocking over a multi-thousand-dollar Chinese vase in the lobby, right?) Bear in mind that every hotel in town accommodates children's needs; a listing without this symbol does not mean "kid unfriendly." Most properties allow kids to stay free with their parents, but the cut-off age varies. Always ask when you're booking.

Chicago Hotels A to Z

Belden-Stratford Hotel

$$ Lincoln Park

This northside hotel is Chicago's best-kept lodging secret. This gracious apartment building offers 25 hotel rooms. The rooms are large, the doorman greets you as if you were a resident, and Chicago's finest French restaurant, **Ambria** (see Chapter 14), is located off the lobby. If you prefer a neighborhood atmosphere and doing as the natives do, this is the place for you. Be sure to ask for a room with a view of Lincoln Park, so that you can watch runners pass and couples stroll as you sip your coffee on a Saturday morning.

2300 N. Lincoln Park West (just north of Fullerton Avenue). ☎ *800-800-6261 or 773-281-2900. CTA: Bus 151 stops at Fullerton in Lincoln Park. Walk west to the hotel. Parking: Valet (with in-out privileges) $25. Rack rates: $139 double. AE, DC, DISC, MC, V.*

Beware, the one-armed man

Movie fans who stay at the Chicago Hilton and Towers should keep their eyes peeled for the one-armed man. Numerous scenes for the movie *The Fugitive* were filmed in the hotel and its Conrad Hilton Suite. For those who really want to stay in style, the suite comes with its own butler, maid, limousine service, and helipad — and goes for $4,000 a night.

Chicago Hilton and Towers

$$ South Loop

Big is not necessarily a bad thing in a hotel. Sprawling over several city blocks, this massive hotel, with 1,545 rooms, is a virtual city within a city. Public areas abound with shops, bars, restaurants, and artwork. Rooms feature cherry-wood furnishings. Many rooms have two bathrooms. The rooms feel spacious, thanks to high ceilings. A club level in the tower provides a higher degree of pampering and has its own check-in. Kitty O'Shea's pub recruits chefs, bartenders, and wait staff under an Irish government exchange program. Buckingham's, the hotel's fine-dining restaurant, specializes in steaks and is known for an outstanding selection of single-malt Scotch. This hotel is ideally located for sightseers — across from Grant Park, five blocks south of the Art Institute of Chicago and a 20-minute walk from the Field Museum of Natural History, John G. Shedd Aquarium, and Adler Planetarium & Astronomy Museum.

720 S. Michigan Ave. (at Balbo Drive) ☎ *800-HILTONS or 312-922-4400. Internet:* www.hilton-chicago.com. *CTA: Buses stop in front of the hotel. Orange, purple, or brown line El to Van Buren (at State Street), then walk 2 blocks west and 3 blocks south. Parking: Valet $22; self $21. Rack rates: $185–$345 double. AE, CB, DC, DISC, JCB, MC, V.*

Chicago Marriott Downtown

$$$ Magnificent Mile

You can't go wrong at the Marriott, located in the heart of the Magnificent Mile near the new North Bridge shopping and entertainment complex. Exceptionally fine rooms of above-average size are more than comfortable. Concierge floors are available for a bit more money. An indoor pool and sun deck, health club, and basketball courts round out the amenities. Although large, at 1,176 rooms, you feel at home here. And, you can go play at nearby DisneyQuest and ESPN Zone and shop 'til you drop at the Nordstrom's mall.

540 North Michigan Ave. (at Grand Avenue). ☎ *800-228-9290 or 312-836-0100. Internet:* www.marriotthotels.com. *CTA: Buses stop in front of the hotel. Parking: Valet (with in-out privileges) $29. Rack rates: $209 double. AE, DC, DISC, JCB, MC, V.*

Central Chicago Accommodations

Belden-Stratford **1**
Best Western River
  North Hotel **20**
Chicago Hilton
  & Towers **38**
Chicago Marriott
  Downtown **23**
City Suites Hotel **2**
Claridge **4**
Courtyard
  by Marriott **24**
The Crowne Plaza Chicago–
  The Silversmith **36**
Doubletree Guest
  Suites **12**
The Drake **6**
Embassy Suites **17**
Fairmont Hotel **33**
Four Seasons Hotel **9**
Hampton Inn &
  Suites **25**
Hilton Garden Inn **21**
Homewood Suites **22**
Hotel Allegro **34**
Hotel Burnham **35**
Hotel Inter-Continental
  Chicago **26**
Hotel Monaco **32**
House of Blues Hotel **27**
Hyatt on Printers
  Row **37**
Hyatt Regency Chicago **29**
Lenox Suites Hotel **19**
Motel 6 **18**
Omni Ambassador
  East **3**

Ⓜ **Subway/El stop**
For stops in the Loop, see
the "Downtown El &
Subway Stations" map
on the Cheat Sheet.

1/4 mi
0.25 km

Lake Michigan

*See also "Near North &
River North Accommodations" map*

E. Delaware Pl.
N. DeWitt Pl.
E. Chestnut St.
E. Pearson
E. Superior
E. Huron St.
E. Erie St.

P.F.C.
Milton Lee
Olive III Park

E. Watton
N. Senaca St.
E. Chicago Ave.
N. Fairbanks Ct.
N.St. Clair
E. Ontario

E. Oak St.
N. Michigan Ave.
Bellevue Pl.
N. Rush St.
N. Wabash Ave.
N. State St.
N. Dearborn St.
N. Clark St.

N. Lake Shore Dr.
N. Astor St.
Goethe St.
E. Elm St.

LINCOLN PARK
LaSalle Dr.
North Blvd.

W. Schiller St.

N. Clark St.
N. Wells St.
Goethe St.
N. Scott St.
W. Elm St.
N. LaSalle St.
Locust St.
N. Chicago Ave.
W. Superior St.
W. Huron St.
W. Erie St.
W. Ontario St.

Lincoln Ave.
N. Eugenie St.
N. Park Ave.
N. Sedgwick St.
N. Franklin St.
N. Orleans St.
Seward Park

Armitage Ave.
W. Wisconsin St.
W. Menomonee St.
N. Hudson Ave.
Cleveland Ave.
W. Blackhawk St.
W. Division St.
Oak St.
N. Sedgwick St.
N. Hudson Ave.

N. Mohawk St.
N. Larrabee St.
N. Howe St.
Orchard St.
N. Burling St.
N. Dayton
N. Fremont
W. Willow St.
W. North Ave.
N. Clybourn Ave.
N. Halsted St.
N. Dayton St.
N. Crosby St.
N. Kingsbury St.
N. Larrabee St.
N. Halsted St.
W. Chicago Ave.

W. Wisconsin St.
N. Bissell St.
N. Sheffield Ave.
Hooker St.
Hickory Ave.
N. Branch St.
Ogden Ave.
N. Milwaukee Ave.

Chicago River

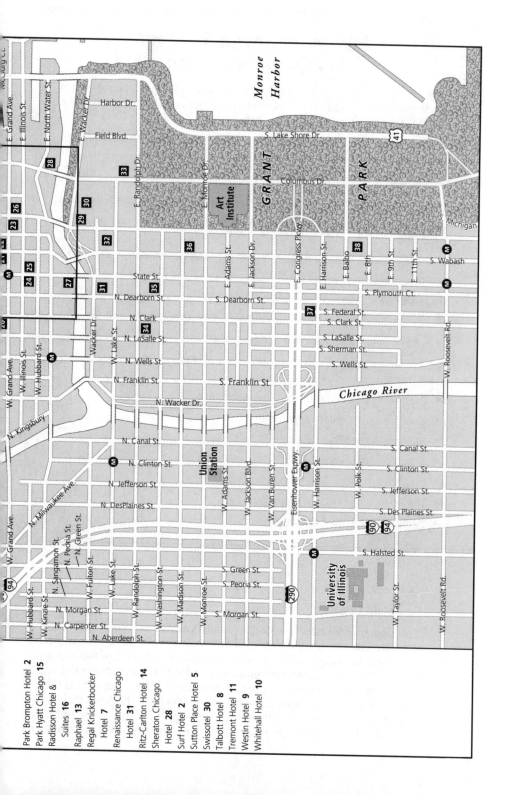

Park Brompton Hotel **2**
Park Hyatt Chicago **15**
Radisson Hotel &
    Suites **16**
Raphael **13**
Regal Knickerbocker
    Hotel **7**
Renaissance Chicago
    Hotel **31**
Ritz-Carlton Hotel **14**
Sheraton Chicago
    Hotel **28**
Surf Hotel **2**
Sutton Place Hotel **5**
Swissotel **30**
Talbott Hotel **8**
Tremont Hotel **11**
Westin Hotel **9**
Whitehall Hotel **10**

New or improved: Chicago hotels worth noting

In the next three years, visitors will have a host of new hotels to choose from in downtown Chicago. If you're planning a future visit, you may want to check out the following (listed in order of completion dates):

- Le Meridien Hotel, 520 N. Michigan Avenue, 311 rooms, completion in April 2001
- Fairfield Inn, 216 E. Ontario Street, 189 rooms, completion in April 2001
- Embassy Suites, 350 E. Illinois Street, 456 rooms, completion in April 2001
- Peninsula Hotel, 730 N. Michigan Avenue, 340 rooms, completion in June 2001
- Baymont Inn and Suites, at Rush and Ontario Streets, 250 rooms, completion in 2002
- Amerisuites, at Kinzie and State Streets, 275 rooms, completion in 2002
- Renaissance by Marriott, 601 N. Dearborn, 314 rooms, completion in 2002
- Hotel Sofitel, Chestnut and Wabash Streets, 415 rooms, completion in 2002
- Marriott Suites, Randolph and State Streets, 357 rooms, completion in July 2003
- Hilton Suites, Fairbanks and Grand Streets, 410 rooms, completion in 2003

And if you're booking one of these hotels, you may ask for one of their recently renovated rooms:

- Doubletree Guest Suites, 198 E. Delaware Place
- Embassy Suites, 600 N. State Street
- Fairmont Hotel, 200 N. Columbus Drive
- Hotel InterContinental, 505 N. Michigan Avenue
- Quality Inn Chicago Downtown, 1 S. Halsted Street
- The Drake Hotel, 140 E. Walton Place
- Whitehall Hotel, 105 E. Delaware Place

Claridge

$$ Gold Coast

This decent, cost-effective lodging makes you feel as if you're staying at an intimate European-style hotel. All 162 rooms are basic but comfortable, decorated in Art Deco style; three of the six suites have wood-burning fireplaces. Best yet, they were renovated in 1998. Rooms above the eighth floor offer superior views of the tree-lined street. One complaint is the limited capacity of the small, slow elevators, which can be a hassle — allow extra time to reach the lobby in the morning and before going out in the evening. Claridge isn't as luxurious as the boutique hotels along the

Magnificent Mile, such as the Tremont Hotel and the Whitehall Hotel — nor is it as pricey. But your vacation dollars stretch even farther here with extras, such as the continental breakfast, newspapers, and limo service (to destinations within a 2-mile radius of the hotel).

1244 N. Dearborn Parkway (one block north of Division Street). ☎ 800-245-1258 or 312-787-4980. Internet: www.claridgehotel.com. *CTA: Buses stop on State Street, 1 block east. El: Red line to Clark/Division. Parking: Valet (with in-out privileges) $25. Rack rates: $150–195 double. Rates include continental breakfast. AE, DC, DISC, JCB, MC, V.*

Courtyard by Marriott Chicago Downtown

$$ River North

This chain offers good deals in the heart of River North, one of Chicago's flashiest tourist areas. Here you're just a short walk from the shops of Michigan Avenue, the Loop, and River North's main strip. Rooms have large desks and two-line phones. Coffee and newspapers (included in the room rate) are available in the lobby, and the hotel has an exercise room, pool, and sun deck. Best yet, you're close to numerous restaurants, the legendary jazz club Andy's (see Chapter 24), and a number of galleries and antique shops.

30 E. Hubbard St. (at State Street). ☎ 800-321-2211 or 312-329-2500. CTA: Red line El to Grand (at State Street), then walk 2 blocks south. Parking: Valet (with in-out privileges) $21; self $17. Rack rates: $139–$199 double. AE, DC, DISC, MC, V.

The Crowne Plaza Chicago/The Silversmith

$$$ Loop

Frank Lloyd Wright would probably be delighted with this smart hotel — there are enough Wright influences to satisfy even his enormous ego. Opened in 1998 as a hotel, the distinctive dark green building was created in 1897 to house silversmiths and jewelers and is a National Historic Landmark. It contains eight floors of guest units (143 rooms) and no two rooms on any floor are alike. Rooms are decorated in Arts and Crafts and Prairie School style, with original 12-foot ceilings, 10-foot windows draped in velvety curtains, and red oak furniture. Desks are designed to accommodate computers. Armoires contain built-in televisions, refrigerators, and CD players. Many rooms have cushioned window seats. Oversize bathrooms have granite countertops and tile-and-granite floors. Adjoining is a branch of Ada's, an upscale delicatessen that stays open until midnight.

10 S. Wabash Ave. (at Madison Street) ☎ 800-2CROWNE or 312-372-7696. CTA: Orange, brown, or green line El to Madison/Wabash, then walk ½ block south, or red line to Washington/State. Parking: Valet (with in-out privileges) $21. Rack rates: $229–$329 double. AE, DC, DISC, MC, V.

You're in good company at the Coq d'Or

Marilyn Monroe, Joe DiMaggio, Jack Benny, and Vince Lombardi carved their initials into the tiny wooden bar of the Cape Cod Room. Management once announced plans to replace the bar, causing such a furor among patrons that it was left in place. Introduce yourself to manager Patrick Bredin, another Drake institution, and take time for a bowl of signature Bookbinder's red snapper soup or oysters at the raw bar.

DoubleTree Guest Suites

$$$ Streeterville

Laid-back comfort and casual attitude characterize DoubleTree Guest Suites, tucked into an elegant street in Streeterville, just a couple blocks east of Michigan Avenue. You're only feet from The Drake, but you have a warm, inviting, immaculate room, plus a separate living room and bedroom and a deluxe bathroom. Park Bistro provides fine dining for adults, while kids will feel welcome at Mrs. Park's tavern, an American bistro. A pool on the 30th floor is surrounded in glass, a great place to watch the fireworks at Navy Pier. The small but very adequate workout room will keep you fit after that Park Bistro meal. Service is gracious but not stuffy. A step up in elegance from other all-suite hotels, you'll be comfortable here, and happily esconced in one of the best neighborhoods in Chicago.

198 E. Delaware Place (at Mies Van Der Rohe Street). ☎ *800-222-TREE* or *312-664-1100. Internet:* www.doubletreehotels.com. *CTA: Red line El to Grand (at State Street). Parking: Valet (with in-out privileges) $23.50. Rack rates: $265 double suite. Rates include full breakfast and evening cocktails. AE, CB, DC, DISC, JCB, MC, V.*

The Drake

$$$$ Magnificent Mile

Staying here is civilization at its finest! This grande dame of Chicago hotels still displays gracious style and boundless charm. Rooms have high ceilings, polished woodwork, marble bathrooms, and every amenity you'd expect, from terry robes to fresh fruit and Swiss chocolates at turndown. Elevators even have velvet seats. Coffee lounges on each floor offer lake views. Besides being a great place to stay, The Drake is a great place to play. A shopping arcade is ideal for browsing. And, there's the Cape Cod Room, a Chicago institution for seafood since 1933. The Coq d'Or piano bar (see Chapter 24) is known for well-made, four-ounce martinis. At the Palm Court, afternoon tea is served around a marble fountain with a harpist accompanying your finger-sandwich eating. A jazz trio plays on weekends.

Near North and River North Accommodations

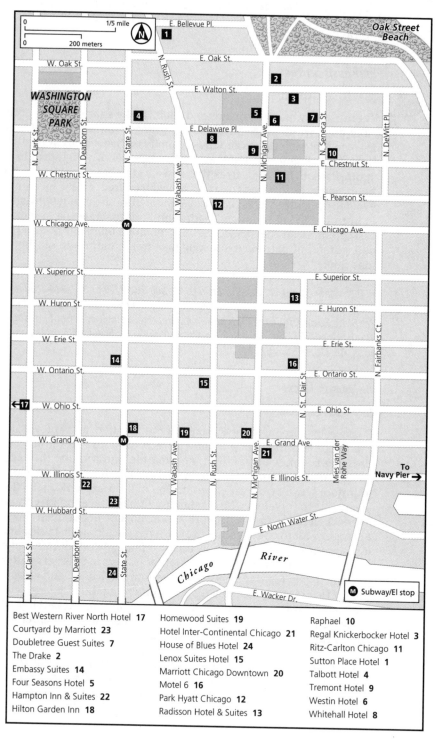

Best Western River North Hotel **17**
Courtyard by Marriott **23**
Doubletree Guest Suites **7**
The Drake **2**
Embassy Suites **14**
Four Seasons Hotel **5**
Hampton Inn & Suites **22**
Hilton Garden Inn **18**

Homewood Suites **19**
Hotel Inter-Continental Chicago **21**
House of Blues Hotel **24**
Lenox Suites Hotel **15**
Marriott Chicago Downtown **20**
Motel 6 **16**
Park Hyatt Chicago **12**
Radisson Hotel & Suites **13**

Raphael **10**
Regal Knickerbocker Hotel **3**
Ritz-Carlton Chicago **11**
Sutton Place Hotel **1**
Talbott Hotel **4**
Tremont Hotel **9**
Westin Hotel **6**
Whitehall Hotel **8**

140 E. Walton Place (at Michigan Avenue). ☎ *800-55-DRAKE or 312-787-2200. CTA: Buses stop on Michigan Avenue, ½ block west. El red line to Chicago/State. Parking: Valet (with in-out privileges) $25. Rack rates: $305–$375 double. AE, CB, DC, DISC, JCB, MC, V.*

Embassy Suites

$$ River North

There's plenty of room for kids and adults in the spacious units at this all-suite hotel with a huge atrium and gushing waterfall. Youngsters enjoy in-room Nintendo games and the proximity to Planet Hollywood, the Hard Rock Café, Rainforest Café, and other kid-friendly, high-profile dining spots. Parents like the extras that make a stay here easy on the pocketbook, such as cooked-to-order breakfasts free every morning, and evening cocktails. Suites have well-equipped kitchens and television sets in both the living room and bedroom. Papagus Taverna, a faux Greek restaurant, is on the street level. A common complaint of hotel guests and restaurant patrons is the long hike to the bathroom on the mezzanine floor.

600 N. State St. (at W. Ontario Street). ☎ *800-362-2779 or 312-943-3800. Internet:* www.embassy-suites.com/es/chi-downtown. *CTA: Red line El to Grand (at State Street), then walk 1 block south. Parking: Valet (with in-out privileges) $28. Rack rates: $169–$379 double suite. Rates include full breakfast and evening cocktails. AE, DC, DISC, JCB, MC, V.*

Fairmont Hotel

$$$ River East

Businessmen frequent the Fairmont for its location, a few blocks north of the Loop, and the exceptionally large rooms. Your room may have a dressing room, walk-in closet, and marble bathroom with a separate shower, enclosed toilet, telephone, and mini-TV. Rooms are no more than four doors away from an elevator. One unit on each of the 37 floors is accessible to travelers with disabilities. Public spaces, clad with marble, are decked out with fine artwork and arrangements of fresh flowers. At Primavera Ristorante, young professional singers wait tables and perform opera, operetta, and show tunes — fun but a bit touristy. Adjoining is a lively sports bar. In the sunken lobby, waiters in tails serve afternoon tea. The highly regarded Entre Nous restaurant is quiet and elegant, and the Art Deco Metropole lounge is building a reputation for jazz. An underground walkway leads fitness buffs to "Mount Chicago," a 110-foot-high climbing wall in the well-equipped Athletic Club Illinois Center — hotel guests can use the facilities for a $10 fee.

200 N. Columbus Dr. (at Lake Street). ☎ *800-527-4727 or 312-565-8000. Internet:* www.fairmont.com. *CTA: Buses stop on Michigan Avenue, 2 blocks west. Brown, orange, or green El lines to Randolph. Parking: Valet (with in-out privileges) $28. Rack rates: $279–$329 double. AE, CB, DC, DISC, JCB, MC, V.*

Four Seasons Hotel

$$$$ Magnificent Mile

In many cities, the local Four Seasons hotel is the best. In Chicago, our Four Seasons Hotel is not only the best in the city — it's the second-best hotel in the country. *Condé Nast Traveler* readers named it the No. 2 hotel in North America in the 2000 Readers' Choice Awards. Spacious guest rooms are packed with extras and served by twice-daily maid service (including delivery of a carafe of water at turndown). The hotel's attractive public areas are lavishly appointed with Italian marble, crystal, intricate wood-work, and plush carpeting. Chandeliers are as common as light bulbs at Motel 6. Connected to the hotel are the 70 shops of 900 North Michigan Avenue, the Magnificent Mile's most upscale mall, otherwise known as the Bloomingdale's mall. Still, you may never venture beyond the hotel's seventh-floor lobby, which holds the Seasons lounge and restaurant. The lounge offers afternoon tea and views of the Magnificent Mile. The restaurant features cutting-edge American cuisine. The hotel's clublike bar, just off the lobby, accommodates cigar smokers. A lavish health spa holds a pool, huge whirlpool, sundeck, and outdoor jogging track.

120 E. Delaware Place (at Michigan Avenue). ☎ *800-332-3442 or 312-280-8800. CTA: Buses stop on Michigan Avenue, ½ block east. Red line El stops at Chicago/State. Parking: Valet (with in-out privileges) $26; self $8.25–$14.25. Rack rates: $402–$525 double. AE, CB, DC, DISC, JCB, MC, V.*

Hampton Inn & Suites Hotel

$ River North

Conveniently located near the Merchandise Mart and Michigan Avenue shops, the Hampton Inn brings welcome relief to the escalating hotel prices in trendy River North. The hotel has a combination of guest rooms, two-room suites, and studios. The residential, warm atmosphere of the hotel puts you close to tourist icons, such as Rainforest Café, Rock-N-Roll McDonald's, Planet Hollywood, and the Hard Rock Café. Children under 18 and third and fourth guests are free. You get a mini-course in Chicago history with a great display of photographs and architectural artifacts. The hotel offers a mix of 100 doubles and 130 suites and is connected by a second-floor skywalk to a branch of Ruth's Chris Steak House.

33 W. Illinois St. (at Dearborn Street). ☎ *800-HAMPTON or 312-832-0330. Internet:* www.hamptoninn-suites.com. *CTA: Buses stop at the corner of Grand and State Streets; red line El to Grand (at State Street), then walk 1 block south and 1 block west. Parking: Valet (with in-out privileges) $20. Rack rates: $119–$169 double. AE, DC, DISC, JCB, MC, V.*

Hotel Allegro

$$ Loop

Located across the street from City Hall, the 483-room Hotel Allegro is splashy, fun, and a great value. The hotel's gimmick is a trumpet player outside each morning at 9:01 a.m. — a wake-up call for Chicago's Loop. Formerly the Bismarck Hotel, the place first opened in 1894 and was rebuilt in 1926, and again in 2000, when it pioneered a flurry of construction in the North Loop. Warm, vibrant colors and bold patterns dominate the public spaces and smallish guest rooms. (Don't be surprised if your room is painted a perky pink-grapefruit color!) Suites have nice amenities, including terry robes, VCRs, and two-person Jacuzzi tubs. You also get melon-and-magenta bedspreads and green throw pillows sprinkled with gold stars. Whirlpools are installed in 31 suites. Guests gather each evening for wine served around a polished black grand piano and limestone fireplace. 312 Chicago restaurant, a colorful extension of the hotel, serves an Italian-American menu.

171 W. Randolph St. (at LaSalle Street). ☎ *800-643-1500 or 312-236-0123. CTA: Buses stop along LaSalle Street; all El lines stop at Washington. Parking: Valet (with in-out privileges) $20. Rack rates: $145–$175 double. Rates include evening wine. AE, CB, DC, DISC, MC, V.*

Hotel Burnham

$$$ Loop

In one of the city's best restorations in years, the Kimpton Group of San Francisco has transformed one of the world's first skyscrapers, D.H. Burnham's Reliance Building (1891), into a super-hip boutique hotel. (Thanks to the same group for creating the Hotel Allegro and Hotel Monaco — both in this chapter!) In the heart of the Loop, just across from Marshall Field's department store, the hotel has 103 rooms and 19 suites — average in size, below average in price. Visitors marvel at huge guest room windows that stretch from floor to ceiling. A playful restaurant on the ground floor allows you to simultaneously dine and admire the restored terrazzo floors and Carrara wainscoting.

1 West Washington St. (at State Street). ☎ *877-294-9712 or 312-782-1111. Internet:* www.burnhamhotel.com. *CTA: Buses stop on State Street. 11, 29, 44, 145, 147, 151; red subway line to Washington/State. Parking: Valet (with in-out privileges), $29. Rack rates: $155–$195 double. AE, DISC, MC, V.*

Hotel Inter-Continental Chicago

$$$ Magnificent Mile

Installed in two adjoining buildings at the foot of the Magnificent Mile, this hotel is both eccentric and lovable. The hotel's south tower was built in 1929 as the Medinah Athletic Club, a luxury men's club. Climbing to the eighth floor, visitors are swept through a melange of architectural styles, from classic Italian renaissance to French Louis XVI, from medieval England to Spain and Mesopotamia. Flourishes include hand-stenciled ceilings, marble columns, brass inlays, and beautiful tapestries and artwork. Service is smooth and rooms are elegant and intimate. Each unit at this 844-room luxury property comes with thick terry robes, a coffeemaker, a refrigerator, a desk, and three dual-line phones. Rooms in the older tower are more classic in style; rooms in the North Tower are modern and more standard. Tucked away on the lobby mezzanine, the Boulevard serves creative Mediterranean cuisine and is one of Chicago's best-kept dining secrets.

505 N. Michigan Ave. (at Grand Avenue). ☎ *800-327-0200 or 312-944-4100. CTA: Buses stop in front of hotel; red El line to Grand/State. Parking: Valet (with in-out privileges) $26.50. Rack rates: $299–$429 double. AE, DC, DISC, JCB, MC, V.*

Hotel Monaco

$$$ North Loop

Rooms at this vibrant makeover of the dowdy Oxford House come complete with a pet. A goldfish in a bowl will be delivered on request and may be kept for the duration of the stay. Gimmicks aside, this sleek hotel, offering 192 guest rooms (including 22 suites, each with two-person whirlpool) is distinguished by its rich decor. Guest rooms are furnished with mahogany writing desks, Art Deco cornice armoires, and lipstick-red quilted headboards. Amenities include coffeemakers and robes. Each evening, wine is served around a limestone fireplace, the centerpiece of Monaco's jewel-box lobby. The registration desk is whimsically modeled after a classic steamer trunk and the adjoining restaurant Mossant is modeled after a Parisian bistro.

225 N. Wabash Ave. (at Wacker Drive). ☎ *800-397-7661 or 312-960-8500. Internet:* www.monaco-chicago.com. *CTA: Buses stop at State and Wacker; purple, brown, orange, or green line El to Lake/State, then walk 1 block north, 1 block east. Parking: Valet (with in-out privileges) $24. Rack rates: $230 double. Rates include evening wine. AE, CB, DC, DISC, MC, V.*

Touring Tarzan's old haunt

Even if you don't stay at the Hotel Inter-Continental Chicago, stop by for a fascinating free architectural tour. Guests and nonguests can take a 30-minute tape-recorded, self-guided walking tour narrated by WGN radio personality Roy Leonard. Leave a driver's license or other identification as security and get a loaner Walkman. Discover the beautiful Venetian-style, junior Olympic-size pool, where Olympic gold medalist and screen actor Tarzan Johnny Weissmuller trained and pioneer body-builder Charles Atlas coached the wealthy. Mobster Al Capone threw a huge poolside party, but only for an episode of *The Untouchables* TV series. Nonguests may use the pool and a state-of-the-art health club for $12 per visit. Changing rooms, saunas, showers, and toiletries are provided.

House of Blues Hotel, a Loews Hotel

$$ North Loop

Part of distinctive Marina Towers, located alongside the Chicago River, House of Blues Hotel is part of a transformation of the complex into an entertainment mecca. House of Blues music club, plus a Chicago branch of the New York steakhouse Smith & Wollensky, wine bar Bin 36, a Crunch Health & Fitness Center, 36-lane AMF Bowling Center, and marina with boat rentals, make this an all-in-one experience. The eclectic decor of the hotel, part of the Loews Hotel group, combines Gothic, Moroccan, East Indian, and New Orleans styles. Hall monitors show live concerts from the House of Blues Music Hall. Upon check-in, guests receive a complimentary music CD. Technology-friendly rooms provide television Internet access. Guest rooms feature interesting furniture, much of which is painted blue, and fabulous Southern folk art.

333 N. Dearborn St. (at the river). ☎ *800-23-LOEWS or 312-245-0333. Internet: www.loewshotels.com. CTA: Buses stop at the corner of State Street and Wacker Drive. Walk 1½ blocks north, 1 block west; red El line goes to Grand/State. Parking: Valet (with in-out privileges) $26. Rack rates: $189–$250 double. AE, CB, DC, DISC, MC, V.*

Hyatt on Printers Row

$$$ South Loop

History meets high-tech at this comfortable hotel. In a now-fashionable area of loft apartments — known as Printers' Row because it was once packed with printing plants — the 161-room hotel fuses the 1896 Morton Salt Building with a century-old printing plant. You're a comfortable walk away from the Art Institute, Grant Park, Sears Tower, Harold Washington Library, and the city's financial district. Guest rooms feature Frank Lloyd Wright-like geometric designs as well as stylish black lacquer furniture and heavy tapestry spreads. While decidedly Old-World European in flavor, this hotel offers amenities, such as VCRs, computer workstations, two telephones per room, and TVs. Adjoining the hotel is the acclaimed Prairie restaurant, which serves innovative Midwestern cuisine.

500 S. Dearborn St. (at Congress Parkway). ☎ *800-233-1234 or 312-986-1234. Internet: www.hyatt.com. CTA: Buses stop at South State Street, across from the Washington Library. Walk 1 block west. Brown El line to Library/Van Buren or red line to Harrison/State. Parking: Valet $23; self $16 (both with in-out privileges). Rack rates: $200–$300 double. AE, CB, DC, DISC, ER, JCB, MC, V.*

Hyatt Regency Chicago

$$$ River East

This sprawling hotel with more than 2,000 rooms is as impersonal as Union Station, bustling with a steady stream of travelers. For the same reason, it is family-friendly — parents don't need to worry unduly about kids acting, well, like kids. With all the hustle and bustle, kids blend right into the general commotion of the place. With its emphasis on conventions and business meetings, the hotel offers in-room conveniences, such as desk, fax, and PC hookups. Beefs: Guest rooms are distributed over two high-rise towers, and can be a long hike from the front desk; soundproofing in some rooms is not all it might be. Bonuses: Food is available through 24-hour room service and at a half-dozen restaurants and cafés. These include Big, Brasserie and Bar, a fine stop for an after-dinner drink that stocks 87 brands of single-malt Scotch, 46 kinds of cognac, 115 armagnacs, and 164 varieties of liqueurs and cordials.

151 E. Wacker Dr. ☎ *800-233-1234 or 312-565-1234. Internet:* www.hyatt.com. *CTA: Buses stop at corner of Wacker Drive and Michigan Avenue, 1 block west. Parking: Valet (with in-out privileges) $26. Rack rates: $185–$240 double. AE, CB, DC, DISC, JCB, MC, V.*

Motel 6

$ Streeterville

Commercials for the bare-bones Motel 6 chain promise to "leave the light on for you:" At the downtown Chicago Motel 6, they leave the chandelier burning. Sconces, silk, damask, and gilt are holdovers from when the property was the French-owned Hotel Richmont. Rooms are budget-size, soap minuscule, and glasses plastic, but the prices are an incredible bargain for a million-dollar location just steps away from trendy North Michigan Avenue. This location marks the first time the low-end chain, usually found at highway off-ramps, has opened a property in the central part of a major city. On the ground floor, budget travelers find Coco Pazzo, a charming sidewalk café with excellent Italian fare at prices that won't eat up all that you saved on lodgings.

162 E. Ontario St. (at St. Clair). ☎ *800-466-8356 or 312-787-3580. CTA: Buses stop on Michigan Avenue, 1 block west; red line El to Grand, then walk 2 blocks north and 4 blocks east. Parking: Valet (no in-out privileges) $16; self $14. Rack rates: $89 double. AE, CB, DC, DISC, MC, V.*

Omni Ambassador East Hotel

$$$ Gold Coast

Traditionalists breathed a sigh of relief when a $20 million revitalization (completed in 1998) left this hotel and its famous restaurant, The Pump Room, vastly improved but basically unaltered. Opened in 1926, the 284-room hotel, in a leafy residential neighborhood just two blocks west of Lake Michigan's famed beaches, features custom furnishings and marble bathrooms. Rooms are clean, tidy, and recently revamped. Standard rooms have two-line phones and minibars, and the 50 suites include 13 ultra-plush "celebrity" units named after famous former guests. On the tiny floor alongside The Pump Room bar, there's dancing to live entertainment.

1301 N. State Parkway (two blocks north of Division Street). ☎ *800-843-6664 or 312-787-7200. Internet:* www.omnihotels.com. *CTA: Buses stop on N. Lake Shore Drive, 2 blocks east. Red El line goes to Clark/Division. Parking: Valet (with in-out privileges) $25.50; self $21. Rack rates: $285 double. AE, CB, DC, DISC, JCB, MC, V.*

Park Hyatt

$$$$ Magnificent Mile

How stunning is this hotel? Stunning enough that Chicago's Pritzker family, owners of the international Hyatt hotel chain, moved in. Part hotel, part condominium building, the 67-story building is a showpiece of the high-end Park Hyatt line, occupying one of the most desirable spots on North Michigan Avenue overlooking Water Tower Square. Decor is sleek and contemporary, and you'll know immediately that you're in Chicago by the elegant black-and-white photographs of the city in each guest room. Relaxing is easy in the 7,000-square-foot pool and spa facility. Guest rooms are oversized. Not as traditionally flowery as the Four Seasons or the Ritz-Carlton, the Park Hyatt has a more masculine style of elegance — not unlike the Giorgio Armani designs you can buy in the boutique on the ground level. The hotel caters to individual business travelers seeking out the ultimate in personalized service and amenities. What might you expect? Sony flat-screen televisions, DVD and CD players, a BRNO desk chair and an Eames chair designed by Ludwig Mies Van Der Rohe and Charles Eames, and four — count them — four two-line phones.

800 North Michigan Ave. (at Chicago Avenue). ☎ *800-233-1234 or 312-335-1234. CTA: Buses stop on Michigan Avenue in front of Water Tower Place; red El line to Chicago/State. Parking: Valet (no in-out privileges) $18. Rack rates: $425–$465 double. AE, CB, DC, DISC, MC, V.*

Raphael

$ Streeterville

This European-flavored boutique hotel, with only 172 rooms and suites, is well known for more than just hospitality. It features live entertainment in one of the neighborhood's most popular piano bars. Rooms and suites, done in Mediterranean style, are spacious and have big picture windows. The 16-story brick building, which fits in comfortably with its tony residential neighbors, occupies a prime location; it's just steps from Water Tower Place and North Michigan Avenue. Above all, the hotel represents good value. Suite prices compare favorably with what you may spend on a standard room at one of the neighboring glitzy properties on or near the Mag Mile. Complimentary coffee is served in the lobby. Guests have discounted privileges at a nearby health club.

201 E. Delaware Place. ☎ *800-821-5343 or 312-943-5000. CTA: Buses stop on Michigan Avenue in front of Water Tower Place. Parking: Valet (with in-out privileges) $25; self $17. Rack rates: $120–$219 double. AE, CB, DC, DISC, MC, V.*

Renaissance Chicago Hotel

$$ North Loop

Returning guests claim that the Renaissance Chicago — retaining a strong following through several name changes — is the most comfortable hotel in the city. A stack of awards appears to back them up. The 565-room, 27-story, luxury hotel built by Stouffer in 1991 features bay windows that offer priceless views of the river and city. Comfortable-but-simple guest rooms are tastefully decorated in dark woods, with rich draperies and fabrics, and plush carpeting. Four club floors offer even more comfortable lodgings (in extra-large rooms), a battery of business amenities, plus concierge service, a private lounge, and breakfast and cocktail-hour hors d'oeuvres are included in the room rates. The hotel has an indoor pool and health club. Cousines Restaurant and Café serves well-rendered Mediterranean specialties. Great Street Restaurant offers casual dining, a spectacular atrium, and wonderful views. The Lobby Court offers evening cocktails and live jazz or piano music. Theater-goers should inquire about packages that include performances in the nearby North Loop theater district.

1 W. Wacker Drive (at State Street). ☎ *800-HOTELS-1 or 312-372-7200. Internet:* www.renaissancehotels.com. *CTA: Buses stop at State and Wacker; brown El line to State/Lake or red line to Washington/State. Parking: Valet $28; self $18 (both with in-out privileges). Rack rates: $179–$310. AE, CB, DC, DISC, JCB, MC, V.*

Ritz-Carlton Chicago

$$$$ Magnificent Mile

Yes, that *was* Oprah heading into the hotel dining room. You may also find Mayor Richard Daley holding a power dinner, or Christie Hefner, Playboy Enterprises CEO. This celebrity magnet is super-luxurious yet large enough, with 431 rooms, to provide anonymity. Guest rooms have handsome cherry-wood furnishings and marble bathrooms; suites are ultra-plush, with glass French doors separating bedroom and living room. Standard amenities include king-size beds, hair dryers, robes, and double-line phones. The Ritz forms part of the Water Tower complex, in the heart of the Magnificent Mile. You can find shoppers taking a respite — perhaps with afternoon tea or an evening aperitif — in the hotel's atrium lobby. Sunday brunch is one of the best in town and includes a separate buffet for kids. Don't miss the gravlax (cured salmon, a Scandinavian delicacy). Despite its upscale ambience, the size and bustle make this hotel a place that parents shouldn't feel uncomfortable taking kids. Their pocketbooks, though, may experience some discomfort.

160 E. Pearson Street (½ block east of North Michigan Avenue, connected to Water Tower Place). ☎ *800-621-6906 or 312-266-1000. CTA: Buses stop in front of Water Tower Place; red El line to Chicago/State. Parking: Valet (with in-out privileges) $27; self $17.50 (no in-out privileges). Rack rates: $355–$425 double. AE, DC, DISC, JCB, MC, V.*

Sheraton Chicago Hotel & Suites

$$ Streeterville

This is a big hotel, but somehow it doesn't feel impersonal. The huge lobby has a friendly piano bar and windows overlooking an esplanade along the Chicago River. Rooms are sizable and comfortable, featuring a sitting area with loveseat and chair. Many of the 1,204 rooms in the 34-story hotel offer spectacular views of Lake Michigan. Guests in 75 tower rooms pay extra for such amenities as robes and access to a club room that serves breakfast and cocktails (included in the room rate). Guests include a large percentage of convention-goers, taking advantage of the property's 120,000 square feet of meeting and convention space. A standout among the hotel's five restaurants and lounges is Streeterville Grille & Bar, serving excellent steaks and chops.

301 E. North Water Street. ☎ *800-325-3535 or 312-464-1000. CTA: Buses stop on Michigan Avenue, 3 blocks west. Parking: Valet (with in-out privileges) $26, self $18. Rack rates: $149–$309 double. AE, DC, DISC, MC, V.*

Sutton Place Hotel

$$$ Gold Coast

Here's an oasis of quiet sophistication off noisy, raucous Rush Street. Housed in a striking 1980s-built geometric granite-and-glass skinned building (which has won awards for architecture and interior design), the 246-room deluxe hotel offers entertainment gadgetry and high-tech conveniences. Each guest room has a stereo TV and VCR (with movie rentals available 24 hours a day), a stereo receiver with a compact disc player (and an in-room selection of CDs), a fully stocked minibar, three telephones (one with a speakerphone), and a dedicated fax or computer hookup. Among 40 luxurious suites are some with balconies, terraces, and sweeping city-and-lake views. You can work out in the fitness suite, or borrow step boxes and a Reebok step video to take back to your room. The bar overlooks the bustle of Rush Street, where the beautiful people drink and dine.

21 E. Bellevue Place (at Rush Street). ☎ *800-606-8188 or 312-266-2100. Internet: www.suttonplace.com. CTA: Buses stop on North Lake Shore Drive, 1 block east; red El line to Clark/Division. Parking: Valet (with in-out privileges) $26. Rack rates: $275–$325 double. AE, CB, DC, DISC, MC, V.*

Talbott Hotel

$$ Magnificent Mile

One of the hidden gems of the bustling Michigan Avenue shopping corridor, the Talbott Hotel combines the charm of an English inn with a location that's hard to beat. Just off the lobby, there's a cozy sitting room where you can curl up in a leather armchair by the fireplace. A bar area and sidewalk café with first-rate people-watching were added recently.

But the real surprise is the rooms — many are exceptionally large and include eat-in kitchens — all at very competitive prices.

20 E. Delaware Street (between Rush and State Streets). ☎ *800-TALBOTT or 312-944-4970. Internet:* www.talbotthotel.com. *CTA: Buses stop on Michigan Avenue, ½ block east; red El line to Chicago/State. Parking: Garage (no in-out privileges) $25; self $19 in the Bloomingdale's building. Rack rates: $189–$329 double. AE, CB, DC, DISC, MC, V.*

Tremont

$$ Magnificent Mile

Chicago's original chic boutique hotel pampers guests with an intimate, romantic ambience and amenities, such as cordials and chocolates on turndown (on request, at no extra charge). Rooms are bright and cheery, and all come with a fax. The lobby has a companionable fireplace. Guests who call room service are connected to Iron Mike's Grille, the boisterous New Orleans-style eatery on the premises where football and cigars reign. Check out the fabulous Bear memorabilia on the upstairs walls.

100 E. Chestnut St. (1 block west of Michigan Avenue). ☎ *800-621-8133 or 312-751-1900. CTA: Buses stop on Michigan Avenue, 1 block east. Red El line to Chicago/State. Parking: Valet, $24. Rack rates: $195–$275 double. AE, CB, DC, DISC, MC, V.*

Westin Hotel

$$$$ Magnificent Mile

Kudos to the Westin for sprucing up this ideally located hotel. For years, it was a fairly average hotel with plenty of potential. Now, with the opening of The Grill, a restaurant that has won rave reviews, the hotel seems on its way to being more than just average. Years of work on the exercise facilities and lobby have eliminated some of its former shabbiness. Ask for a tower lake view room, which is larger than standard, and features upgraded bathrooms and turndown service.

909 N. Michigan Ave. (at Delaware Place). ☎ *800-WESTIN-1 or 312-943-7200. CTA: Buses stop on Michigan Avenue. Parking: Valet (with in-out privileges) $30. Rack rates: $329 double. AE, CB, DC, DISC, JCB, MC, V.*

IENDLY

Time waits for no one

Kids are fascinated by the interactive sculpture at Columbus Drive and Illinois Street, near the Sheraton Chicago Hotel & Suites. It is a giant horizontal clock, 70 feet in diameter. The raised granite numerals that serve as benches are swept clean every 59 minutes by the relentless minute hand.

Whitehall Hotel

$$ Magnificent Mile

European style and ambience abound in this hideaway hotel tucked into a side street off Michigan Avenue. After being shuttered for several years, this landmark hotel in the heart of Chicago's most fashionable shopping district has made a quiet comeback after a multimillion-dollar renovation. Developed in 1928 as a prestigious apartment building, the 221-room property was later converted to a European-style boutique hotel. Off the small, paneled lobby are a piano bar and the Rose Garden Tea Room, which serves British-style afternoon tea. Modernized guest rooms and suites have three multiline telephones (with fax and PC capability), Crabtree & Evelyn toiletries, and terry robes. Rates include the morning newspaper. The stylish, comfortable accommodations feature mahogany furnishings, including armoires and Chippendale desks. Among the eight luxury suites, appointed in 18th-century English style with Asian touches, are two with outdoor terraces and knockout skyline views. The fully equipped fitness center supplies exercise bikes for in-room use. The hotel restaurant, a casual European bistro, serves reasonably priced lunch fare and a dinner menu created by nationally known Chef Jesse Llapitan. The adjoining lounge has a piano bar and cabaret entertainers.

105 E. Delaware Place (just west of Michigan Avenue). ☎ *800-323-7500 or 312-944-6300. CTA: Buses stop on Michigan Avenue, ½ block east; red El line to Chicago/State. Parking: Valet (with in-out privileges) $24. Rack rates: $285–$330 double. AE, DC, DISC, JCB, MC, V.*

Runner-up Accommodations

Best Western River North Hotel

$ **River North** This former motor lodge surprises you with its attractive interior, offering moderately priced lodging within easy walking distance of one of the busiest nightlife and restaurant zones of the city. *125 W. Ohio St. (at LaSalle Street).* ☎ *800-528-1234 or 312-787-3100. Internet:* www.bestwestern.com. *CTA: Red El line to Grand/State. Parking: Free parking for guests (1 car per room). Rack rates: $109–$141 double. AE, CB, DC, DISC, JCB, MC, V.*

City Suites Hotel

$ **Near North** This affordable 45-unit hotel is spotlessly clean, although worn and a bit decrepit, and offers suites with sleeper sofas, armchairs, and desks. *933 W. Belmont Ave. (at Sheffield Avenue).* ☎ *800-248-9108 or 773-404-3400. Internet:* www.cityinns.com. *CTA: Red line El to Belmont. Parking: Adjacent lot (with in-out privileges) $8. Rack rates: $105 double. AE, DC, DISC, MC, V.*

Urban golf among the skyscrapers

Adjacent to the Swissotel, the **Illinois Center Golf Course and Driving Range** is a nine-hole, par-three course (complete with a hole that has an island green). It opened on 31 acres of prime downtown real estate — an innovative use of available land — when the building boom went bust a few years ago. See Chapter 17 for a full description.

Hilton Garden Inn

$$$ Near North   In an enviable location near the North Bridge development, this sparkling new hotel puts you close to DisneyQuest, ESPN Zone, a Virgin Megastore, and Nordstrom's mall. *10 E. Grand Ave. (at State Street).* ☎ *800-HILTONS or 312-595-0000. CTA: Red El line to Grand/State. Parking: Valet (with in-out privileges), $27.50. Rack rates: $289 double. AE, DC, DISC, MC, V.*

Homewood Suites

$$$ Near North   Located in the North Bridge development, you'll be right at home in this simple-yet-comfy hotel with one- and two-bedroom suites. *40 E. Grand Ave. (at Wabash Street).* ☎ *800-CALL-HOME or 312-644-2222. Internet: www.homewood-suites.com. CTA: Red line El to State/Grand. Parking: Valet (with in-out privileges), $26. Rack rates: $259 double. AE, DC, DISC, MC, V.*

Lenox Suites Hotel

$$ Magnificent Mile   Although this hotel is a little dowdy by Michigan Avenue standards, shoppers love its location, only one block west of the shopping mecca. *616 N. Rush St.* ☎ *800-44-LENOX or 312-337-1000. CTA: Buses stop on Michigan Avenue, 1 block east. Red line El to Grand (at State Street), then walk 3 blocks east. Parking: Valet (with in-out privileges) $21.50. Rack rates: $199 double. AE, CB, DC, DISC, JCB, MC, V.*

Park Brompton Hotel

$ Near North   This 52-room hostelry in a leafy residential neighborhood near Wrigleyville has the ambience of an English inn, and larger suites have butler's pantries with microwave, refrigerator, and wet bar. *528 W. Brompton St. (at Lake Shore Drive).* ☎ *800-727-5108 or 773-404-3499. Internet: www.cityinns.com. CTA: Buses stop on Marine Drive, ½ block east; red El line to Addison, walk several blocks east to Lake Shore Drive and 1 block south. Parking: Self-parking in nearby garage (no in-out privileges) $7. Rack rates: $95–$105 double. Rates include continental breakfast. AE, DC, DISC, MC, V.*

Radisson Hotel & Suites

$$ **Streeterville**   One rare feature of this recently renovated hotel is a rooftop, outdoor swimming pool. The sleeping rooms have great views too because they start on the fourteenth floor. *160 E. Huron Street. (just east of Michigan Avenue).* ☎ *800-333-3333 or 312-787-2900. CTA: Buses serving many routes stop on Michigan Avenue, ½ block west. Parking: Valet (no in-out privileges) $25. Rack rates: $159–$279 double. AE, CB, DC, DISC, JCB, MC, V.*

Regal Knickerbocker Hotel

$$$ **Streeterville**   After a $15-million renovation, this hotel is trying to make a comeback as a stylish member of the Regal group — it's not there yet, but the 305-room hotel has made big strides in sprucing up its rooms and does offer good value. *163 E. Walton St. (just east of Michigan Avenue).* ☎ *800-621-8140 or 312-751-8100. Internet: www.regalhotels.com/chicago. CTA: Buses stop on Michigan Avenue, ½ block west; red El line to ChicagoState. Parking: Valet (with in-out privileges) $26; self $18.85. Rack rates: $235–$275 double. AE, DC, DISC, MC, V.*

Surf Hotel

$ **Near North**   One of a trio of small hotels owned (like City Suites Hotel and Park Brompton Hotel) by Neighborhood Inns of Chicago, this 55-room property also offers comfortable rooms at low-end rates in a quiet residential neighborhood. *555 W. Surf Street (at Broadway).* ☎ *800-727-5108 or 773-404-3499. Internet: www.cityinns.com. CTA: Buses stop 1 block west. Parking: Self-parking in two nearby garages (one offers in-out privileges; the other doesn't) $9.75. Rack rates: $105–$139 double. Rates include continental breakfast. AE, CB, DC, DISC, MC, V.*

Swissotel

$$$ **River East**   Spacious guest rooms feature superior views created by this hotel's modernistic triangular glass design. *323 E. Wacker Drive (at Columbus Drive).* ☎ *800-654-7263 or 312-565-0565. CTA: Buses stop at Wacker Drive and Michigan Avenue, 3 blocks west; brown, orange, or green El lines to Randolph. Parking: Valet (with in-out privileges), $26. Rack rates: $229–$309 double. AE, CB, DC, DISC, JCB, MC, V.*

Hotel Index by Neighborhood

Gold Coast

The Claridge ($$)
Omni Ambassador East
  Hotel ($$$)
The Sutton Place Hotel ($$$)

Loop

Chicago Hilton and Towers ($$)
The Crowne Plaza Chicago–The
  Silversmith ($$$)
Hotel Allegro ($$)
Hotel Burnham ($$$)
Hotel Monaco ($$)

House of Blues Hotel ($$)
Hyatt on Printers Row ($$$)
Renaissance Chicago Hotel ($$$)

Magnificent Mile

Chicago Marriott Downtown ($$$)
The Drake Hotel ($$$$)
Four Seasons Hotel ($$$$)
Hotel Inter-Continental
    Chicago ($$$)
Lenox Suites Hotel ($$)
Park Hyatt ($$$$)
Ritz-Carlton Chicago ($$$$)
Talbott Hotel ($$)
The Tremont ($$$)
Westin Hotel Michigan
    Avenue ($$$$)
The Whitehall Hotel ($$$)

Near North/Lincoln Park

Belden-Stratford Hotel ($$)
City Suites Hotel ($)
Park Brompton Hotel ($)
Surf Hotel ($)

River East

Fairmont Hotel ($$$)
Hyatt Regency Chicago ($$)
Swissotel ($$$)

River North

Best Western River North
    Hotel ($)
Courtyard by Marriott Chicago
    Downtown ($$)
Embassy Suites ($$)
Hampton Inn & Suites Hotel ($)
Hilton Garden Inn ($$$)
Homewood Suites ($$$)

Streeterville

Doubletree Guest Suites ($$$)
Motel 6 ($)
Radisson Hotel & Suites ($$)
The Raphael ($)
Regal Knickerbocker Hotel ($$$)
Sheraton Chicago Hotel &
    Suites ($$)

Hotel Index by Price

$$$$

The Drake Hotel
    (Magnificent Mile)
Four Seasons Hotel
    (Magnificent Mile)
Park Hyatt Hotel
    (Magnificent Mile)
Ritz-Carlton Chicago
    (Magnificent Mile)
Westin Hotel Michigan Avenue
    (Magnificent Mile)

$$$

Chicago Marriott Downtown
    (Magnificent Mile)
The Crowne Plaza Chicago–The
    Silversmith (Loop)
DoubleTree Guest Suites
    (Streeterville)

Fairmont Hotel (River East)
Hilton Garden Inn (River North)
Homewood Suites (River North)
Hotel Burnham (Loop)
Hotel Inter-Continental Chicago
    (Magnificent Mile)
Hotel Monaco (North Loop)
Hyatt on Printers Row
    (South Loop)
Hyatt Regency Chicago
    (River East)
Omni Ambassador East Hotel
    (Gold Coast)
Regal Knickerbocker Hotel
    (Streeterville)
The Sutton Place Hotel
    (Gold Coast)
Swissotel (River East)
The Whitehall Hotel
    (Magnificent Mile)

$$

Belden-Stratford Hotel
(Lincoln Park)
Chicago Hilton and Towers
(South Loop)
The Claridge (Gold Coast)
Courtyard by Marriott Chicago
Downtown (River North)
Embassy Suites (River North)
Hotel Allegro (Loop)
House of Blues Hotel
(North Loop)
Hyatt Regency Chicago
(East River)
Lenox Suites Hotel
(Magnificent Mile)
Radisson Hotel & Suites
(Streeterville)
Renaissance Chicago Hotel
(North Loop)

Sheraton Hotel & Suites
(Streeterville)
Surf Hotel (Near North)
The Tremont (Magnificent Mile)

$

Best Western Inn River North
(River North)
City Suites Hotel (Near North)
Hampton Inn & Suites Hotel
(River North)
Motel 6 (Streeterville)
Park Brompton Hotel
(Near North)
The Raphael (Streeterville)

Chapter 9

Tying Up the Loose Ends

. . . .

In This Chapter

▶ Buying travel insurance

▶ Renting a car

▶ Making entertainment reservations

▶ Packing wisely

. . . .

The little things mean a lot: having tickets to a great opera or the latest Steppenwolf or Goodman Theater production, getting a reservation at that restaurant you've heard so much about, or having the right clothing so you're not constantly freezing or sweating.

Organizing everything before you go can save you precious time in Chicago — time otherwise spent waiting in line, trying to get tickets, calling around town, buying the socks, long underwear, or sweater you forgot to bring, and dealing with all the other annoyances that plague the unprepared traveler. This chapter helps you make sure you cover everything from buying travel insurance to packing comfortable walking shoes.

Deciding About Travel Insurance

Three kinds of travel insurance are available: trip cancellation, medical, and lost luggage. Trip cancellation insurance is a good idea if you paid a large portion of your vacation expenses up front. I hate to say it, but trip cancellation insurance is also wonderful to have if you or a family member gets sick or dies, and then you can't travel. The other two types of insurance, medical and lost-luggage insurance, don't make sense for most travelers. Your existing health insurance should cover you if you get sick while on vacation. *Before you leave home,* call your insurer to see whether you are fully covered away from home and what procedures you need to follow if you need to visit a doctor or make a trip to the emergency room. This is especially important if you belong to an HMO.

Your homeowner's insurance should cover stolen luggage if you have off-premises theft. Check your existing policies before you buy any additional coverage. The airlines are responsible for $1,250 on domestic flights if they lose your luggage; if you plan to carry anything more valuable than that, keep it in your carry-on bag.

Some credit cards (American Express and certain gold and platinum Visas and MasterCards, for example) offer automatic flight insurance against death or dismemberment in case of an airplane crash. If you feel you need more insurance, then try one of the companies I've listed. But don't pay for more insurance than you need. For example, if you only need trip-cancellation insurance, don't purchase coverage for lost or stolen property. Trip cancellation insurance costs approximately 6 to 8% of the total value of your vacation. Among the reputable issuers of travel insurance are

- ✔ **Access America,** 6600 W. Broad Street, Richmond, VA 23230 (☎ 800-284-8300; Internet: www.accessamerica.com).

- ✔ **Mutual of Omaha,** Mutual of Omaha Plaza, Omaha, NE 68175 (☎ 800-228-9792; Internet: www.mutualofomaha.com).

- ✔ **Travel Guard International,** 1145 Clark Street, Stevens Point, WI 54481 (☎ 800-826-1300; Internet: www.travel-guard.com).

- ✔ **Travel Insured International, Inc.,** P.O. Box 280568, East Hartford, CT 06128 (☎ 800-243-3174; www.travelinsured.com).

Getting Sick Away from Home

This is the stuff you hate to even think about. What if you get sick during your trip? It happens. And if it happens to you, you'll be happier if you gave it a few minutes of thought before you left home. Bring all your medications with you, as well as a prescription for more if you might run out. If you have health insurance, be sure to carry your identification card in your wallet. Bring an extra pair of contact lenses in case you lose one. And don't forget over-the-counter products for common travelers' ailments, such as upset stomach, headaches, or diarrhea.

If you suffer from a chronic illness, talk to your doctor before traveling. For conditions such as epilepsy, diabetes, or a heart ailment, wear a **Medic Alert Identification Tag,** which immediately alerts any doctor to your condition and gives him or her access to your medical records through Medic Alert's 24-hour hotline. Membership is $35, plus a $15 annual fee. Contact the Medic Alert Foundation, P.O. Box 1009, Turlock, CA 95381-1009 (☎ 800-825-3785; Internet: www.medicalert.org).

If you're really worried about getting sick away from home, consider buying medical insurance (see the section on travel insurance earlier in the chapter). Travel medical insurance will cover you more completely than your existing health insurance, but again, weigh the expense against the likelihood that something catastrophic can happen.

Say you do get sick. Your first step is to ask the concierge at your hotel to recommend a local doctor. Most large hotels can recommend someone at any hour. If you can't get a doctor to help you right away, try an emergency room. Many have walk-in clinics for emergency cases that are not life-threatening. You may not get immediate attention, but you won't pay the high price of an emergency room visit (usually a minimum of $300 just for signing your name, on top of whatever treatment you receive). See the appendix for listings of local hospitals.

If you're staying in downtown Chicago, the closest hospital will likely be **Northwestern Memorial Hospital,** 251 E. Huron Street (☎ **312-926-2000;** Internet: www.nmh.org), right off North Michigan Avenue. Their physician referral service is ☎ **312-926-8400.** The emergency department (☎ **312-926-5188**) is at 250 E. Erie Street near Fairbanks Court. The hospital has an excellent reputation.

Renting a Car: Pros and Cons

Do you need to rent a car in Chicago? The answer is a qualified "No." A car can be a liability. Parking can be expensive, while street parking and metered parking are scarce. If you drive Chicago's expressways, you'll start to understand why many complain that the road system no longer handles the increased volume of traffic and will be less equipped to do so as time passes. Gridlock is becoming more frequent and intense.

All that said, Chicago is not as often the nightmare for the driver that, for example, New York and London are. Anyone who has sat fuming in Manhattan's snarled crosstown traffic or on London's ancient and narrow streets may find driving in downtown Chicago a breeze. More often than not traffic *does* move, even in the heart of the Loop or along the Magnificent Mile. Still, the major arteries in and out of the city usually are jammed during the misnamed *rush hour,* which is more like three hours. All of which brings me to that qualified "No."

A car is not necessary if you plan to stay downtown and confine your touring to the outlying neighborhoods. Public transportation — bus, El (an abbreviation of "elevated") train, and subway — is good and mostly reliable. As long as you stick to busy routes during daytime, you should be safe. (Avoid long rides into unfamiliar areas late at night.) Beyond that, taxis are plentiful and pretty much affordable for short runs. On the other hand, if you want to explore or have business in the outlying suburbs (and there is plenty to see, including a drive along the lake shore — see Chapter 21), a car is a must.

Getting the best rate

And you thought airfares were complicated! So are car-rental rates. They can depend on the size of the car, how long you keep it, where and when you pick it up, how far you drive it, and a number of other factors, including the time of year.

Asking the right questions can save you a ton of money. Weekend rates are usually lower than weekday rates and sometimes start as early as noon on Thursday; be sure to find out. If you're keeping the car for more than four days, the weekly rate may be cheaper than four or five days at the daily rate. If you'd like to drop off the car at a different location than the one where you picked it up, most companies charge a steep fee; others, notably National, do not. And don't forget to ask if the rate is different at the airport and in town.

When you call to book a car from O'Hare or Midway airport, ask what the rate would be if you picked up the car from a downtown location. Rates sometimes are considerably lower downtown. Financially, you might be better off taking the train into the city — plenty of rental car companies have offices within a block or two of the major El stops. Don't forget to ask about deals for members of AAA, AARP, frequent-flier programs, trade unions, and other organizations to which you belong. You may be entitled to a discount of 5 to 30%.

Snaring a deal on the Web

Spare yourself the annoying chore of comparing rates on each company's Web site by using a search engine. One useful resource, **Yahoo Travel** (Internet: http://travel.yahoo.com/travel; choose "Reserve car"), allows you to look up rental prices for any size car at more than a dozen companies in hundreds of cities. You enter the size of car you want, the pickup and return dates and times, and the city where you want to rent, and the server returns a price. It can even make your reservation for you. (If you're taking advantage of a promotional rate, you'll probably have to do some calling. However, you can at least get a sense of the undiscounted price.)

Identifying additional charges

On top of the standard rental prices, optional charges apply to most car rentals. Insurance alone can double the daily cost of a rental, so make sure you need the coverage before you purchase it. Particularly if you own a car, you may not need to concern yourself with insurance — check with your insurance agent at home and read the fine print on your credit card agreement to see if you already have coverage.

Collision Damage Waiver (CDW), which requires the rental company to pay for damage to the car in a collision, is illegal in some states, but many credit card companies also cover damage. It can be as much as $10 a day, so be sure to check beforehand.Car-rental companies also offer additional *liability* insurance (if you harm others in an accident), *personal accident* insurance (if you harm yourself or your passengers), and *personal effects* insurance (if your luggage is stolen from your car). If you have insurance on your car at home, you are probably covered for most of these unlikely events. If your policy doesn't cover you for rentals, or if you don't have auto insurance, you can consider the additional coverage (the car-rental companies are liable for certain base amounts, depending on the state). I usually come down on the conservative side of things: Although the likelihood of getting into an accident may be slim, the cost of an accident could inflict serious financial damage if you don't have the insurance. If you look at it that way, the extra $20 or so a day won't seem like much.

Some companies also offer *refueling* packages, in which you pay for an entire tank of gas up front. The price is usually fairly competitive with local gas prices, but you don't get credit for any gas remaining in the tank. If you reject this option, you pay only for the gas you use, but you have to return it with a full tank or face sky-high charges (as much as $4 a gallon) for any shortfall. If you know you're a procrastinator and are likely to forget to refuel until you're on your way to the airport with time running out, then take advantage of the fuel purchase option. Otherwise, skip it.

Before you start, know the date and time you expect to pick up and return the car, the applicable discounts, and whether you need insurance. Be sure the reservations agent knows you're willing to be flexible (if you are) and be sure you ask for the grand total, including taxes, fees, and surcharges, not just the daily rate. Here are some national chains to get you started on your search:

- ✔ **Alamo** (☎ **800-462-5266**; Internet: www.goalamo.com)
- ✔ **Avis** (☎ **800-331-1212**; Internet: www.avis.com)
- ✔ **Budget** (☎ **800-527-0700**; Internet: www.budgetrentacar.com)
- ✔ **Enterprise** (☎ **800-736-8222**; Internet: www.pickenterprise.com)
- ✔ **Hertz** (☎ **800-654-3131**; Internet: www.hertz.com)
- ✔ **National** (☎ **800-227-7368**; Internet: www.nationalcar.com)

Sitting Pretty: Getting Tickets

Need a pair of theater seats front and center? Or a table at the hottest restaurant — preferably not next to the kitchen? If you have your sights set on a special show and a trendy restaurant, it wouldn't hurt to make arrangements long before you leave for Chicago. But you can usually get a table at most restaurants with only a day or two of notice — sometimes even with a same-day phone call. For the latest and greatest theater tickets, a good ploy is to show up at the box office around noon on the day you want to see the show. You can often pick up a cancellation. This is definitely the case at the Lyric Opera, where patrons have a long-standing tradition of turning in unused subscription tickets at the box office before the show. You can purchase those tickets and often obtain great seats.

In Chicago, you can buy half-price tickets on the day of the performance at one of the Hot Tix booths operated by the Chicago League of Theatres. For more details on the Chicago arts scene, see Chapter 23. For more on obtaining Hot Tix tickets, see Chapter 22.

Staying Informed: The Latest News

Chicago's two metropolitan dailies — Chicago Tribune and Chicago Sun-Times — and a widely distributed suburban daily, the Daily Herald, have bulky weekend sections packed with entertainment and events listings. So do the city's free alternative newspapers — the long-established *Chicago Reader* and the newer, edgier *New City*. Glossy city magazines *Chicago* and *North Shore* also have comprehensive listings, as do free publications, such as *Where*, but keep in mind that *Where* is advertising-driven and the "reviews" are biased. Of course, you'll also want to search the Web.

Check out these sources:

- ✔ **Chicago Tribune** (☎ 312-222-3232; Internet: www.chicago.tribune.com) publishes a weekend tabloid insert, *Friday,* that's full of listings and reviews. The section is known for excellent restaurant reviews.

- ✔ *Weekend,* the Friday entertainment section of the **Chicago Sun-Times** (☎ 312-321-3000; Internet: www.suntimes.com), is packed with listings. Most famous are the movie reviews by critic Roger Ebert; the restaurant review section is also good.

- ✔ **Daily Herald** (☎ 847-427-4300; Internet: www.dailyherald.com), published in suburban Arlington Heights and distributed throughout the city, has a fat weekend entertainment section, *Time Out!,* published on Friday.

- ✔ The free **Chicago Reader** (☎ 312-828-0350; Internet: www.chicagoreader.com) is a hippie-era alternative newspaper that has become "respectable" (mainstream). Published on Thursday and distributed in the city's restaurants, cafes, and bookstores, the *Reader* contains Chicago's most comprehensive entertainment listings and reviews, covering a wide range of tastes and lifestyles.

✔ Gritty **New City** (Internet: www.newcitychicago.com) strives to be what the *Reader* once was. Published on Thursday, its pages are full of the offbeat and the irreverent.

✔ **Chicago Magazine** (☎ 312-222-8999; Internet: www.chicagomag.com), the premier city magazine, covers lifestyles, culture, theater, Chicago gossip, and other entertainment and is a reliable source of restaurant reviews.

✔ **North Shore** (☎ 847-486-0600) is a magazine that covers the suburbs and publishes Chicago restaurant listings.

✔ **Centerstage Chicago** (Internet: www.centerstage.net/chicago) offers an online menu of music, food, dancing, theater, art, and bars.

✔ **Chicago Architecture Foundation** (☎ 312-922-TOUR; Internet: www.architecture.org) offers a wide variety of city tours — on foot, by bicycle, and on water.

✔ **Chicago Bulls'** official site (Internet: www.nba.com/bulls) tells all you want to know about the NBA team's struggles in the post-Jordan era. Boo-hoo!

✔ **Chicago Transit Authority** (☎ 312-836-7000; Internet: www.yourcta.com) distributes bus, El, and subway schedules and maps.

✔ **Cool Chicago Links** (Internet: www.enteract.com/atrovato.local/chicago.html) covers the arts, entertainment, radio, TV, weather, and sports. Metromix, sponsored by the Chicago Tribune, is a great site for keeping abreast of new restaurants, clubs, bars, and shows (Internet: www.metromix.com).

World's Greatest Newspaper

Tune in to one of Chicago's most popular radio stations, WGN - 720 AM, which is owned by the Chicago Tribune Company and has a studio in the *Tribune's* showcase window along North Michigan Avenue, just north of the Michigan Avenue Bridge that spans the Chicago River. The newspaper is especially proud of the station's call letters — WGN ("World's Greatest Newspaper").

The Tribune Shop, on street level at the newspaper, sells reproductions of newspapers with famous headlines — "War Ends," "Bulls Repeat," and the like. Ask for the newspaper issued during the 1948 election with the headline that loudly (and incorrectly) screamed, "Dewey Defeats Truman." Democrats especially love this souvenir. The shop is located at 435 N. Michigan Avenue (☎ 317-222-3080).

Chicago's colorful politics

Read the newspapers, listen to the news, and you'll get a glimpse into Chicago's ward politics and political machine ("vote early and often" was a phrase coined in the Windy City) and the not-so-complimentary nicknames that Chicago gives its politicians.

Corrupt Alderman "Bathhouse" John Coughlin earned his nickname because he formerly labored in a public bathhouse. Snippy Mayor Jane Byrne was known as "Attila the Hen" and "Crazy Jane." Slick-tongued, deal-making Alderman Edward Vrodolyak was known as "Fast Eddie." Not-so-slick-tongued Mayor Eugene Sawyer was dubbed "Mayor Mumbles." Mayor Anton Cermak was labeled "Pushcart Tony" because of his former job as a teamster.

The Right Stuff: Packing Wisely

The classic packing advice is to start your packing by laying out on your bed everything you think you need. Then get rid of half of it. As a woman, I hate this advice because I always wind up needing something I left behind. To me, the key is to check out the Web address www.weather.com and see the long-range forecast. Then imagine what you would wear in your own city in that weather, and pack it. Leave room in the suitcase. Never pack until bulging because you will undoubtedly buy items while traveling.

If you are trying to bring only a small bag, such as a roller bag, you won't be able to leave much space for items you may purchase in Chicago. If that's the case, a good trick is to pack an empty nylon duffel bag. On the way home, you can stuff it with your souvenirs and other loot.

Sun, rain, wind: Packing for a Chicago day

Chicago's famously changeable weather calls for some special packing tips:

- ✔ Always pack a sweater when planning to visit Chicago. Even in summer, you can run into a cool evening by the lake or a theater or restaurant where the air-conditioning reaches polar levels.

- ✔ If you're visiting in the winter, be sure to pack some sort of head-gear. You may be concerned about looking unstylish, but believe me, you'll appreciate this advice later. Don't worry about fashion. When it gets cold in Chicago, no one goes without head covering.

> ✔ If you're comfortable wearing shorts, you'll want to pack them for a spring or fall trip as well as for a summer visit. (Some folks do tend to rush the season, and you may see some people strolling along the Mag Mile in shorts during a February mild spell.)
>
> ✔ Even in summer, a lightweight jacket is always a good idea because the Windy City can get breezy at any time of year.

Unless you are planning a formal night out, you can leave the high heels and suits and ties at home. Most restaurants, even pricier ones, have become more casual. For men, a dress shirt, a jacket, and tie will more than suffice for any night out. (In fact, dress pants and a shirt with a sweater are acceptable almost anywhere.) For women, a long skirt with a nice sweater or blouse can work as well. A few of the top restaurants and clubs (the Pump Room at the Omni Ambassador East Hotel is a notable example) enforce a dress code. If you plan to visit these spots, you need at least one dressy outfit.

 Gift shops carry lots of clothes — from cheesy logo fare to designer-label fashion. They also have raincoats, umbrellas, swimwear, and other weather-related items that you may forget to pack. But be aware that you're likely to pay a premium!

Choosing your suitcase

When choosing your suitcase, think about the kind of traveling you'll be doing. A bag with wheels is handy if you'll be mostly on hard floors but not on uneven surfaces or many stairs. A fold-over garment bag helps keep dressy clothes wrinkle-free, but a garment bag may be unnecessary on a casual vacation. Hard-sided luggage protects break-able items better, but weighs more than soft-sided bags.

When packing, start with the biggest, hardest items (usually shoes), and then fit smaller items in and around them. Pack breakable items between several layers of clothes, or keep them in your carry-on bag. Put things that could leak — shampoo, sunscreen, moisturizer — in plastic zipper bags, and throw in a few extra plastic bags for dirty laun-dry. Lock your suitcase with a small padlock (available at most luggage stores, if your bag doesn't already have one), and put identification tags on the inside and outside.

You're allowed two pieces of carry-on luggage, a limit most airlines have begun enforcing strictly, especially on crowded flights. In fact, one bag is preferable should you board late and find the overhead bins full (as they always seem to be). Ask the reservations clerk or travel agent for the exact dimensions allowed and expect to be forced to check a bag at the gate if you try to sneak on an extra-large piece.

Should you have a long flight (or delays, which are becoming routine), it's nice to have some creature comforts. Women may bring a cozy wrap, such as a lightweight wrap, plus thick socks to wear should your feet swell. Neck rests, eye covers, and nasal saline sprays are a comfort to both men and women.

In your carry-on bag that you know won't have to be checked (and possibly delayed or lost), pack anything irreplaceable, such as your return ticket, passport, expensive jewelry, contact lenses or glasses, and prescription medication. Also bring along anything breakable, a book or magazines, a personal stereo with headphones, a bottle of water, and a snack in the likely event that you don't like the airline food. Leave a little space for the sweater or jacket should the airplane get cold.

Part III
Settling into Chicago

The 5th Wave   By Rich Tennant

"The closest hotel room I could get you to the Magnificent Mile for that amount of money is in Cleveland."

In this part . . .

*B*eing in a new city can be a bit like groping around in the dark. Distances are longer or shorter than they appeared on the map, and north, south, east, and west can get mixed up easily. If you manage to set some points of reference, however, you can get your bearings wherever you roam. Reading through this part will have you navigating around the city like a native. And believe me, even the natives don't know everything about this city! You can find your way from the airport into the city and figure out transportation and neighborhoods. Maybe you'll even find yourself giving directions to hapless tourists on the street!

Chapter 10

Orienting Yourself in Chicago

In This Chapter

▶ Getting from point A to point B (from the airport to your bed)

▶ Discovering the lay of the land: The city's layout and neighborhoods

▶ Finding information while you're in Chicago

*F*inding your way around the Windy City is a breeze. For openers, whenever you spot Lake Michigan dead ahead — the lake is pretty hard to miss — you know you're facing east. In this part of the book, you'll find out how to reach the city from the airports, pick up the finer points of orienting yourself, and get the scoop on Chicago's neighborhoods.

Arriving in Chicago

Because Chicago is at the hub of the interstate highway system, many visitors arrive by car. In addition, Amtrak serves Chicago relatively well, even in this era of diminished train travel. Nonetheless, Chicago's airports provide most of the city's visitor activity. Each day, several hundred thousand air travelers fly in and out of Chicago.

Chicago has two major airports, O'Hare International and Midway. Despite their combined vast capacity, the city has outgrown them both. For years, the creation of a third airport has been a political football, with plans afoot to locate it in Chicago's far south suburbs, in neighboring Indiana, and even offshore on a pod in Lake Michigan.

Sometime in the new millennium, Chicago will get that third airport. Until then, the city must struggle with what it has. Though at times frustrating and daunting, O'Hare was revitalized over the past decade and has become more user-friendly. Over the same period, Midway has gone from a virtually abandoned facility to a frenetically busy airport struggling to shoehorn travelers into its limited public spaces.

Time-honored tradition of being stuck at O'Hare

If you find yourself spending significant time at O'Hare, planned or unexpected, check out the visitor services. Information booths are available on the lower levels of Terminals 1, 2, and 3, outside the lower-level customs area, and on the upper level of Terminal 5. (By the way, there's no Terminal 4.) They're open daily from 8:15 a.m. to 8 p.m. Pick up a map that shows where everything is. Or phone ☎ 773-686-2200 for an extensive menu of airport information.

The airport has shops, restaurants, and other diversions that include satellites of two Chicago museums. The **Museum of Broadcast Communications** has a 70-seat theater in Terminal 2, where a 1½-hour compilation of TV shows from its archives runs in a continuous loop. Artifacts from the museum's collection of vintage radios and TV sets are on display.

Travelers with youngsters in tow head for the interactive **Kids on the Fly Children's Museum** in Terminal 2, near the security checkpoint. Hand-on exhibits focus on aviation, travel, and geography.

Some of the Windy City's signature food and drink is available at O'Hare. Pizzeria Uno, Gold Coast Dogs, and Lou Mitchell's Express (a satellite of Chicago's best breakfast spot) are in Terminal 5; Goose Island, the city's best-known microbrewery, operates in Terminal 3.

By plane to O'Hare Airport

Sprawling O'Hare International Airport has the dubious distinction of being one of the world's busiest air-travel hubs. Although traffic at Midway has grown spectacularly over the last decade, O'Hare is by far the city's major airport.

O'Hare's statistics read like something out of the *Guinness Book of Records*. The airport sprawls across 7,700 acres, has 162 gates in four terminal buildings, serves more than 65 airlines, and handles about 190,000 passengers a day — 69 million a year.

Many visitors grumble that they're greeted by unprotected luggage carousels, lines for cabs, grouchy cops, repeated loudspeaker threats to tow illegally parked cars, and tiresome bus rides to rental-car lots deep in the hinterland.

Good things take place at O'Hare, too. A link to Chicago's subway system dodges gridlocked traffic, shuttling you downtown in about 45 minutes for only $1.50. If you prefer a cab (lines are not always long), an airport employee who's in charge of making sure the cab line moves efficiently will pair strangers willing to share rides and cut costs. And should weather unexpectedly lock you in, a pedestrian tunnel means that good food, comfortable accommodations, and an array of services are only a short walk away at the excellent on-site O'Hare Hilton Hotel.

The trek between terminals can be long, but an elevated people-mover system, opened in 1993 as part of $2 billion in improvements, whisks passengers at 35 mph between the terminals and long-term Parking Lot E. Stations are located at each terminal and at the remote parking lot.

If you leave O'Hare for another U.S. destination, you often encounter long lines that wind up to the ticket counters like a conga line at a wedding reception. Avoid them with curbside check-in, available on domestic flights only.

Getting into the city

The **Chicago Transit Authority** (☎ 312-836-7000) subway is the cheapest and often fastest way downtown, but not necessarily the safest. In 1997, as an economy measure, the CTA eliminated conductors from trains. Many believe this compromises safety. Travelers should avoid the subway during quieter times, such as late at night. Rush and daylight hours are safe enough.

To reach the El (the word *El* is short for "elevated" train), follow the signs displayed near baggage-claim areas and in arrival halls. They guide arriving passengers through a series of ped-ways (served by escalators, elevators, and moving walkways) to the CTA blue line train stop.

Early to bed, early to rise

O'Hare Hilton Hotel (☎ **800-HILTONS** or 773-686-8000), within the airport, couldn't be more convenient for travelers with early flights. The 858 guest rooms are not only well appointed but are also absolutely soundproof, despite being virtually on the runways.

Even if you're not a guest, you can work out at the 10,000-square-foot health club, which has a pool, whirlpool, steam room, and sauna. The fee of $9 a day includes towels, shampoo, conditioner, and hair dryers.

The Hilton is also home to the **Gaslight Club,** an establishment in the Playboy Club genre. **Andiamo** is a full-service restaurant that serves three meals daily and supplies the Hilton's **"Food on the Fly"** program (☎ **773-601-1733**). Hot sandwiches and entrees, mostly priced under $10, are a great alternative to airline food.

A cab ride downtown costs about $33, half that if you share. Join the queue (if there is one) at the cabstand, and when you reach the head of the line, tell the starter (the airport employee in charge of making the cab line move efficiently) you want to share a ride. You and three other passengers can each pay a flat rate of $15. The number for **Yellow Cab** is ☎ **312-540-9098,** for **Checker Cab** ☎ **312-243-2537.** Airport buses, operated by **Continental Air Transport/Airport Express** (☎ **312-454-7800**), cost $15.50. They stop at most downtown hotels and are a wonderful option. Limousine service runs about $45. **American Limousine** (☎ **800-762-6888** or 630-920-8888) doesn't require a reservation but does suggest passengers call ahead.

Renting a car — or not?

If you plan to stay in downtown Chicago, a rental car can be a liability. Vacant parking meters are tough to find, parking is expensive, and navigation can be a hassle. You're better off using a cab or public transportation (bus or subway).

If your trip involves travel to the 'burbs or beyond, you need to rent a car at O'Hare. Unlike some airports with on-premises rental offices, O'Hare uses remote lots served by shuttle buses. Beyond the time it normally takes to complete your rental transaction, allow an extra 15 to 30 minutes for the shuttle and waiting time. (See Chapter 9 for the ins and outs of renting a car.)

Also expect to be hit with heavy taxes and surcharges on top of the quoted rate. They include the 18% sales tax and a $2.75 transaction fee Local numbers and average daily costs for a midsize car at press time were: **Alamo** ☎ **847-671-7662;** $55/day, $190/week; **Avis** ☎ **773-825-4600;** $48/day, $180/week; **Budget** ☎ **773-686-4951;** $30/day, $212/week; **Dollar** ☎ **773-686-2030;** $57/day, $254/week; and **Thrifty** ☎ **847-928-2000**); $40/day, $220/week.

By plane to Midway Airport

Midway (☎ **773-838-0600**) almost died in the 1980s, but the addition of flights by ATA and Southwest Airlines revived Midway Airport. Today, the airport is undergoing major reconstruction. While closer to downtown, the construction is making the airport hard to navigate. Under optimum conditions, the trip from downtown using surface routes (car, cab, or shuttle bus) can take less than half an hour. But those conditions seldom prevail, and by the time you negotiate the construction around the airport entrance, the journey often takes as long as the trip from O'Hare.

The **CTA** also serves Midway. The orange line trip to Midway is much shorter than the blue line ride to O'Hare. But the walk from airport terminal to subway terminal is a long one that lacks O'Hare's moving sidewalks — a long haul when you're struggling with luggage.

Cab rides to Midway are about $5 cheaper than to O'Hare. Cab sharing is available (ask the starter at the booth outside the main entrance), but only if you're going downtown. The airport shuttle van to downtown hotels is cheaper, too, at $11 one way. Most major car-rental companies also have counters at Midway, but their lots are remote. Most parking is also in remote lots served by shuttle buses.

Midway has fewer flights than O'Hare and is served by fewer airlines. Traffic still exceeds the capacity of its facilities, though. Baggage carousels are jammed in beside ticket counters. Security gates and the main food court are squeezed into adjacent areas, and frequently infringe on each other. Midway is often a noisy, frenzied mess.

By Train

Nearly every transcontinental Amtrak route runs through or to Chicago's sprawling Union Station. The cavernous loading and unloading area lies below street level in the heart of the Loop. During the day, you should have no problem hailing a cab curbside. At night, you may want to call for a taxi from inside the station. Across the street from Union Station is Northwestern Station, the hub of METRA train service to the suburbs.

Understanding the Lay of the Land

Here's an easy way to keep yourself oriented in Chicago: The lake is always to the east. "The lake," of course, is Lake Michigan, which disappears into the horizon like some huge inland sea. As my friend from London said while staring trancelike at the lake, "You . . . can't . . . see . . . across it." When in doubt, remember that the lake is to the east, and barring some unforeseen natural disaster, it always will be.

The Chicago River forms a "Y" that divides the city into three sections: north side, west side, and south side (what would be the east side, of course, is the lake). The Loop, the business and financial center of the city, is located just south of the Chicago River. The main shopping district is North Michigan Avenue, also known as the Magnificent Mile,

Yes, Virginia, that is a lake

Lake Michigan is 22,300 square miles in size and reaches depths of over 900 feet. The other Great Lakes are Erie, Superior, Ontario, and Huron. Each of the lakes is honored with a street on the east-west corridor intersecting the Michigan Avenue shopping district. The U.S.-Canada international boundary runs through all the Great Lakes, except Lake Michigan, which lies wholly in U.S. territory.

which stretches north of the Chicago River, not too far east of the lake. On the west side is Bucktown/Wicker Park, the Randolph Street Market District, and many outlying residential neighborhoods.

As a former part of the Northwest Territories, Chicago is laid out in a grid system, with point zero located at the intersection of State and Madison Streets, within the Loop. State Street divides east and west addresses and Madison divides the north and south. Some diagonal streets may throw you off, though. And some streets end unexpectedly, only to take up again a block or two farther along. Here are some key points to remember:

✔ The focal point of the city's numbering system is the intersection of State and Madison Streets, in the heart of the Loop. Madison Street runs east-west and is the north-south divider. State Street runs north-south and is the east-west divider.

✔ The Loop is the heart of downtown. Its approximate boundaries are the Chicago River to the north, Congress Street to the south, Halsted Street to the west, and Wabash Avenue to the east.

✔ Numbered streets always run east-west. Numbers get higher as you travel from north to south beginning at 12th Street (also known as Roosevelt Road). East-west streets north of Madison Street have names, not numbers.

✔ All north-south streets also have names, not numbers.

✔ The first few streets south of Madison are named for American presidents in the order of their terms. In order, they're Madison, Monroe, Adams, Jackson, Van Buren, Harrison, Polk, and Taylor.

✔ Streets north of Madison follow a grid system. Division Street, for example, is an east-west street that is approximately 12 blocks north of Madison and is numbered 1200 North. The same grid system applies to north-south streets. For example, Halsted Street, approximately 8 blocks west of State Street, is numbered 800 west.

Chicago by Neighborhood

Chicago is a city of neighborhoods. And because it's so ethnically diverse, in many cases they're ethnic neighborhoods. Prominent Chicago neighborhoods, from south to north, include

✔ **The Loop:** Chicago's downtown is named after the elevated train track that circles the financial district. The main attractions include riding the El and visiting the Chicago Board of Trade and Mercantile Exchange, where you can watch traders in the pit doing their thing — whatever it is, it has always been beyond me!

✔ **Chinatown:** Chicago's Chinese enclave is compact and the main thoroughfares are along short stretches of Cermak Road (also known as 22nd Street) and Wentworth and Archer Avenues. Here you can find good restaurants (such as **Three Happiness,** 209 W. Cermak Road, ☎ **312-842-1964**), interesting tearooms, and shops.

✔ **Near West:** Former warehouses have been converted to living and working space just west of the Kennedy Expressway. The area includes Greektown and Oprah's workplace, Harpo Studios, plus a host of hip restaurants and bars.

✔ **Magnificent Mile:** The northern length of Michigan Avenue is Chicago's version of Fifth Avenue, Oxford Street, and Rodeo Drive. The Mag Mile stretches from the Chicago River to the Oak Street Beach. Anchoring the south end are the distinctive Wrigley Building and Gothic Tribune Towers; at the north end is The Drake Hotel. Highlights include the John Hancock Center Observatory, Fourth Presbyterian Church, Water Tower Place, Chicago Place mall, Terra Museum of American Art, and The Shops at North Bridge.

✔ **Streeterville:** Adjoining the Magnificent Mile, Streeterville is a booming neighborhood of trendy restaurants, bars, and tucked-away boutiques and galleries. Streeterville is bounded by Michigan Avenue to the west, Lake Michigan to the east, the Chicago River to the south, and Oak Street to the north.

✔ **River North:** Go gallery hopping and visit the site of some of the city's hippest restaurants and clubs. Some 70 galleries are located in an area dubbed "SuHu" (two of its major east-west streets are Superior and Huron). The neighborhood is bounded by Chicago Avenue to the north, the Chicago River to the west and south, and State Street to the east.

✔ **Near North:** A feast of restaurants, bars, and boutique shops just west and north of the Magnificent Mile, including the famous rows of bars on Rush and Division Streets. Great goings-on for going out.

✔ **Gold Coast:** The bastion of Chicago's old money, this beautiful neighborhood has many 19th-century homes and runs along Lake Shore Drive north of Michigan Avenue.

✔ **Bucktown/Wicker Park:** The area is said to be home to the third-largest concentration of artists in the country. In recent years, the area has become somewhat gentrified, with waves of hot new restaurants, alternative culture, and loft-dwelling yuppies rolling in. The focal point of the neighborhood is the intersection of Milwaukee and North Avenues.

✔ **Lincoln Park:** The young and the restless, families just starting out, and anyone else who can afford it inhabit Chicago's most popular neighborhood. On the neighborhood's far eastern edge is the park for which the neighborhood is named — Lincoln Park — which includes the nation's oldest zoo and two museums. The neighborhood of Lincoln Park includes many of Chicago's most popular bars, restaurants, theater companies, and retail shops.

✔ **Wrigleyville:** Named after Wrigley Field, the neighborhood surrounding the ballpark is filled with "three flats" and "five flats" — apartment buildings with three or five floors of apartments — and sports bars. It is also where many young people just launching their careers in Chicago choose to live.

✔ **Andersonville:** This formerly Swedish enclave stretches along three or four blocks of North Clark Street immediately north of Foster Avenue. On Saturdays, a bell-ringer makes his rounds as storekeepers ceremonially sweep sidewalks with corn brooms. Here you'll also find the Swedish-American Museum, a pair of Scandinavian delis, a Swedish bakery, and two good Swedish restaurants.

✔ **Hyde Park:** Home of the University of Chicago, Hyde Park is an oasis of liberal thinking and intellectualism, hemmed in on all sides by some of Chicago's most crime-ridden neighborhoods. The Museum of Science and Industry is the main attraction here, with Rockefeller Chapel at the University of Chicago a close second.

Street Smarts: Where to Get Information After You Arrive

After you're in Chicago, one of the easiest ways to gather information is to visit the **Chicago Office of Tourism** in the Chicago Cultural Center, 78 E. Washington Street (☎ **312-744-2400**). It's open weekdays from 10 a.m. to 6 p.m., weekends 10 a.m. to 5 p.m. Printed materials, including the **Chicago Visitor's Guide,** are available free. While you are at this historic building, take a free, guided tour and admire the rare marble, mosaics, and Tiffany stained glass. You also can enjoy a variety of free entertainments, including movies, music performances, art exhibitions, and guest speakers. During peak seasons, tours of Chicago's diverse neighborhoods depart from the center.

Another walk-in visitor center operated by the Chicago Office of Tourism is in the historic **Water Tower Pumping Station,** 186 E. Pearson Street (☎ **312-744-8783**). Open daily from 7:30 a.m. to 7 p.m., the tourist office distributes printed materials and is a primary stop for trolley and bus tours. **Hot Tix,** where theatergoers can purchase discounted tickets, is here too (see Chapter 3).

The **Illinois Marketplace at Navy Pier,** 600 E. Grand Avenue (☎ **312-832-0010**), stays open late to accommodate visitors to Chicago's most popular tourist attraction. Hours are Sunday through Thursday from 10 a.m. to 10 p.m., and on Friday and Saturday from 10 a.m. to midnight. The marketplace has guidebooks and maps, and brokers tickets for Lake Michigan boat rides and dinner cruises that depart from the pier.

Geared to business travelers, the **Chicago Convention and Tourism Bureau** office at McCormick Place on the Lake, 2301 S. Lake Shore Drive (☎ **312-567-8500**), has information on Chicago's major points of interest. It's open weekdays from 8 a.m. to 5 p.m.

The **Thompson Center** (☎ **312-814-6667**) is in the State of Illinois Building, 100 W. Randolph Street, across from City Hall. There's a rack of printed information, including the **Chicago Visitor's Guide,** in the lobby. Illinois Tourism operates the center, which is also the place to stop for information about attractions elsewhere in the state. Materials are available 24 hours a day; the booth is staffed on weekdays from 8 a.m. to 4:30 p.m.

Chapter 11

Getting Around Chicago

• •

In This Chapter

▶ Using public transportation

▶ Cabbing it

▶ Hoofing it: Exploring the city on foot

• •

*Y*ou don't need a car to explore Chicago. You are better off without one, in fact. Parking is expensive, street parking is tough to find, and the volume of traffic is at its limit. The good news: Public transit is pretty far-reaching. Even better news: Your own two feet are often the best way to get up close and check out Chicago from street level. In this chapter, I cover the various forms of transportation and reveal the best ways to get around the city.

Riding the Rails and the Roads

When in Chicago, do as Chicagoans do and take the train or the bus. Chicago Transit Authority (CTA) subway and elevated trains connect most of the city's key attractions and provide fast, cheap transportation between downtown and O'Hare and Midway Airports. Buses are also ideal for getting around, though subject to the same gridlock as automobiles during rush hours.

Bussing it

CTA buses are a convenient, cheap way to explore downtown Chicago and many of its ethnic neighborhoods. Buses stop about every two blocks — look for blue CTA bus stop signs that list bus numbers and routes. On most routes, buses run every day, every 10 to 20 minutes through late evening. For exact times on various routes, call the CTA at ☎ 312-836-7000.

Chicago buses and trains accept dollar bills, but do not give change. A ride costs $1.50; a 30-cent transfer is good for two additional rides on any route within a two-hour period. Feed bills into a machine next to the driver, drop coins into a fare box, or insert transfer cards and transit passes into another machine alongside the driver. The fare for children age 7 to 11 is 75 cents, plus 10 cents for a transfer.

CTA **visitor passes** are a convenient budget-stretching idea. For $5, a one-day pass offers unlimited rides on CTA buses and trains for 24 hours from the first time you use it. You can also buy passes good for two days ($9), three days ($12), and five days ($18). Passes are sold at visitor centers, Hot Tix booths, select museums, both airports, Union Station, and other locations around town. For advance sales, call ☎ **888-YOUR-CTA** or visit their Web site at www.yourcta.com.

Be sure to equip yourself with one of the excellent free route maps available at all CTA stations. The maps pinpoint major sightseeing attractions and hotels in relation to bus and train routes. If you're unsure which bus or train runs to your destination, call the CTA information line (☎ **800-YOUR-CTA**). Tell the attendant your point of origin and destination, and he or she will give you a route. The line is staffed daily from 5 a.m. to 1 a.m.

Locals know how to get around the city and suburbs on buses. CTA buses (routes 1 through 204) run in the city and nearby suburbs. PACE buses run throughout the suburbs, connect with the CTA, and accept CTA transfer cards, transit cards, and passes.

Riding high and going underground

CTA rail system, also referred to as the "El" or "L" (short for elevated), has elevated tracks, surface tracks, and underground tracks — often all on the same line. The fare is $1.50, and you need a pass, as tokens have been eliminated. All stations sell passes during open hours. There's no central station, but the Loop is the center of the system. Stations are named for the streets where they are located.

The blue line runs between O'Hare and downtown; the orange line runs between Midway and downtown. Chicago's main subway and El lines include:

- ✔ **Blue line:** Runs west-northwest to O'Hare airport.
- ✔ **Brown line:** Zig-zags on a north-south route.
- ✔ **Green line:** Runs along Wabash and Lake Streets and travels west-south.
- ✔ **Orange line:** Runs southwest and serves Midway Airport.
- ✔ **Purple line:** Provides express service to Evanston.
- ✔ **Red line:** Runs along State Street and heads on a north-south route.

Do-it-yourself sightseeing

You can spend $20 to $40 on a guided tour, or you can do it yourself for $1.80. Why only $1.80? The CTA fare is $1.50, plus 30 cents for a transfer, which is good for the return trip if you use it within two hours. Here are some of the city's best sightseeing routes:

✔ **Brown line** (20-minute ride; Monday through Saturday). Ride from the Loop to Belmont Station. You get a bird's-eye view of downtown, gentrified loft districts, and a number of historic neighborhoods. Start at the big El station at Clark and Lake Streets and get on the northbound train.

✔ **No. 151 Sheridan bus** (trip duration 30 minutes; daily). Pick up the 151 downtown on Michigan Avenue (the bus stops every two blocks on the avenue) and ride it north to Belmont. You cover Lake Shore Drive and Lincoln Park. If you take it south, you cover State Street and wind up at Union Station.

✔ **No. 146 Marine-Michigan bus** (trip duration 20 minutes; daily). This express bus allows you to take in North Michigan Avenue, State Street, and Museum Campus. Pick up the bus on Sheridan and Diversey going south. (You can also pick up the 146 along Michigan Avenue, although it has fewer stops than the 151.) You see the Harold Washington Library, the Art Institute, the Chicago Cultural Center, and the landmark Water Tower.

✔ **No. 10 Museum of Science and Industry bus** (35 minutes; weekends year-round, daily in summer and winter holiday season). From North Michigan Avenue at Water Tower (the stop is in front of Borders Books & Music on Michigan Avenue across from Water Tower Place), ride south to the museum campus. You see Grant Park, the Art Institute, the University of Chicago, and Chinatown.

Most trains run daily every 5 to 25 minutes through late evening. The red line and blue line (Congress branch) run 24 hours. For information, call the CTA at ☎ 312-836-7000 or go to www.chicagotransit.com.

Metra operates commuter trains on 12 lines between the suburbs and several downtown Chicago terminals. The system is separate from the CTA, with its own fares. Service is frequent during rush hours, otherwise every one to three hours. Most routes run daily. On some lines, Metra offers heavily discounted weekend passes to encourage leisure travelers to use the system. Trains leave for the suburbs from Union Station (where Amtrak is also based) and Northwestern Station (also known as the Ogilvy Transportation Center) in the Loop. If you are taking a Metra train, make sure to ask which station your train leaves from. For information, contact **Metra Passenger Services** (☎ 312-322-6777; Internet: www.metrarail.com).

Backseat Riding: Taking a Cab

In areas with plenty of pedestrian traffic, such as the Loop, North Michigan Avenue, and River North, taxis are easy to hail. If you can't find one, head for the nearest major hotel; should the doorman find you one, a $1 or $2 tip is in order.

Outside downtown and late at night, cabs are fewer and harder to flag down. To call ahead for a ride, try **Yellow Cab** (☎ **312-540-9098**) or **Checker Cab** (☎ **312-243-2537**).

 The fare schedule recently increased, making cabbing it a slightly more expensive option. The cost is $1.90 for meter start-up, plus 20 cents for each additional ⅛ of a mile, 20 cents for each 36 seconds of time elapsed, and 50 cents per additional passenger aged 12 to 65.

Hoofing It

You can cover great ground on foot while avoiding gridlock and crowded subway trains. Chicago is a good walking city and as safe as most major cities. Use common sense. Walk only where you feel safe. (Rule of thumb: If you don't feel safe, you probably aren't. Get into a cab immediately.) You can feel confident and comfortable on foot in areas such as North Michigan Avenue (and the intersecting streets), Streeterville, River North, Rush Street, Gold Coast, and Lincoln Park neighborhoods. During the day, the Loop is crowded with business-people and you can find safety in numbers. At night, the Loop tends to empty out, except around the North Loop Theater District, where plenty of people and cabs congregate.

Some of my favorite walks are right in the heart of downtown. The Magnificent Mile, for example, is a window shopper's delight that also offers some architectural gems. On the lakefront, you can stroll past the long string of high-rise apartment buildings (including some architecturally significant ones by Mies Van der Rohe around 900 N. Lake Shore Drive). Or take advantage of the CTA bus system and ride to Lincoln Park, then do some walking and explore the excellent free attractions, including Lincoln Park Zoo.

Chapter 12

Money Matters

In This Chapter

▶ Discovering where to get cash

▶ Dealing with a stolen wallet

*M*oney, money, money. This chapter discusses the merits of various forms of money (don't leave home without it!) and how to deal with the worst-case scenario — a stolen wallet.

Dollars and Cents: Where to Get Cash

Two major ATM networks are **Cirrus** (☎ 800-424-7787 or 800-4CIRRUS) and **Plus** (☎ 800-843-7587). Check the back of your card for the name of your bank's network. Often, you'll find it is linked to at least two or three different networks.

In Chicago, **Bank One** (with its blue and white logo) has a large network of ATMs. On Michigan Avenue, there are Bank One ATMs in the John Hancock Center Observatory building and in the Bank One building on Michigan and Ontario Street (near the northwest corner of the intersection). If you are not a Bank One customer, the charge to use the ATM is $1.50. If you are a Bank One customer, there is no charge. Bank One is a member of the MAC, Cash Station, and Cirrus networks.

When using the ATM, exercise the same caution that you would at home (for example, protect your password). Don't be complacent, just because you're in a busy foot-traffic area — that makes running off with your money easier, not harder.

What to Do If Your Money Gets Stolen

Almost every credit card company has an emergency 800 number that you can call if your wallet or purse is stolen. The issuing bank's 800 number is usually on the back of the credit card — though that doesn't help you much if the card was stolen. Call toll-free information (☎ 800-555-1212) for the number. Citicorp Visa's U.S. emergency number is ☎ 800-336-8472. American Express cardholders and traveler's check holders can call ☎ 800-221-7282 for all money emergencies. MasterCard holders should call ☎ 800-307-7309. Making a list of these numbers and stashing them in your suitcase is also a good idea.

The credit card company may be able to wire you a cash advance off your credit card immediately, and, in many places, can deliver an emergency credit card in a day or two. If you opt to carry traveler's checks (see Chapter 3), be sure to keep a record of their serial numbers separate from the checks — again, stash the list in your suitcase — so you're ensured a refund in just such an emergency.

Odds are that if your wallet is gone, the police won't be able to recover it for you. However, after you realize that it's gone and you cancel your credit cards, call the police to fill out a report. (In Chicago, ☎ 311 is the non-emergency police number.) Your credit card company or insurer may require a police report number.

Playing it safe

Don't make it easy for pickpockets and purse-snatchers. Here are some things to keep in mind:

✔ Don't carry your wallet in the back pocket of your pants. Known as the "sucker pocket," your back pocket is easy for thieves to grab or even cut with a blade.

✔ Don't carry a purse or bag on the side of your body closer to the road. If you do, a thief can easily grab it and make a quick getaway.

✔ Use a small cloth pouch as a mock pocket. Pin the pouch on the inside of your clothing and carry your large bills and state ID or driver's license in the pouch — that way, even if your wallet or purse is snatched, you'll have enough cash to get around and won't have the hassle of replacing your ID or driver's license.

Part IV
Dining in Chicago

The 5th Wave By Rich Tennant

"I'd give you a hot dog with everything, but I'm out of Fruit Loops."

In this part . . .

Dining out is one of Chicago's favorite sports. With 6,000 restaurants, the city has enough variety to keep a galloping gourmet on the run. Chicagoans tend to latch on to restaurants, enabling the established favorites to hold their own longer here than in other big cities, such as New York, where shifting restaurant sands swallow up all but the most hallowed dining spots. In Chicago, out-of-the-way gems exist in outlying neighborhoods for when you want to take a culinary safari. And, the trendy restaurant scene is always on the move, keeping the hip crowd on their toes.

Whether you're into the tried-and-true, restaurant hopping, or table hopping in see-and-be-seen spots, you can find a good introduction to Chicago restaurants in this part. I describe Chicago's best restaurant areas, specialties, and deals, as well as complete reviews of my favorite places. And, if you're on the street and in desperate need of a quick bite, you can find answers in a whole chapter devoted to snacking.

Chapter 13

The Lowdown on the Chicago Dining Scene

· ·

In This Chapter

▶ Discovering the major dining neighborhoods

▶ Experiencing Chicago's culinary favorites

▶ Eating your way around the globe: Ethnic cuisine

▶ Dressing for dinner

▶ Making reservations

· ·

Chicago is no longer the meat-and-potatoes place that it was back when the Chicago stockyards and packing houses fed the nation. Today, dining in Chicago is as sophisticated as dining in New York, San Francisco, and other cosmopolitan cities.

Yes, Chicago still offers the famous deep-dish pizza that was invented here in the 1940s. **Gino's East** (see Chapter 14) and other Chicago pizzerias continue to draw big crowds. Thousands of pizza pies are sold as carry-ons to deep-dish diehards flying out of O'Hare.

Yes, you can find excellent steakhouses. Chicago's highest grossing restaurant is **Gibson's** (1028 N. Rush; ☎ 312-266-8999), a clubby, dark-wood den of cigars, fine red wine, and gargantuan steaks. A few steakhouse chains have put down stakes in Chicago, including **Ruth's Chris Steak House** (4312 N. Dearborn Street at Hubbard Street; ☎ 312-321-2725) and **Smith & Wollensky** (318 N. State Street; ☎ 312-670-9900). Old favorites include **Eli's The Place for Steak** (215 E. Chicago Avenue near Michigan Avenue; ☎ 312-642-1393), which is also the place for cheesecake, and **Gene & Georgetti**, (500 N. Franklin Street at Illinois Street; ☎ 312-527-3718).

Many hotels are handing over restaurant operations to independent restaurateurs — often celebrity chefs — who must compete in the marketplace. In many cases they provide room service, too. Notable Chicago examples: **Iron Mike's Grille** (Tremont Hotel), **Mossant** (Hotel Monaco), and **Atwood Café** (Hotel Burnham). See Chapter 14 for more information.

But Chicago is much more than pizza and steak. You can find everything from rooftop chic (**Everest,** 440 S. La Salle Street at Van Buren Street; ☎ **312-663-8920**) to basement brash at **Billy Goat Tavern** (430 N. Michigan Avenue; ☎ **312-222-1525**). Mexican food doesn't get any better than **Frontera Grill** (445 N. Clark; ☎ **312-661-1434**), where the museum-quality Mexican art completes an atmosphere that matches the level of the cuisine. And a bit off the beaten track farther north, **Arun's** (4156 N. Kedzie; ☎ **773-539-1909**) offers exquisite Thai food and desserts so beautiful that tears come to your eyes.

Scoping the Major Dining Destinations

Restaurants reflect the neighborhoods in which they're located. In the **Loop,** restaurants are tailored to an expense-account business crowd. Around the **Magnificent Mile,** you find plenty of outdoor dining where stylish people go to see and be seen. In the burgeoning **Randolph Street Market District,** where Oprah's Harpo Studios and many graphic designers and production companies make their home, a whole row of hip new restaurants has popped up in this former warehouse and market area. In the **Bucktown/Wicker Park** neighborhood, home to a large concentration of artists, you can find eclectic fare and restaurants with cutting-edge decor. **River North,** the gallery district, is where you find the city's largest concentration of dining spots. In **Lincoln Park** and on the **North Side,** you find locals hanging out at their neighborhood favorites, which tend to change less frequently. To get your bearings in terms of Chicago's neighborhoods, see Chapter 10.

One of Chicago's hottest new areas, the **Randolph Street Market District,** has sprouted among the cabbages and turnips of the produce market of West Randolph Street. It's about a $5 cab ride from the Mag Mile. The young and the beautiful flock to this "urban chic" neighborhood, with such restaurants as **Marché** (833 W. Randolph Street; ☎ **312-226-8399**), **Blue Point Oyster Bar** (741 W. Randolph Street; ☎ **312-207-1222**), **Red Light** (820 W. Randolph Avenue; ☎ **312-33-8880**), and **Vivo** (830 W. Randolph; ☎ **312-733-3379**), which offers a stylish loft setting.

Sampling Chicago's Local Favorites

When Jay Leno brings his *Tonight Show* to Chicago, he often heads for **Mr. Beef on Orleans** for an Italian beef or sausage sandwich (see Chapter 15). Don't miss these Chicago favorites — juicy beef or spicy grilled sausage served on a chewy roll and dressed with sweet or hot peppers.

Curse of the Cubs

Billy Goat Tavern patrons soon hear the tale of the Cubs' curse, cast after the late "Billy Goat" Siannis and his mascot, a goat, were ejected from Wrigley Field during the 1945 World Series. The Cubs lost the Series and have never made it back. Present owner Sam Siannis has removed the curse, but so far, it's to no avail. Somewhere in hamburger heaven an old Greek and his goat are chuckling.

Although the famed Maxwell Street market has relocated, you can still buy trademark pork chop sandwiches along **Halsted Street.** Other don't-miss Chicago treats include double cheeseburgers at **Billy Goat Tavern** (see Chapter 15), All-Beef Vienna hot dogs and fries smothered in cheddar cheese at **Gold Coast Dogs** (see Chapter 15), and ribs at **Twin Anchors** (see Chapter 14) and worth-the-trip outposts in Oak Park (**Robinson's No. 1 Ribs**) and Evanston (**Hecky's Barbecue**) (see Chapter 14 for more information).

Around the World, Restaurant-Style

Dining in Chicago is a patchwork of ethnic diversity stitched from cuisines from around the globe. Looking for the cuisine of Cuba or China? Of Japan or Jamaica? Of Laos or Lithuania? Find them all and many more in the Windy City, where sending your taste buds on a multinational culinary adventure is easy.

Italian, Chicago-style

At the south end of the Loop, Taylor Street is as Italian as spaghetti and meatballs. Here in Chicago's own "Little Italy" (which, sadly, is shrinking due to encroaching urban renewal), the neighborhood wears its ethnicity boldly.

Check out the red-white-and-green decor of **Mario's Italian Lemonade,** a little stand at 1070 W. Taylor Street. Pans of rich pizza bread, crusty loaves, and amaretto cookies fill the air with wonderful smells at **Scafuri Bakery** (1337 W. Taylor Street; ☎ 312-733-8881). And stores still sell imported olive oil, sausages, cheeses, and wines. You may even run into Italian-American celebrities like Tony Bennett dining at old neighborhood favorites, such as the **Rosebud Café** (1500 W. Taylor Street, near Ashland Avenue; ☎ 312-942-1117). And, as in the old days in this neighborhood, black-shawl-draped elderly women gossip on stoops, and men in cloth caps linger over strong coffee.

Italian restaurants, old and new, are sprinkled throughout the city. A Loop landmark for more than 70 years, **Italian Village** (71 W. Monroe Street, at Dearborn Street; ☎ 312-332-7005) is actually three restaurants in one and a favorite for pre- and post-theater dining. Stylish **Coco Pazzo** (300 W. Hubbard Street; ☎ 312-836-0900) features the cooking of Tuscany. Just off the Magnificent Mile, **Bice Ristorante** (158 E. Ontario; ☎ 312-664-1474) offers top food and great people-watching from a sidewalk dining area. Intimate **Pane Calde** (72 E. Walton Street, between North Michigan Avenue and North Rush Street; ☎ 312- 649-0055) has a wide-ranging menu that changes daily, and River North's **Centro** (710 N. Wells Street, between Huron and Superior Streets; ☎ 312-988-7775) serves up a mean penne in vodka sauce.

Forget about "one potato, two potato." The **Mashed Potato Club** (316 W. Erie at Orleans Street; ☎ 312-255-8579) offers *104* different kinds of smashed spuds topped with everything from asparagus to zucchini.

It's all Greek to me

Greektown is a great destination for a large group, where long tables and family-style dining reign. Greektown, which received a facelift in 1996 around the time of the Democratic Convention in Chicago, occupies a few blocks of Halsted Street north of Jackson Boulevard and offers a zesty mix of Greek restaurants, nightclubs, and grocery stores. Greektown restaurants serve such Mediterranean staples as Greek salad, *saganaki* (flaming cheese), and *baklava* (a dessert made with thin layers of pastry, nuts, and honey), as well as the ubiquitous gyros plate or sandwich. One of the most attractive is **Pegasus,** 130 S. Halsted (☎ 312-226-3777), where a rooftop garden offers a panoramic view of the Chicago skyline. Another favorite of mine is **Santorini** (800 W. Adams Street; ☎ 312-829-8820) — although most of the restaurants in the neighborhood offer the same lively atmosphere and similar fare.

Best of the wurst

Hearty German good fellowship (known as *gemutlichkeit*) flows — along with mounds of plump sausages — at several German restaurants. Among these is **The Berghoff** (17 W. Adams Street; ☎ 312-427-3170) in the Loop.

The largest concentration of German food and culture is found in the Lincoln Square neighborhood. Business is often transacted in German at **Meyer's Delicatessen** (4750 N. Lincoln Avenue; ☎ 773-561-3377) and the **Merz Apothecary** (4716 N. Lincoln Avenue; ☎ 773-949-0900), with its fragrant European herbs and toiletries. The **Chicago Brauhaus** (4732 N. Lincoln Avenue; ☎ 773-784-4444) resembles a Munich beer hall and offers schnitzel, smoked pork loin, *Koenigsberger klopse* (meatballs in caper sauce), and other German specialties.

Tips about tipping and taxes

How much should you tip? Throughout the United States, the standard tip is 15 percent of the total before tax is added; 20 percent is considered a generous tip. If you prefer, you can strike a reasonable compromise by figuring 15 percent of the total, tax included. Chicago's food tax is substantial. Restaurants levy an 8.75 percent state tax, plus a 1 percent city tax. I find it easiest to look at the tax and double it, and then leave that amount for the tip.

Do remember that everyone needs to make a living and tips are the majority of the wages of waiters and waitresses. They usually receive well below base minimum-wage pay because management expects that the difference will be made up in tips. Unless service is atrocious, leave at least the minimum 15 percent gratuity. Of course, if your waiter or waitress goes the extra mile, 20 percent is not out of line. Conversely, if the service was sloppy and uncaring, reduce the tip accordingly. But don't fall into the trap of blaming the wait staff for poor food. They didn't prepare it. If there is a problem, address it with the manager.

Dim sum and then some

Chicago's Chinatown is located about 20 blocks south of the Loop and about two long blocks west of the McCormick Place convention complex. Some 50 restaurants, plus bakeries, markets, and import houses are strung along a few blocks of Cermak Road and Wentworth Avenue. Perennially popular restaurants include **Three Happiness** (209 W. Cermak Road; ☎ 312-842-1964; and 2130 S. Wentworth Avenue; ☎ 312-791-1228), known for its bountiful dim sum cart, and **Emperor's Choice** (2238 S. Wentworth Ave.; ☎ 312-225-8800), which serves superior seafood. Elsewhere in the city, head for River North to try the satay bar at **Ben Pao** (52 W. Illinois Street at Dearborn Street; ☎ 312-222-1888).

Samplings from around the world

A Vietnamese enclave known as Little Saigon centers on Argyle Street and North Sheridan Road, about a 20-minute cab ride going north from downtown. You find a number of restaurants here that feature **Vietnamese** and **Laotian** specialties, as well as markets offering Oriental vegetables, exotic spices, and hand-painted teapots. Even the El station on Argyle sports a red, pagoda-style roof.

Go just to the east and a bit north of Little Saigon to find Andersonville, a formerly **Scandinavian** neighborhood with eateries such as **Svea Restaurant,** 5236 N. Clark Street (☎ 773-275-7738), and **Ann Sather** (see Chapter 14). They serve traditional pea soup, potato sausage, Swedish meatballs, and Swedish pancakes with tart lingonberries.

Mind if I smoke?

Unlike New York and California, Chicago still allows smoking in restaurants. City ordinances require that all restaurants provide nonsmoking sections. How comfortable and effective they are for nonsmokers depends on the ventilation and the distance between designated smoking and nonsmoking areas. Sometimes nonsmoking sections are in a separate room, away from smokers; often the sections adjoin.

Check out the Swedish American Museum Center, a pair of Scandinavian delis, and **Swedish Bakery**, 5348 N. Clark Street (☎ 773-561-8919) — a must-visit if you're in the area. Middle Eastern food is also becoming popular in the area, with several excellent bakeries and restaurants.

Other major enclaves in Chicago that offer ethnic cuisine include a **Lithuanian** area around Marquette Park on the Southwest side; a concentration of **Indian** shops and restaurants along Devon Avenue; and **Ukrainian Village** (on the west side, near Chicago Avenue and Oakley Boulevard), where you find borscht and cabbage rolls. Sections of North Milwaukee Avenue are "Main Street" for Chicago's huge **Polish** population (the second-largest urban concentration after Warsaw's), with storefront restaurants, such as **Home Bakery** (2931 N. Milwaukee Avenue at Central Park Avenue; ☎ 773-252-3708).

Dressing Up and Dressing Down

As "Casual Day" has taken hold in corporate America, restaurant dress codes, too, have become more casual. With a few exceptions — the **Pump Room** (see Chapter 14) is a notable one — Chicago restaurant dress codes are relaxed and many top spots allow jeans and sports shirts. If a man wears a tie and a woman a cocktail dress, you may feel slightly overdressed in all but the most formal Chicago restaurants. Still, I find it better to be slightly overdressed than slightly underdressed. In most places, women can feel comfortable in black pants, a sweater, and boots, and men in dress pants and a sweater. In the summertime, a sundress with cardigan and sandals for women and khakis and golf shirt for men should suffice in most places. If you're concerned, call ahead and ask if the restaurant has a dress code.

Reserving a Table

Some restaurants are so popular with walk-in diners that they choose not to accept reservations. To avoid a long wait, plan an early or late lunch (say, 11:30 a.m. or 1:30 p.m.) or an early or late dinner (before 7 p.m. or after 9:30 p.m.). Exceptions at dinner include restaurants close to theaters, where you can usually get a table easily around 8 p.m., after the crowds have left to make the curtain.

In cases where I recommend reservations, I do urge that you take the few minutes to make them — especially for dinner. In popular restaurants you may still have to wait up to an hour, even with reservations. Without them, forget it.

Time-savers

Busy, diner-type restaurants (with booths, tables, and counter seats) usually don't take reservations. Be willing to take a seat at the counter, and you may be seated immediately. The counter is not as intimate or private as a table, but it works for a single diner, a couple, or, in a pinch, a threesome. This strategy usually works, for example, at Lou Mitchell's, the Loop's most popular breakfast spot, which often has long lines.

Chapter 14

Chicago's Best Restaurants

. . . .

In This Chapter

▶ Getting the lowdown on some of Chicago's best restaurants

▶ Checking out restaurants by location, cuisine, and price

▶ Indexing restaurants for easy reference

. . . .

*I*f you crave variety, you came to the right town. No matter what your dining pleasure, you're pretty much assured of finding exactly what you want somewhere in Chicago. If you want cheap but good food, you can find it. If you want top-drawer restaurants owned by celebrity chefs, then you can find those, too. You can also find just about every ethnic cuisine you can imagine. And there's no shortage of spots that kids are bound to enjoy, or of candlelit bistros that are perfect for romantic evenings.

Decide what kind of food you want to eat or pick the neighborhood you plan to visit, and then check the indexes that appear at the end of the chapter, following the reviews of my favorite eateries.

To help you budget, each listing includes a main-course price range and a dollar-sign icon. Prices per person include appetizer, main course, dessert, and coffee — but not tax, tip, or drinks. The price brackets and their dollar sign ratings are

$ (dirt cheap) = under $25

$$ (inexpensive) = $25 to $35

$$$ (moderate) = $35 to $45

$$$$ (expensive) = $45 to $60

$$$$$ (astronomic) = over $60 (If you have to ask how much, then you shouldn't eat here!)

Use these dollar sign ratings to get a rough idea of how much you're likely to spend on a meal, but don't rely only on them. Certainly, you can get $$ meals at $$$ restaurants — and vice versa — depending on what you order. Remember, too, that many restaurants offer specials and prix fixe meals that the dollar signs don't reflect.

As you peruse the listings, check the maps to see a restaurant's location. The map in this chapter shows the location of many of the restaurants listed in Chapters 13 and 15, in addition to the restaurants listed in this chapter. The indexes at the end of the chapter help you select a restaurant by location, price, or type of cuisine.

My Favorite Chicago Restaurants

Ambria

$$$$ Lincoln Park   FRENCH

Ambria is one of Chicago's finest restaurants. Housed in the stately Belden-Stratford Hotel (now mostly condominiums), Chicago's classical French restaurant consistently maintains a high standard. You find deals being brokered and couples celebrating anniversaries in the wood-paneled, clublike atmosphere. Service is exemplary, from the charming hostess who makes you feel comfortable in the upscale French atmosphere, to the professional wait staff. The food, from roasted rack of lamb, to medallions of New Zealand venison, is superb. Order a souffle for dessert when you order your main course (so they have time to prepare this light-as-air French classic).

2300 Lincoln Park West (at Belden Avenue). ☎ *773-472-0076. CTA: Bus 151 to Belden Avenue. Reservations recommended. Main courses: $22–$35; fixed-price meals $48–$64. AE, DC, DISC, MC, V. Open: Mon–Thurs 11:30 a.m.–11 p.m., Fri–Sat 11:30 a.m.–midnight, Sun 5–9 p.m.*

Ann Sather

$ Andersonville and North Side   SWEDISH

Gooey, buttery-soft homemade cinnamon rolls are reason enough to visit this mecca of Swedish delights. So are thin Swedish pancakes with lingonberry sauce, and maybe a side of mild Swedish potato sausage. This popular breakfast spot is especially busy on weekends — you may have to wait, but lines move quickly. Hearty, inexpensive lunches include chopped beefsteak, roast pork loin, and meatballs. In the heart of the Andersonville neighborhood, Ann Sather's is bright and cheerful, decorated with paintings from a Swedish fairy tale. A sister restaurant (the original Ann Sather's) is at 929 W. Belmont Avenue (☎ **773-348-2378**).

5207 N. Clark St. ☎ *773-271-6677. CTA: Bus 22 to North Clark and Foster, ½ block away. Reservations not accepted. Main courses: Breakfast $4.25–$6; Lunch $6–$11. AE, DISC, MC, V. Open: Mon–Fri 7 a.m.–3:30 p.m., Sat–Sun 7 a.m.–5:30 p.m.*

Arun's

$$$$$ North Side THAI

Stunningly beautiful Thai food and a prix-fixe menu make this the best Thai restaurant in the city. For my money, this restaurant may be the best Thai restaurant in the country. Tucked away in a far north and west neighborhood, the restaurant's unassuming exterior cloaks a spectacular interior. This restaurant recently switched to a prix-fixe-only menu for $75. Expensive, but worth it. On any given night, you may sample hot-and-sour shrimp soup, three-flavored red snapper, or garlic prawns. And the desserts are a work of art.

4156 N. Kedzie (at Irving Park Road). ☎ *773-539-1909. CTA: Blue line to Irving Park Road, then transfer to eastbound bus 80; or brown line to Irving Park, then transfer to westbound bus 80. Reservations recommended. Main courses: Prix-fixe menu only for $75 per person. AE, CB, DC, DISC, MC, V. Open: Tues–Sat 5–10 p.m., Sun 5–9:30 p.m.*

Atwood Cafe

$$ Loop ECLECTIC

Colorful and offbeat, this stylish eatery in the Hotel Burnham is interesting, fun, and has fantastic food. One of the best new dining sites in the Loop, this romantic spot is filled with nooks and cranies and sofalike seats. Don't miss the mussels in a garlicky tomato sauce with crusty grilled homemade bread. The bar is small, so you're allowed to take drinks and sit in cozy chairs around the fireplace in the hotel lobby.

1 W. Washington St. (at State Street). ☎ *312-368-1900. CTA: Bus 151 to Washington and Michigan, then walk west. Reservations recommended. Main courses: $14–$25. AE, DISC, MC, V. Open: Breakfast, Mon–Fri 7–10 a.m., Sat 8–10:30 a.m., Sun brunch 8 a.m.–3 p.m.; Lunch Mon–Sat 11:30 a.m.–3 p.m.; afternoon tea Mon–Sun 3–5 p.m.; dinner Mon–Sun 5:30–10 p.m.; bar open Mon–Sun 11 a.m.–11 p.m.*

Bice

$$ Streeterville ITALIAN

This sleek, flashy restaurant just east of Michigan Avenue serves homemade pasta and other Northern Italian fare. It's often busy, but the bar is stylish and pleasant enough to rest your weary feet after a long day of shopping or touring. Many prefer to sit outside, where you can watch passers-by.

158 E. Ontario Street. ☎ *312-664-1474. CTA: Buses stop on Michigan Avenue, 1 block west. Reservations recommended. Main courses: $5–$14. AE, DC, MC, V. Open: Mon–Sat 11 a.m.–11 p.m., Sun 11 a.m.–9 p.m.*

Dining in the Loop and Near North

Atwood Cafe **29**
Bice **14**
Bistro 110 **7**
Bistro Zinc **4**
Blackhawk Lodge **12**
Café Iberico **9**
Centro **11**
Chez Joël **27**
Cyrano's Bistro & Wine Bar **15**
Flat Top Grill **1**
Frontera Grill & Topolobampo **44**
Gibson's Steakhouse **5**
Gino's East **10**
Harry Caray's **20**
Harvest on Huron **13**
Heaven on Seven **30**
Hubbard Street Grill **18**
Iron Mike's Grille **8**
Joe's Seafood, Prime Steak and Stone Crab **17**
Kamehachi **2**
Lou Mitchell's **26**
Mossant **21**
Nine **22**
Pump Room **3**
The Saloon **6**
Shaw's Crab House **19**
Sushi Wabi **24**
Trattoria No. 10 **28**
Vivo **23**
Wishbone **25**
Zinfandel **16**

Subway/El stop

For stops in the Loop, see the "Downtown El & Subway Stations" map on the Cheat Sheet.

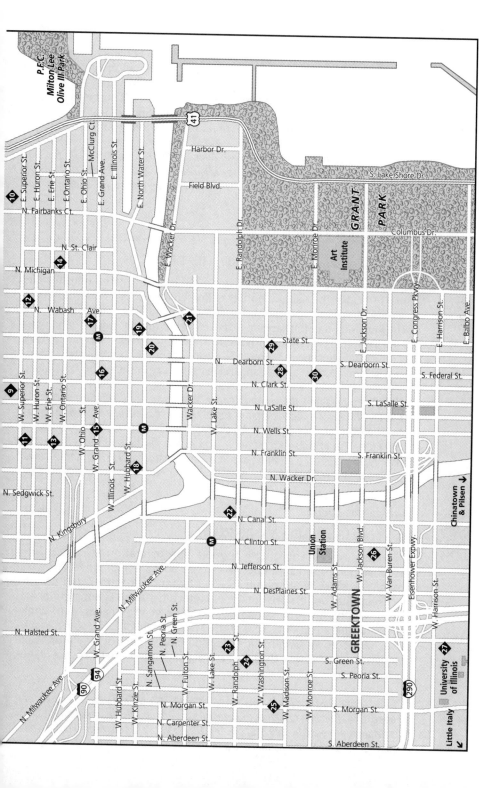

Bistro 110

$$ Magnificent Mile AMERICAN

The neighborhood crowd gathers at Bistro 110 for its changing weekly specials, posted on a chalkboard on one wall of the restaurant (you can also check out the temperature and other local news). You can get a grilled piece of fish, steak, or roasted veggie platter. Because it's a neighborhood crowd, the atmosphere is relaxed and kid-friendly. Sunday brunch is a popular ritual. Get there early — or be prepared for a long wait.

110 E. Pearson St. (just west of Michigan Avenue). ☎ *312-266-3110. CTA: Red line to Chicago/State; 151 bus to Water Tower. Main courses: $12–$29. AE, CB, DC, DISC, MC, V. Open: Mon–Thurs 11:30 a.m.–11 p.m., Fri–Sat 11:30 a.m.–midnight, Sun 11 a.m.–10 p.m.*

Bistro Zinc

$-$$$ Gold Coast and North Side BISTRO

The curving zinc bar, where you find hard-boiled eggs on offer for customers to eat at the bar and bottles of French liqueur, such as Chartreuse, is the most striking feature of this French bistro. The Southport Avenue restaurant has a cafe that offers more casual dining, plus a velvet-curtained formal dining room with red-leather banquettes. The smaller Gold Coast restaurant has one large, tile-floored room with a bar area. Salade frisee, salade niçoise, skate fish, and escargot are some of the specialties.

3443 N. Southport Ave. (between Belmont Avenue and Addison Street). ☎ *773-281-3443. CTA: Brown line to Belmont. Reservations recommended. Main courses: Cafe, $7–$13; restaurant, $10–$17. AE, DC, MC, V. Open: Cafe Tues–Thurs 5–10 p.m., Fri 5–11 p.m., Sat 11 a.m.–11 p.m., Sun 11 a.m.–9 p.m. Restaurant Tues–Thurs 5:30–10 p.m., Fri–Sat 5:30–11 p.m., Sun 5–9 p.m. Second location at 1131 N. State St. (near Rush Street).* ☎ *312-337-1131.*

Blackhawk Lodge

$$$ Magnificent Mile AMERICAN

This cozy restaurant offers a good approximation of a northern Wisconsin lodge and supper club — more upscale than most Wisconsin versions. A screened-in porch area is pleasant in summer, and the fireplaces and big booths are comfy in wintertime. Food is substantial and homey. The highly professional wait staff serve crab cakes, corn chowder, trout, and steak — typical of the Midwestern fare. The warm atmosphere, large crowd (where kids blend in easily), and homey food make this a good place to take the kids for a big night out — because the dishes are a bit pricey.

41 E. Superior St. (at Wabash Avenue). ☎ *312-280-4080. Reservations recommended. CTA: Red line to Chicago/State; buses stop on Michigan Avenue, 1 block east. Main courses: $16–$28. AE, CB, DC, DISC, MC, V. Open: Mon–Fri 5–10 p.m., Sat 5–10 p.m., Sun 11–3 p.m. and 5–9 p.m.*

Café Absinthe

$$$ Bucktown/Wicker Park   ECLECTIC

Café Absinthe doesn't look like much from the outside (in fact, you enter from the alleyway), but the romantic interior is the perfect place to linger over a meal with a date. Draperies divide the tables, creating privacy for a tete-a-tete. Food is interesting and changes weekly. Features may include seared tuna or beef tenderloin. Dessert is as exotic as the rest of the meal — if it's available, try the passion-fruit tart with baked meringue.

1954 W. North Ave. ☎ *773-278-4488. Reservations recommended. CTA: Blue line to Damen. Main courses: $15–$22. AE, DC, DISC, MC, V. Open: Mon–Thurs 5:30–10 p.m.; Fri–Sat 5:30–11 p.m.; Sun 5:30–9 p.m.*

Café Iberico

$ River North   SPANISH

Sure, this place is loud. And boisterous. And crowded. But the food is fresh, authentic, and inexpensive. You may try going in the off hours, such as very late at night (after 10 p.m.) or early (at 4 p.m., after a day of shopping or touring). Tapas (appetizer-size portions perfect for sharing) include baked goat cheese, grilled octopus, and tortilla española. Order a pitcher of sangria and join in the fun. Great for a group and it stays open late.

739 N. LaSalle St. (between Chicago Avenue and Superior Street. ☎ *312-573-1510. Reservations accepted during the week for parties of six or more. CTA: Red line to Chicago/State. Main courses: $8–$13; tapas $3.50–$5. DC, DISC, MC, V. Open: Mon–Thurs 11 a.m.–11 p.m., Fri 11 a.m.–1:30 a.m.; Sat noon–1:30 a.m.; Sun noon–11 p.m.*

Centro

$$$ River North   ITALIAN

Plentiful platters of pasta, an impressive rendition of chicken Vesuvio, and a penne in vodka sauce to die for make this one of Chicago's most popular Italian restaurants. The lively crowd makes the decibel level rise, but if you sit outside, you may get some relief.

710 N. Wells St. (between Huron and Superior Streets). ☎ *312-988-7775. Reservations recommended. CTA: Brown line to Chicago. Main courses: $12–$30. AE, DC, DISC, MC, V. Open: Mon–Thurs 11 a.m.–11 p.m.; Fri 11 a.m.–11:30 p.m.; Sat noon–11:30 p.m.; Sun 4–10 p.m.*

Charlie Trotter's

$$$$$ Lincoln Park   NOUVELLE

Welcome to foodie Mecca. Charlie Trotter's is a destination, not just a restaurant. Located in a 1908-built brownstone, the food outshines the restaurant's setting. Highly stylized items and lush ingredients make for

Dining in Lincoln Park and Wrigleyville

Ambria **6**
Ann Sather **5**
Arun's **1**
Bistrot Zinc **3**
Charlie Trotter's **7**
Mia Francesca **4**
Tango Sur **2**
Twin Anchors **8**

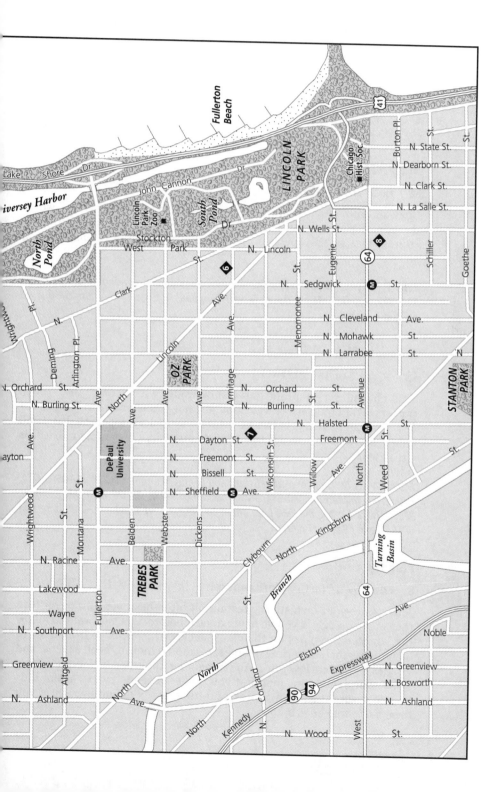

complex dishes that are innovative, improvisational, and harmonious. The grand menu degustation ($115) changes daily, and a vegetable menu is $90. Table Four by the kitchen allows for the best viewing and must be booked well in advance for $150/person, which includes the price of the meal.

816 W. Armitage (near Halsted Street). ☎ *773-248-6228. Internet:* www. charlietrotters.com. *Reservations required. CTA: Brown line to Armitage. Fixed-price dinners: $90–$115. AE, CB, DC, DISC, MC, V. Open: Tues–Sat from 6 p.m.*

Chez Joël

$$ Little Italy   BISTRO

Cozy and romantic, this tiny piece of France in Little Italy is well worth the trip. A pretty garden is a wonderful setting in the summer. Main courses may be fish specials, steak frites, braised lamb shank, and coq au vin.

1119 W. Taylor. ☎ *312-226-6479. Reservations recommended. Main courses: $12–$22. AE, DC, MC, V. Open: Mon–Fri 11 a.m.–3 p.m.; Mon–Thurs 5–10 p.m.; Fri–Sat 5–11 p.m.*

Cyrano's Bistro & Wine Bar

$$ River North   BISTRO

This charming restaurant has yellow walls, gilt mirrors, and French posters — after a glass of wine, you just may think you're in France. For $25, you can have a prix-fixe feast that may include lobster salad, lamb chops, and a lemon-orange tart. A four-course lunch special for $10.95 is a real deal.

546 N. Wells St. (between Ohio Street and Grand Avenue). ☎ *312-467-0546. CTA: Brown line to Merchandise Mart. Main courses: $9–$22. AE, DC, DISC, MC, V. Open: Mon–Thurs 11:30 a.m.–2:30 p.m. and 5:30–10 p.m.; Fri 11:30 a.m.–2:30 p.m. and 5–10:30 p.m.; Sat 5–11 p.m.*

Flat Top Grill

$ Old Town/North Side/Randolph St. Market District   ASIAN

This create-your-own stir-fry restaurant often has lines, but never fear, they move quickly. If you've never done it before, you may want to follow the suggested recipes on the giant blackboards. Choose from over 70 ingredients including rice, noodles, seafood, chicken, beef, sauces, and veggies — for one low price. And remember, the price includes multiple visits to the food line. If at first you don't succeed, try, try again. Kids love to create their own dishes, and the price is definitely right if you have a few wee ones in tow.

319 W. North Ave. ☎ *312-787-7676. CTA: 76 bus stops on North Avenue. Open: Mon–Thurs 5 –10 p.m., Fri 11:30 a.m.–3 p.m. and 5–11 p.m., Sat 11:30 a.m.–11 p.m., Sun 11:30 a.m.–10 p.m.; 1000 W. Washington Blvd.* ☎ *312-829-4800. CTA: The neighborhood is a $5 cab ride form downtown. Open: Mon–Thurs 11 a.m.–10 p.m., Fri–Sat 11 a.m.–11 p.m., Sun 11 a.m.–9 p.m.; 3200 N. Southport Ave.* ☎ *773-665-8100. CTA: Brown line to Southport. Open: Mon–Wed 5 p.m.–10 p.m., Thurs 11:30 a.m.–3 p.m. and 5–10 p.m., Fri 11:30 a.m.–3 p.m. and 5–11 p.m., Sat 11:30 a.m.–11 p.m., Sun 11:30 a.m.–10 p.m. Internet:* www.flattopgrill.com. *Main courses: one price, lunch $8; dinner $11. AE, DC, DISC, MC, V.*

Frontera Grill/Topolobampo

$$–$$$$ **River North**   **MEXICAN**

Owners Rick and Deann Bayless travel extensively throughout Mexico gathering authentic regional recipes for what is arguably one of America's best Mexican restaurants. Topolobampo is more upscale, and you can order off its menu at its sister eatery, Frontera Grill. Try the signature *tacos al carbon* (precursor of Americanized fajitas) or chili-marinated stuffed quail with smoky red beans, enchiladas, browned potatoes, and tangy cabbage. If you're unable to decide among the innovative offerings, try the chef's tasting dinner — five courses for $45.

445 N. Clark St. (between Illinois and Hubbard streets). ☎ *312-661-1434. Reservations recommended at Topolobampo, not accepted at Frontera Grill. CTA: Red line to Grand (at State Street). Main courses: $7–$19. AE, DC, DISC, MC, V. Open: Tues–Fri 11:30 a.m.–2:30 p.m. and 5–10 p.m.; Sat 11:30 a.m.–2:30 p.m. and 5–11 p.m.*

Gibson's Steakhouse

$$$$ **Gold Coast**   **STEAKHOUSE**

Chicagoans come here to see and be seen, and the food isn't bad either. Photos of celebs decorate the Art Deco rooms. The bar has its own life, with the who's who of the city mingling and mixing. Everything is larger than life, from the patrons to the martinis, which come in ten-ounce glasses. Entrees are also giant sized and well-aged steaks are the star of the show. This is Chicago's highest-grossing restaurant (and the 11th highest-grossing restaurant in the country), so call well in advance for reservations.

1028 N. Rush St. (at Bellevue Place). ☎ *312-266-8999. CTA: Red line to Clark/Division. Reservations recommended. Main courses: $22–$30. AE, CB, DC, DISC, MC, V. Open: Daily 3 p.m.–midnight (bar open later).*

Gino's East

$ **Magnificent Mile**   **PIZZA**

Chicago's famous pizzeria serves up deep-dish pizzas in the classic style. And, patrons are welcome to scrawl on the graffiti-covered walls and furniture, making this a favorite among kids. This pizza is so filling that one piece is more than a meal for many. Three or more pieces is enough to send you into cholesterol overdrive.

160 E. Superior St. (at Rush Street). ☎ *312-943-1124. CTA: Red line to Clark/State. Reservations not accepted. Main courses: Deep dish pizza from $11–$18. AE, CB, DC, DISC, MC, V. Open: Mon–Thurs 11 a.m.–10 p.m.; Fri–Sat 11 a.m.–midnight; Sun noon–10 p.m.*

Harry Caray's

$$ River North   ITALIAN/STEAKHOUSE

Holy cow! One of Chicago's most flamboyant eateries is larger than life, like its namesake, legendary baseball broadcaster Harry Caray. From the huge baseball bat outside to showcases filled with uniforms, helmets, cards, and photographs, this is Valhalla for those who follow America's favorite pastime. (Have you ever hurled a baseball from a pitcher's mound to home plate? To get an idea of the distance, take a look at the bar at Harry Caray's restaurant. It measures 60 feet, 6 inches, the exact distance from hill to plate.) The food is pretty good, too — steaks, chops, pasta with red sauce, and such Italian basics as chicken Vesuvio, cheese ravioli, and calamari. The bar offers homemade thick-cut potato chips that can be addictive. Be careful not to ruin your appetite!

33 W. Kinzie St. (at Dearborn Street). ☎ *312-828-0966. Reservations recommended for lunch, accepted for dinner only for parties of 8 or more. CTA: Brown line El to Merchandise Mart, or red line El to Grand (at State Street). Main courses: $8–$30. AE, DC, DISC, MC, V. Open: Lunch weekdays; sandwich menu/bar only Sat 11:30 a.m.–4 p.m. and Sun noon–4 p.m.; dinner daily.*

Harvest on Huron

$$ River North   ECLECTIC

A great wine list makes Harvest on Huron's bar as appealing as the restaurant. And in fact, you may want to come here for the nightlife alone. In my opinion, though, the food deserves as much attention as the hip crowd. Roasted breast of guinea hen and grilled tuna are excellent choices. As is fitting for a restaurant in Chicago's gallery district, the walls are covered in fabulous art.

217 W. Huron (between Wells and Franklin Streets). ☎ *312-587-9600. Reservations recommended for dinner. CTA: Brown line to Franklin. Main courses: $12–$26. AE, DC, DISC, MC, V. Open: Mon–Fri 11:30 a.m.–2:30 p.m.; Mon–Thurs 5:30–10:00 p.m.; Fri–Sat 5:30 p.m.–12 a.m.*

Heaven on Seven

$$ Loop CAJUN

Tucked away on the seventh floor of the Garland Building, you can find what may well be the best Cajun and Creole cooking north of New Orleans. Don't miss the acclaimed gumbo, po' boy sandwiches (try the oyster and soft-shell crab versions), hoppin' John (black-eyed peas), and spicy jambalaya. Sweet potato pie and bread pudding are top desserts. Coffee comes with chicory. Although many regulars prefer the original, the restaurant has a trendy new location on the Magnificent Mile at 600 N. Michigan Ave., at Rush and Ohio Streets (☎ 312-280-7774). It's open Sunday to Thursday from 11 a.m. to 10 p.m., Friday and Saturday from 11 a.m. to 11 p.m.

111 N. Wabash Ave. (at Washington Street). ☎ 312-263-6443. CTA: Orange, brown, or green line to Madison/Wabash, then walk 1 block north. Reservations not accepted. Menu items: $2.75–$10. No credit cards. Open: Mon–Fri 7 a.m.–5 p.m., Sat–Sun 10 a.m.–3 p.m., first & third Fri of each month 5:30–9 p.m.

Hubbard Street Grill

$$ River North AMERICAN

Colorful, big, and busy (but not noisy), Hubbard Street Grill is a great lunch spot. A bowl of soup can be a meal when combined with the bread basket. Salads, burgers, grilled fish, and more complete the menu. The scene is less lively at dinner, but right after work you can find a crowd of casual diners. Roasted half chicken and whitefish share the bill with filet mignon.

351 W. Hubbard St. ☎ 312-222-0770. CTA: Red line to Clark/Grand. Reservations not necessary. Main courses: $10–$25. AE, DC, DISC, MC, V. Open: Mon–Thurs 11:30 a.m.–9 p.m.; Fri 11:30 a.m.–10 p.m.; Sat 5–10 p.m. (weekdays, lunch is served until 5 p.m.).

Iron Mike's Grille

$$$ Magnificent Mile STEAKHOUSE

For many Chicago football diehards, the glory days of former Coach Mike Ditka are still alive and well. From the football memorabilia to the menu's "duck cigars" appetizer, this place is all guy. (For the uninitiated, duck cigars are a hand-rolled pastry filled with a duck and mushroom mixture.) Local celebs and a sleek crowd gather here. Televisions in the bar allow you to drink Scotch and watch the Bears while praying for "Da Coach" to come home to Chicago. Upstairs, cigar smoking reigns in the lounge area. The hamburger here can feed two and is one of the city's best.

100 E. Chestnut St. (in the Tremont Hotel, between Michigan and Rush). ☎ 312-587-8989. CTA: Red line to Chicago/State or 151 bus to Water Tower. Reservations accepted. Main courses: $12–$33 (less at breakfast and lunch). AE, DC, DISC, MC, V. Open: Mon–Thurs 7 a.m.–11 p.m.; Fri–Sat 7 a.m.–midnight; Sun 7 a.m.–10 p.m.

Jane's

$$ Bucktown-Wicker Park   ECLECTIC

I almost hate to write about Jane's. It's my favorite restaurant — and a local secret. Casual and chic, the restaurant is located in an old house that was gutted, so it's open to the ceiling. The walls are decorated with ever-changing work by local artists. In the winter, soft yellow light makes the place cozy; in the summer, you can sit outside at sidewalk tables. Wicker Park residents pack the place, so you usually wind up squeezing into the bar area to wait. But the experience is worth it. Try Jane's version of salade niçoise, with grilled ahi tuna. Seared sea bass is also a fave.

1655 W. Cortland St. (1 block west of Ashland Avenue). ☎ *773-862-5263. CTA: Blue line to Damen (walk three blocks north on Damen Avenue, four blocks east on Cortland). Reservations available on a limited basis. Main courses: $8–$21. MC, V. Open: Mon–Thurs 5–10 p.m.; Fri 5–11 p.m.; Sat 11 a.m.–11 p.m.; Sun 11 a.m.–10 p.m.*

Joe's Seafood, Prime Steak and Stone Crab

$$$ Magnificent Mile   SEAFOOD/STEAKHOUSE

Here's a little piece of Miami Beach transplanted to the North Bridge area. The only outpost of famed Joe's Stone Crab of Miami Beach opened here in late 2000. If you've never had stone crab, Joe's may be just the thing. The crab claws are flown in from Florida and cracked perfectly so as to preserve the delectable meat. (**Note:** The claws are served cold.) Sides include creamed spinach and hash browns. The key lime pie is the best I've ever had — and believe me, I've tasted many. If you get hooked, never fear. You can order stone crabs from Joe's over the Web and they'll arrive via Fed Ex the next day, packed in dry ice.

60 E. Grand Ave., at the corner of Grand and Rush (behind Marriott Hotel). ☎ *312-379-5637. Internet: www.leye.com. CTA: Red line to State/Grand. Reservations recommended and available on limited basis. Main courses: $15–$50 (depends on market price). AE, CB, DC, DISC, MC, V. Open: Mon–Thurs 11:30 a.m.–10 p.m.; Fri–Sat 11:30 a.m.–11 p.m.; Sun 4 p.m.–10 p.m.*

Kamehachi

$$ Old Town   SUSHI

When my sushi-loving friends and I debate the merits of Chicago sushi spots, we always come back to Kamehachi. The atmosphere is fun and the sushi is fresh. In the fast-changing restaurant world, Kamehachi's record is impressive. This family-owned restaurant has been going since 1967, when it opened Chicago's first sushi bar. If you have a group, call ahead and book the tatami room, where you can make plenty of noise and linger over dinner. Otherwise, ask for a table upstairs where you can watch the good-looking crowd.

Dining and Nightlife in Bucktown/Wicker Park

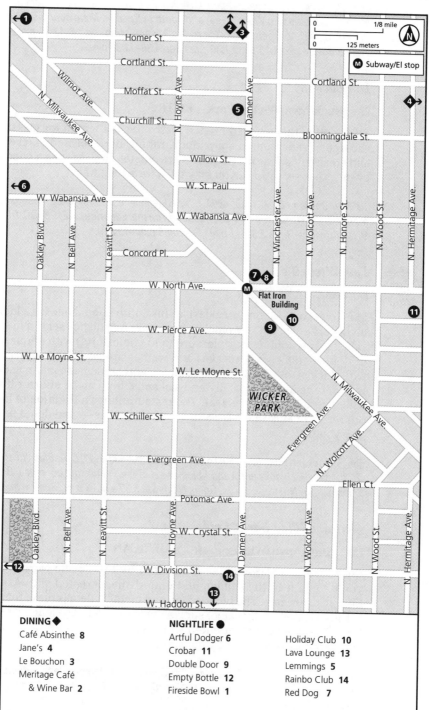

Homer St.

Cortland St.

Moffat St.

Churchill St.

Wilmot Ave.

N. Milwaukee Ave.

N. Hoyne Ave.

N. Damen Ave.

Cortland St.

Bloomingdale St.

Willow St.

W. St. Paul

W. Wabansia Ave.

W. Wabansia Ave.

Oakley Blvd.

N. Bell Ave.

N. Leavitt St.

Concord Pl.

N. Winchester Ave.

N. Wolcott Ave.

N. Honore St.

N. Wood St.

N. Hermitage Ave.

W. North Ave.

Flat Iron Building

W. Pierce Ave.

W. Le Moyne St.

W. Le Moyne St.

WICKER PARK

W. Schiller St.

Hirsch St.

Evergreen Ave.

N. Milwaukee Ave.

Evergreen Ave.

N. Wolcott Ave.

Ellen Ct.

Potomac Ave.

Oakley Blvd.

N. Bell Ave.

N. Leavitt St.

N. Hoyne Ave.

W. Crystal St.

N. Damen Ave.

N. Wolcott Ave.

N. Wood St.

N. Hermitage Ave.

W. Division St.

W. Haddon St.

0   1/8 mile
0   125 meters

M Subway/El stop

DINING ◆
Café Absinthe **8**
Jane's **4**
Le Bouchon **3**
Meritage Café
    & Wine Bar **2**

NIGHTLIFE ●
Artful Dodger **6**
Crobar **11**
Double Door **9**
Empty Bottle **12**
Fireside Bowl **1**

Holiday Club **10**
Lava Lounge **13**
Lemmings **5**
Rainbo Club **14**
Red Dog **7**

1400 N. Wells St. (at Schiller Street). ☎ *312-664-3663. Internet:* www.kamehachi.com. *Reservations recommended. CTA: No. 22 Clark Street bus to Clark and North Avenue, walk west to Wells Street and south to Schiller. Main courses: $8–$15. AE, DC, DISC, MC, V. Open: Mon–Thurs 11:30 a.m.–2 p.m. and 5–12:30 p.m.; Fri–Sat 11:30 a.m.–2 p.m. and 5 p.m.–1:30 a.m.; Sun 4:30–11:30 p.m.*

Le Bouchon

$$ Bucktown/Wicker Park   BISTRO

This idyllic, tin-ceilinged French bistro packs them in for classics like escargot, French onion soup, duck, rabbit, herb-roasted chicken, fish, and steak frites. The fruit desserts are outstanding. At such a good price, even with reservations, you may be in for a long wait.

1958 N. Damen. ☎ *773-862-6600. CTA: Blue line to Damen. Reservations recommended. Main courses: $15–$50 (depends on market price). AE, CB, DC, DISC, MC, V. Open: Mon–Thurs 5:30–11 p.m.; Fri–Sat 5 p.m.–12 a.m.*

Lou Mitchell's

$ Loop   AMERICAN

Plan to eat at least one breakfast at this South Loop diner. It's a long-time favorite, known for airy omelets and other egg dishes served in sizzling skillets. You double your pleasure (and cholesterol) with Mitchell's use of double-yolk eggs. Pancakes and waffles are good, too. Orders come with thick slabs of toasted Greek bread and homemade marmalade. The wait can be long, especially on weekends, but can be shorter if you're willing to take a counter seat. The restaurant has a tradition of handing out boxes of Milk Duds to waiting female patrons — and donut holes for everyone.

565 W. Jackson Blvd. (at Jefferson Street). ☎ *312-939-3111. CTA: Blue line to Clinton St., then walk 2 blocks north and 1 block west. Reservations not accepted. Breakfast items: $2–$7. No credit cards. Open: Mon–Sat 5:30 a.m.–3 p.m., Sun 7 a.m.–3 p.m.*

Meritage Wine Bar & Café

$$$ Bucktown/Wicker Park   AMERICAN

Chef Jonathan Harootunian is inspired by the Pacific Northwest and you'll taste it in the salmon and crab dishes, created with Asian and European accents. The blond wood and metallic details make this a cozy setting. There's daily game, such as venison and excellent seared scallops. The West Coast–oriented wine list is heavy on Bordeaux blends, with more than 20 wines by the glass.

2118 N. Damen. ☎ *773-235-6434. CTA: Blue line to Damen. Reservations recommended. Main courses: $15–$23. AE, DC, MC, V. Open: 5:30–11 p.m.; Fri–Sat 5:30 p.m.–12 a.m.; Sun 5–10 p.m.*

Mia Francesca

$$ North Side and Little Italy   ITALIAN

The place is crowded, noisy, overly warm — and people love it. Thanks to the generous helpings of pasta at reasonable prices, you always have a wait. My longest wait was one hour and 45 minutes, so pace yourself so you don't wind up drinking a bit too much on an empty stomach at the bar. That potential pitfall aside, it's hard not to love the food. The menu changes weekly and might include thin-crust pizza appetizers, four-cheese ravioli, linguine with seafood, and farfalle with ham, peas, and wild mushrooms. A second location is open in Little Italy with the same menu and less frenetic atmosphere. Francesca's on Taylor is located at 1400 W. Taylor Street (☎ 312-829-2828).

3311 N. Clark St. (just north of Belmont Avenue). ☎ *773-276-8700. Internet:* www.miafrancesca.com. *CTA: Red line to Belmont. Reservations not accepted. Main courses: $9–$23. AE, MC, V. Open: Sun–Thurs 5–10:30 p.m.; Fri–Sat 5–11 p.m.*

Mossant

$$ North Loop   BISTRO

Mossant, modeled after a Parisian bistro, serves the best fries in the city. The pommes frites (with Dijon mayonnaise for dipping) accompany mussels steamed in Muscadet. Executive Chef Mehdi Spadavecchia aims to revive bistro classics. He says, "I love food that is simple, balanced, and not overly rich — food like your mother used to cook, if she was French." The decor features red leather booths, whimsical vintage French posters, and artwork that plays on the hat theme, celebrating Mossant's namesake Parisian milliner.

In Hotel Monaco, 225 N. Wabash Ave. (near the junction of East Wacker Drive and South Water Street). ☎ *312-236-9300. CTA: Buses stop at State and Wacker; walk 1 block south. Purple, brown, orange, or green line to Lake/State, then walk 1 block south. Reservations recommended. Main courses: $15–$25. AE, DC, DISC, MC, V. Open: Breakfast and lunch weekdays 7–10:30 a.m. and 11:30 a.m.–2:30 p.m.; brunch Sat–Sun 8 a.m.–2 p.m.; dinner daily 5–10 p.m.*

Nine

$$$ Loop   SEAFOOD/STEAKHOUSE

Chicago's trend-setters are flocking to Nine in droves. Crowd pleasers such as plasma TV screens in the seductive lounge and the boys restroom, a circular "ice bar" just for champagne and caviar, and an upstairs Ghost Lounge, whose signature drink is a glow-in-the-dark Midori martini, make Nine a scene any night of the week. The icy, metallic look of mirrored tiles and stainless steel are warmed with the use of ash wood in the décor. And the food is based on straightforward favorites of steak

and seafood. You'll find Chilean sea bass, ahi tuna, a 22-ounce veal porterhouse, and filet mignon on the menu — most with an interesting twist
(the sea bass is wrapped in pancetta and is highly recommended!).

*440 W. Randolph St. ☎ 312-575-9900. CTA: 125 and 129 bus to Randolph and Canal;
Green line. Reservations recommended well in advance. Main courses: $14–$32.
AE, DC, DISC, MC, V. Open: Lunch: Mon–Fri 11 a.m.–2 p.m.; Dinner: Mon–Wed
5:30–10 p.m.; Thurs 5:30–11 p.m.; Fri and Sat 5:30 p.m. to midnight. Ghost Bar: Thurs
and Fri 9 p.m.–2 a.m.; Sat 9 p.m.–3 a.m.*

Pump Room

$$$ Gold Coast FRENCH

A $2 million restoration has brought Chicago's most famous restaurant
back to life. Once the bastion of stars whose appearance in Booth One
would guarantee a photo in the newspaper the next morning, the Pump
Room is slightly less star-filled these days — but the room has been
restored to its former glory, in the original cobalt blue and gold décor.
The jury is still out on the cuisine, as the chef who re-opened the place
left in February 2001. However, things are looking good for the Pump
Room. Service is now provided by a well-trained crew, and the food pro-
vides some creative twists on old classics, including veal sweetbreads
with Idaho potatoes and foie gras and Muscovy duck in a mango sauce.

The Pump Room has a dress code — and it's enforced. Men must wear
jackets after 4 p.m., and no jeans are allowed.

*1301 N. State Pkwy. ☎ 312-266-0360. CTA: Buses stop on Lake Shore Drive, several
blocks east. Reservations recommended. Main courses: $23–$34. AE, DC, DISC,
MC, V. Open: Breakfast: daily 6:30–10:30 a.m.. Lunch: Mon–Sat 11:30 a.m.–2:30 p.m.
Dinner: Mon–Thurs 6–10 p.m.; Fri and Sat 5 p.m. to midnight; Sun 5–10 p.m. Brunch
Sun 11 a.m.–2:30 p.m.*

The Saloon

$$$ Streeterville STEAKHOUSE

The Saloon is all that a steakhouse should be. It has a warm, cheery look
and is usually filled with happy, animated carnivores attacking high-
quality cuts of flavorful beef. You can't go wrong with steaks, suitably
marbled and dry-aged, but many regulars go for pork chops prepared in
the restaurant's smoker. Be sure to try a side of bacon-scallion mashed
potatoes. The potable of choice is a "Bloody Bull," made with beef bouil-
lon and garnished with anchovy-and-blue-cheese-stuffed olives.

*200 E. Chestnut St. (at Mies van der Rohe Way). ☎ 312-280-5454. CTA: Buses stop on
Michigan Avenue, 1 block west. Reservations recommended. Main courses: $12–$27.
AE, DC, DISC, MC, V. Open: Mon–Sat 11 a.m. to midnight, Sun 11 a.m.–10 p.m.*

Shaw's Crab House and Blue Crab Lounge

$$ River North SEAFOOD

You'd swear you stepped into a 1940s-era restaurant on the Atlantic Coast at Shaw's. Fresh seafood is the specialty, with fried smelt, sautéed sea scallops, and grilled fish among the fare. The adjoining Blue Crab Lounge offers an excellent raw bar and jazz or blues — although some of us are entertained simply by watching the shuckers do their thing.

21 E. Hubbard St. (between State Street and Wabash Avenue). ☎ *312-467-9449. Internet:* www.shaws-chicago.com. *CTA: Red line to State/Grand. Reservations accepted for the main dining room. Main courses: $15–$30. AE, CB, DC, DISC, MC, V. Open: Mon–Thurs 11:30 a.m.–10 p.m.; Fri–Sat 11:30 a.m.–11 p.m.; Sun 5–10 p.m.*

Sushi Wabi

$$ Randolph Street Market District SUSHI

Chicago's hippest sushi restaurant attracts the young and the restless and rewards them with interesting sashimi and sushi, plus maki rolls like the "dragon" — rolled eel and avocado with tempura shrimp as the dragon's head and tail. Exposed brick walls, butcher block tables, and a 19-seat sushi bar set the atmosphere. Desserts are excellent and put green tea and red bean ice cream to new and creative uses.

842 W. Randolph. ☎ *312-563-1224. Transportation: $5 cab ride from the Loop. Reservations recommended. Main courses: $10–$15. AE, DC, DISC, MC, V. Open: Lunch Mon–Fri 11:30 a.m.–2 p.m., dinner Sun and Mon 5–11 p.m., dinner Tues–Sat 5 p.m.–midnight.*

Tango Sur

$ North Side ARGENTINE

This upbeat storefront restaurant, located in one of my favorite neighborhoods, often has lines outside for the mouth-watering Argentine barbecue. Tango music provides the backdrop for the imported Argentine beef, mixed grill of short ribs, sweetbreads, chorizo, and morcilla (blood sausage) with chimichurri (parsley, garlic, and olive oil). Empanadas are a specialty. Afterwards, head down the block to Cullen's for a drink, or catch a movie at Chicago's most charming old-time theater, the Music Box, where an organist plays before the show.

3763 N. Southport (south of Irving Park Road). ☎ *773-477-5466. CTA: Brown line to Belmont, walk north. Reservations not accepted. Main courses: $4.29–$18. AE, DC, DISC, MC, V. Open: Mon–Fri 11:30–1 a.m., Sat 11:30–2 a.m., Sun 11:30 a.m.–11:30 p.m.*

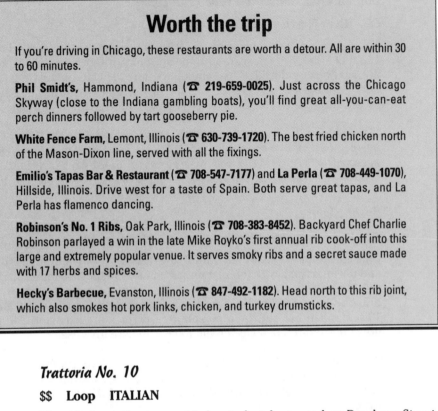

Worth the trip

If you're driving in Chicago, these restaurants are worth a detour. All are within 30 to 60 minutes.

Phil Smidt's, Hammond, Indiana (☎ 219-659-0025). Just across the Chicago Skyway (close to the Indiana gambling boats), you'll find great all-you-can-eat perch dinners followed by tart gooseberry pie.

White Fence Farm, Lemont, Illinois (☎ 630-739-1720). The best fried chicken north of the Mason-Dixon line, served with all the fixings.

Emilio's Tapas Bar & Restaurant (☎ 708-547-7177) and **La Perla** (☎ 708-449-1070), Hillside, Illinois. Drive west for a taste of Spain. Both serve great tapas, and La Perla has flamenco dancing.

Robinson's No. 1 Ribs, Oak Park, Illinois (☎ 708-383-8452). Backyard Chef Charlie Robinson parlayed a win in the late Mike Royko's first annual rib cook-off into this large and extremely popular venue. It serves smoky ribs and a secret sauce made with 17 herbs and spices.

Hecky's Barbecue, Evanston, Illinois (☎ 847-492-1182). Head north to this rib joint, which also smokes hot pork links, chicken, and turkey drumsticks.

Trattoria No. 10

$$ Loop ITALIAN

This ideal pre-theater spot is located underground on Dearborn Street. The dimly lit rooms have a warm orangey glow and ceramic floor tiles, giving the place a Tuscan feel. The real bargain here is the wonderful (and cheap) after-work buffet. In the dining room, pasta reigns. Ravioli (try the butternut squash version) is supreme.

10 N. Dearborn St. (between Madison and Washington Streets). ☎ *312-984-1718. CTA: Red or blue line to Dearborn. Reservations recommended. Main courses: $12–$27. AE, DC, DISC, MC, V. Open: Mon–Thurs 11:30 a.m.–2 p.m. and 5:30–9 p.m.; Fri 11:30 a.m.–2 p.m. and 5:30–10 p.m.*

Tuscany on Taylor

$$ Little Italy ITALIAN

This restaurant is the real thing, one of the most reliable restaurants in Little Italy, with green checkered tablecloths and waiters who wax poetic over pasta. Some of the meals are so rich, you won't need dessert. By the end of the meal, you'll feel like part of the family. Other Tuscan fare includes pizzas, veal, chicken, and a risotto of the day.

1014 W. Taylor St. (between Racine Avenue and Halsted Street). ☎ *312-829-1990. Internet:* www.stefanirestaurants.com. *CTA: Blue line to Polk. Reservations* recommended. Main courses: $9.50–$27. AE, DC, DISC, MC, V. Open: Mon–Fri 11 a.m.–3:30 p.m.; Mon–Thurs 5–11 p.m.; Fri–Sat 5 p.m.–midnight; Sun 2–9:30 p.m.

Twin Anchors

$ Old Town   BARBECUE

Although it keeps classy company in a neighborhood of elegant brownstones, this eatery is strictly a rib joint. Done in dark mahogany and serviceable Formica, it has been around since the days when the Untouchables battled to clean up the city. Sinatra was an occasional patron, and you'll find Ol' Blue Eyes featured prominently on the walls and the jukebox. Meaty slabs of slow-cooked baby back ribs are fall-off-the-bone tender. You can also get steaks and chicken — but ribs are what keep people coming back.

1655 N. Sedgwick St. (1 block north of North Avenue). ☎ 312-266-1616. CTA: Brown line to Sedgwick. Reservations accepted only for parties of 6 or more. Main courses: $7.50–$17. AE, DC, DISC, MC, V. Open: Mon–Thurs 5–11 p.m.; Fri 5 p.m.–12 a.m.; Sat 12 p.m.–12 a.m.; Sun 12–10:30 p.m.

Vivo

$$$ Randolph Street Market District   ITALIAN

In 1991, this restaurant was a pioneer, constructed in an old warehouse in the produce market just west of the Loop. Today, the Market District has become one of the city's dining hot spots, with about ten restaurants scattered among the onions and tomatoes. The glitterati still gather at Vivo, which remains glamorous *and* affordable. The daily spread of antipasti is always worth sampling, as is gazpacho dotted with tiny shrimp. You can't go wrong with pasta or with roasted lamb chops, served with white beans.

Vivo's most requested seating is a solitary table poised atop an old elevator shaft and is booked by celebrities and the romantically inclined. Call well in advance to reserve this special place.

838 W. Randolph (at Halsted). ☎ 312-733-3379. Reservations recommended. Transportation: $5 cab ride from the Loop. Main courses: $11–$21. AE, DC, DISC, MC, V. Open: Lunch weekdays 11:30 a.m.–2:30 p.m., dinner Mon–Wed and Sun 5:30–10 p.m., Thurs 5:30–11 p.m., Fri and Sat 5:30 p.m. to midnight.

Wishbone

$ Randolph Street Market District   CAJUN/SOUTHERN

Primitive art decorates this bright, open restaurant that's always bustling. It's one of the few restaurants in Chicago that draws a highly diverse crowd, from Harpo Studios employees (Oprah is headquartered just around the corner) to families, suits, and creatives. The breakfast is outstanding — try the salmon cakes. Dinner offerings may include pan-fried chicken, jambalaya, or chicken etoufee.

1001 W. Washington St. (at Morgan Street). ☎ *312-850-2663. Transportation: $5 cab ride from the Loop. Reservations accepted only for parties of six or more (no reservations accepted on Sun). Main courses: $5.50–$14. AE, DC, DISC, MC, V. Open: Mon 7 a.m.–3 p.m.; Tues–Thurs 7 a.m.–10 p.m.; Fri 7 a.m.–11 p.m.; Sat 8 a.m.–11 p.m.; Sun 8 a.m.–2:30 p.m.*

Zinfandel

$$ River North AMERICAN

Take a tour of America — each month Chef Susan Goss supplements her menu with offerings from a different region — from the Low Country cooking of South Carolina to Pennsylvania Dutch specialties to the soul food of Hawaii. On the regular menu, don't miss deviled cod cakes, braised pot roast, Oklahoma-style smoked barbecued spare ribs, and garlic mashed potatoes. Buttermilk biscuits cooked to order in an iron skillet are tops. Susan does the cooking, elaborating on recipes handed down from her grandmother; husband Drew buys the wine, assembling an extensive and appealing list.

59 W. Grand Ave. (between Dearborn and Clark Streets). ☎ *312-527-1818. CTA: Red line to Grand (at State Street). Reservations recommended. Main courses: $15.50–$19. AE, DC, MC, V. Open: Mon–Fri 11:30 a.m.–2 p.m.; Mon–Thurs 5–10 p.m.; Fri–Sat 5–11 p.m.; Sat (brunch) 10:30 a.m.–2 p.m.*

Index of Restaurants by Neighborhood

Andersonville

Ann Sather (Swedish, $)

Bucktown/Wicker Park

Café Absinthe (Eclectic, $$$)
Jane's (Eclectic, $$)
Le Bouchon (Bistro, $$)
Meritage Café and Wine Bar
   (American, $$$)

Gold Coast

Bistro Zinc (Bistro, $$$)
Gibson's Steakhouse
   (Steakhouse, $$$$)
Pump Room (French, $$$$)

Lincoln Park

Ambria (French, $$$$)
Charlie Trotter's
   (Nouvelle, $$$$$)

Little Italy

Chez Joel (Bistro, $$)
Francesca's on Taylor (Italian, $$)
Tuscany on Taylor (Italian, $$)

Loop

Atwood Café (Eclectic, $$)
Heaven on Seven (Cajun, $$)
Lou Mitchell's (American, $)
Mossant (Bistro, $$)
Nine (Seafood/Steakhouse, $$$)
Trattoria No. 10 (Italian, $$)

Magnificent Mile

Bistro 110 (American, $$)
Blackhawk Lodge (American, $$$)
Gino's East (Pizza, $)
Iron Mike's Grille
　(Steakhouse, $$$)
Joe's Seafood, Prime Steak and
　Stone Crab (Seafood, $$$)

North Side

Arun's (Thai, $$$$$)
Bistro Zinc (Bistro, $–$$$)
Flat Top Grill (Asian, $)
Mia Francesca (Italian, $$)
Tango Sur (Argentine, $$)

Old Town

Flat Top Grill (Asian, $)
Kamehachi (Sushi, $$)
Twin Anchors (Barbecue, $)

Randolph Street Market District

Flat Top Grill (Asian, $)
Sushi Wabi (Sushi, $$)

Vivo (Italian, $$$)
Wishbone (Cajun/Southern, $)

River North

Café Iberico (Spanish, $)
Centro (Italian, $$$)
Cyrano's Bistro and Wine Bar
　(Bistro, $$)
Frontera Grill/Topolobampo
　(Mexican, $$–$$$$)
Harry Caray's (Italian/
　Steakhouse, $$)
Harvest on Huron (Eclectic, $$)
Hubbard Street Grill
　(American, $$)
Shaw's Crab House and Blue Crab
　Lounge (Seafood, $$)
Zinfandel (American, $$)

Streeterville

Bice (Italian, $$)
The Saloon (Steakhouse, $$$)

Index of Restaurants by Cuisine

American

Bistro 110 (Magnificent Mile, $$)
Blackhawk Lodge (Magnificent
　Mile, $$$)
Hubbard Street Grill (River
　North, $$)
Lou Mitchell's (Loop, $)
Meritage Café and Wine Bar
　(Bucktown/Wicker Park, $$$)
Zinfandel (River North, $$)

Argentine

Tango Sur (North Side, $)

Asian

Flat Top Grill (Old Town, North
　Side, and Randolph Street
　Market District, $)

Barbecue

Twin Anchors (Gold Coast, $)

Bistro

Bistro Zinc (Gold Coast and North
　Side, $–$$$)
Chez Joël (Little Italy, $$)
Cyrano's Bistro & Wine Bar (River
　North, $$)
Le Bouchon (Bucktown/Wicker
　Park, $$)
Mossant (Loop, $$)

Breakfast

Ann Sather (Andersonville and
　North Side, $)
Lou Mitchell's (Loop, $)
Wishbone (Randolph Street
　Market District, $)

Cajun/Creole/Southern

Heaven on Seven (Loop and
  Magnificent Mile, $$)
Wishbone (Randolph Street
  Market District, $)

Eclectic

Atwood Café (Loop, $$)
Café Absinthe (Bucktown/Wicker
  Park, $$$)
Harvest on Huron (River
  North, $$)
Jane's (Bucktown/Wicker
  Park, $$)

French

Ambria (Lincoln Park, $$$$)

Italian

Bice (Magnificent Mile, $$)
Centro (River North, $$$)
Harry Caray's (River North, $$)
Mia Francesca (North Side, $$)
Trattoria No. 10 (Loop, $$)
Tuscany on Taylor (Little Italy, $$)
Vivo (Randolph Street Market
  District, $$$)

Mexican

Frontera Grill/Topolobampo
  (River North, $$–$$$$)

Nouvelle

Charlie Trotter's (Lincoln
  Park, $$$$$)

Pizza

Gino's East (Magnificent Mile, $)

Seafood

Joe's Seafood, Prime Steak and
  Stone Crab (Magnificent
  Mile, $$$)
Nine (Loop, $$$)
Shaw's Crab House and Blue Crab
  Lounge (River North, $$)

Spanish

Café Iberico (River North, $)

Steakhouses

Gibson's Steakhouse (Gold Coast,
  $$$$)
Harry Caray's (River North, $$)
Iron Mike's Grille (Magnificent
  Mile, $$$)
Joe's Seafood, Prime Steaks and
  Stone Crab (Magnificent
  Mile, $$$)
Nine (Loop, $$$)
The Saloon (Streeterville, $$$)

Sushi

Kamehachi (Old Town, $$)
Sushi Wabi (Randolph Street
  Market District, $$$)

Swedish

Ann Sather (Andersonville and
  North Side, $)

Thai

Arun's (North Side, $$$$$)

Index of Restaurants by Price

$

Ann Sather (Swedish,
  Andersonville and North Side)
Bistro Zinc (Bistro, North Side)
Flat Top Grill (Asian, Old Town,
  North Side, and Randolph
  Street Market District)
Gino's East (Pizza,
  Magnificent Mile)
Lou Mitchell's (American, Loop)
Tango Sur (Argentine, North Side)
Twin Anchors (Barbecue,
  Old Town)

Wishbone (Cajun/Southern,
    Randolph Street Market
    District)

$$

Atwood Café (Eclectic, Loop)
Bice (Italian, Streeterville)
Bistro 110 (American,
    Magnificent Mile)
Chez Joël (Bistro, Little Italy)
Cyrano's Bistro & Wine Bar
    (Bistro, River North)
Frontera Grill/Topolobampo
    (Mexican, River North)
Harry Caray's (Italian/Steakhouse,
    River North)
Harvest on Huron (Eclectic,
    River North)
Heaven on Seven (Cajun, Loop)
Hubbard Street Grill (American,
    River North)
Jane's (Eclectic, Bucktown/
    Wicker Park)
Kamehachi (Sushi, Old Town)
Le Bouchon (Bistro,
    Bucktown/Wicker Park)
Mia Francesca (Italian, North Side,
    and Francesca on Taylor in
    Little Italy)
Mossant (Bistro, Loop)
Shaw's Crab House and Blue Crab
    Lounge (Seafood, River North)
Sushi Wabi (Sushi, Randolph
    Street Market District)
Trattoria No. 10 (Italian, Loop)
Tuscany on Taylor (Italian,
    Little Italy)
Zinfandel (American, River North)

$$$

Bistro Zinc (Bistro, Gold Coast,
    and North Side)
Blackhawk Lodge (Bistro,
    Magnificent Mile)
Café Absinthe (Eclectic,
    Bucktown/Wicker Park)
Centro (Italian, River North)
Iron Mike's Grille (Steakhouse,
    Magnificent Mile)
Joe's Seafood, Prime Steak and
    Stone Crab (Seafood,
    Magnificent Mile)
Meritage Café and Wine Bar
    (American, Bucktown/
    Wicker Park)
Nine (Seafood/Steakhouse, Loop)
The Saloon (Steakhouse,
    Streeterville)
Vivo (Italian, Randolph Street
    Market District)

$$$$

Ambria (French, Lincoln Park)
Frontera Grill/Topolobampo
    (Mexican, River North)
Gibson's Steakhouse (Steakhouse,
    Gold Coast)
Pump Room (French, Gold Coast)

$$$$$

Arun's (Thai, North Side)
Charlie Trotter's (Nouvelle,
    Lincoln Park)

Chapter 15

On the Lighter Side: Top Picks for Snacks and Meals on the Go

. . . .

In This Chapter

▶ Stopping and snacking

▶ Sleuthing out Chicago's best street eats

▶ Grabbing a quick meal

. . . .

*B*eing a tourist can really take it out of you. Sometimes all you want is to rest your aching feet and re-energize with a quick snack. Unlike New York, Chicago doesn't have battalions of pushcart food vendors (thankfully — it keeps the sidewalks clear and cuts down on greasy smells), but it does have great portable food and quick eats. Maybe you've burned off your lunch more quickly than expected. Or maybe you only have an hour to squeeze in a meal before a show. You're in luck. Chicago's best snacking places are right here.

Snacking with the Pros

Chicago street eats span meat-eater favorites to icy delights — from world-famous Chicago hot dogs to burgers and sandwiches.

Carnivore favorites

Local carnivore favorites include Italian beef and Italian sausage sandwiches. My favorite spot for these specialties is **Mr. Beef on Orleans,** 666 N. Orleans Street, between Erie and Huron Streets (☎ 312-337-8500). This hole-in-the-wall eatery has a counter up front and seating at picnic benches in the rear. When Jim Belushi and Jay Leno are in Chicago, they stop by, as do local media celebs. There are two main decisions to make: Whether you want an Italian beef (juicy, thinly sliced, piled high) or an

Italian sausage (charbroiled and spicy), and whether you want toppings of hot or sweet peppers. Each sandwich is packed into a chewy roll. If you can't decide, order a combo.

Another good choice is **Al's Italian Beef,** with branches at 169 W. Ontario Street at Wells Street, River North (☎ 312-943-3222), and 1079 Taylor Street, between Aberdeen and Carpenter, Little Italy (☎ 312-226-4017).

Refreshing Italian ice

For those on the low-fat route, you'll find **Mario's Italian Lemonade** in Little Italy, 1070 W. Taylor Street (no phone). From May to late October, the stand sells refreshing Italian ice — cups of shaved ice doused with syrup (traditional lemon flavor and a variety of others). **Tom and Wendee's Homemade Italian Ice,** 1136 W. Armitage Avenue at Clifton Street, Lincoln Park (☎ 773-327-2885), sells a version made with fresh fruit rather than syrup.

World-famous Chicago hot dogs

"Hot dogs" in Chicago mean **Vienna All-Beef franks** served with mustard, green relish, chopped onion, sliced tomato, hot peppers, and celery salt. Ketchup is optional, but not for purists. Two popular chains sell these delicious dogs. **Gold Coast Dogs** has 15 locations, including the original at 418 N. State Street (☎ 312-527-1222), 159 N. Wabash Avenue (☎ 312-917-1677), and the mezzanine level of Union Station (☎ 312-258-8585). Gold Coast Dogs also offers cheese fries made from Idaho potatoes topped with a glob of Wisconsin cheddar.

Byron's serves Vienna All-Beef hot dogs at three locations: 1017 W. Irving Park Rd. (☎ 773-281-7474), 1701 W. Lawrence (☎ 773-271-0900), and 680 N. Halsted (☎ 312-738-0968).

Sandwiches on the go

Chicagoans in the know head for **Potbelly Sandwich Works.** The warm, crusty homemade bread can be loaded up with all sorts of meats, cheeses, and veggies. The shakes are fantastic, too. Yes, there's even a potbellied stove inside and all sorts of Old West–type memorabilia. They're located at 190 N. State St., at Lake Street, in the Loop (☎ 312-683-1234), and 2264 N. Lincoln Avenue, between Belden and Webster, (☎ 773-528-1405).

Also in the Loop (in the Sears Tower, to be exact) is **Mrs. Levy's Delicatessen,** a retro deli that displays signed photographs of famous patrons. Staples such as knishes, blintzes, and soups are made daily from scratch. Sandwiches are piled high and include such standards as corned beef, beef brisket, and pastrami; soup choices include sweet-and-sour cabbage, chicken matzo ball, and mushroom barley. You can find it on the mezzanine level of the Sears Tower, 233 S. Wacker Drive (☎ 312-993-0530).

Corner Bakery offers cafeteria-style dining and sandwiches, soups, salads, pastas, and pizzas. (Plus, check out the bakery items — hard to resist!) Thirteen locations are spread around the downtown area. Two of the larger ones are located at 676 N. St. Clair at Erie Street (☎ 312-266-2570) and 1121 N. State Street, near Cedar Street (☎ 312-787-1969).

Foodlife, located on the mezzanine level of Water Tower Place, 835 N. Michigan Avenue (☎ 312-335-3663), takes the concept of "food court" to a higher level. First, you find more healthy alternatives to fast food. About 12 kiosks offer everything from barbecue chicken to Asian stir-fry, from pizza to low-fat Caesar salad. Miracle Juice Bar offers fresh juice and smoothies; Sacred Grounds offers espresso beverages to jolt you back into action. The entire area seats 400.

Grabbing a Burger

You cannot have lived through the late 20th century without hearing the phrase, "Cheeborger, cheeborger, chip, chip. No Coke — Pepsi." John Belushi's crabby, Greek, short-order cook (a staple of *Saturday Night Live*), was inspired by Chicago's **Billy Goat Tavern,** 430 N. Michigan Ave. (☎ 312-222-1525). The Billy Goat is a hangout for newspaper writers from the nearby Tribune and Sun-Times buildings. You can get beer and greasy food fast. And it's a real Chicago experience.

I would be remiss in writing about Chicago if I omitted McDonald's (because the company headquarters is in suburban Oak Brook). In fact, the chain's most profitable franchise is located in the heart of downtown. **Rock-N-Roll McDonald's** is at 600 N. Clark St., at Ohio Street (☎ 312-664-7940). Fifties and sixties memorabilia decorates the place. The food is, well, McDonald's.

Breaking for Coffee

Now that a **Starbuck's** is on every corner, you don't have to go far for your caffeine fix. Downtown, "Club Starbucks" — as natives like to call this branch — is where the "in" crowd goes to talk on cell phones and rest between shopping excursions to Barney's and Prada, 932 N. Rush Street, between Oak and Walton Streets (☎ 312-951-5436).

My favorite cafe hangout is **Uncommon Grounds,** 1214 W. Grace Street at Clark Street (☎ **773-929-3680**), which serves up fine breakfasts and sandwiches, plus wine and beer. In fact, a good portion of this book was written there, so you know you can hang out for hours without anyone bothering you!

Part V
Exploring Chicago

The 5th Wave   By Rich Tennant

"We do offer an authentic William 'The Refrigerator' Perry football jersey for sale, we just don't have a wall large enough to display it on."

In this part . . .

In this part, I guide you through Chicago's attractions. Chapter 16 points out the major sights. In Chapter 17, I indicate additional attractions, should you have the time, energy, and inclination. For those of you who want to take a piece of Chicago home with you, flip to Chapter 18 for my advice on shopping. And if this jumble of things to do and see is just too much for you, Chapter 19 boasts five ready-made itineraries, depending on how many days you have in Chicago and what your interests are.

Chapter 16

Chicago's Best Sights

· ·

In This Chapter

▶ Getting a handy list of the most popular destinations

▶ Scanning your options: From top spots to off-the-beaten-path

· ·

Chicago is many things: Lincoln Park, with the nation's oldest zoo, plus miles of running and biking paths; diverse neighborhoods, so far-flung that most visitors can only get to one or two; and Wrigley Field, the friendly confines of the Chicago Cubs. But Chicago is so much more. As in most big cities, here you can see great paintings and sculpture and hear opera and classical music. Chicago, though, has charms other cities don't offer: blues clubs to hang at until the wee hours, beach activities on the shores of Lake Michigan, and those famous garlic- and hot pepper-laden Chicago hot dogs.

In this chapter, I describe the city's most popular attractions followed by indexes organized by neighborhood and type of attraction. "The Top Sights" list is arranged alphabetically. Look for the kid-friendly icon on those sights that are particularly entertaining for the junior visitor. My list contains what generally are regarded as the "Big Five" — Art Institute of Chicago, Adler Planetarium & Astronomy Museum, Field Museum of Natural History, John G. Shedd Aquarium, and Museum of Science and Industry. These certainly are worthy of their fine reputations. But I also include other worthwhile attractions, as well as a few off-the-beaten-path surprises.

For locations of the various attractions described in this chapter, see the "Central Chicago Attractions" map in this chapter, unless otherwise noted.

Taking advantage of museum free days

The city's major museums all have free admission days. So schedule yourself correctly and you can save yourself some dollars while immersing yourself in the best culture Chicago has to offer.

✔ **Monday:** Chicago Historical Society

✔ **Tuesday:** Adler Planetarium, Art Institute of Chicago, Museum of Contemporary Art (first Tuesday of the month only), Nature Museum of the Chicago Academy of Sciences, Terra Museum of American Art

✔ **Wednesday:** Field Museum of Natural History

✔ **Thursday:** DuSable Museum of African-American History, Museum of Science and Industry, John G. Shedd Aquarium (Oceanarium admission extra), Chicago Children's Museum (5 to 8 p.m. only)

✔ **Always Free:** Chicago Cultural Center, Garfield Park/Lincoln Park Conservatory, Lincoln Park Zoo, Newberry Library, Oriental Institute Museum, David and Alfred Smart Museum of Art

The Top Sights

Adler Planetarium & Astronomy Museum
Museum Campus, South Lake Shore Drive

The first planetarium in the Western Hemisphere launched itself into the new millennium with a $40 million facelift. The new addition wraps itself around the 1920-built planetarium like a high-tech glass visor. And high-tech it is: Star Pavilion includes four exhibition galleries, including the world's first StarRider virtual reality theater, which propels visitors on an exhilarating voyage of discovery into the infinity of space. Visitors participate in the journey by operating controls in the armrests of their seats. **Galileo's,** the pavilion's new cafe, offers stunning views of Chicago's skyline and a wide selection of salads, soups, and sandwiches. Definitely worth a visit, especially if you have kids and want to check out the mind-blowing StarRider Theater. Allow at least two hours at the Adler, or wrap it into a day at the Museum Campus (see the "Mixing fish, fossils, and outer space: Museum Campus" sidebar, in this chapter).

1300 S. Lake Shore Dr. ☎ *312-922-7827. Internet:* www.adlerplanetarium. org. *CTA: Red line El to Roosevelt; Bus No. 12 or 146 to planetarium entrance. Admission: $5 adults, $4 seniors and children 4–17. Free to all Tues. Open: Mon–Thurs 9 a.m.–5 p.m.; Fri 9 a.m.–9 p.m.; Sat–Sun 9 a.m.–6 p.m.*

Art Institute of Chicago

South Michigan Avenue near the Loop

Chicago's pride and joy is a warm, welcoming museum, a world-class institution that never seems stuffy. (You can get an idea of the museum's sense of whimsy during the holidays when the famous lion sculptures that guard its entrance sport Santa hats.) A diverse museum like the New York's Metropolitan Museum of Art and Paris's Louvre, the Art Institute has several different departments with their own exhibition spaces and impressive collections. Highlights include well-known works, such as a St. John the Baptist by Guido Reni, Seurat's *Grande Jatte, Paris Street: Rainy Day* by Gustave Caillebotte; and two icons of American isolation, Edward Hopper's *Nighthawks* and Grant Wood's *American Gothic.*

The size and scope of the Art Institute's collections can be overwhelming. First-timers do well to take a Collection Highlight Tour (Tuesday and Saturday at 2 p.m.; other days, 1 p.m.). They're free and last about an hour, concentrating on a few major works. A highlight tour for kids runs on Saturdays, and there are fun seek-and-find programs for children. If you're going it on your own, don't miss the outstanding French Impressionist collection and the Thorne Miniature Rooms — 68 exquisite chambers that chronicle decorative arts through the centuries. Watch for major touring shows, for which reservations are usually required. The bustling gift shop is a great place to shop for jewelry, glassware, books, and quality reproductions. Reserve at least two hours for the museum and try to go at off times, such as weekdays, or early in the morning or late in the day.

111 S. Michigan Ave. ☎ 312-443-3600. CTA: Green, brown, purple, or orange line El to Adams, or red line El to Monroe or Jackson. Bus No. 3, 4, 60, 145, 147, or 151 to Monroe and South Michigan Avenue, then walk 1 block. Open: Mon and Wed–Fri 10:30 a.m.–4:30 p.m.; Tues 10:30 a.m.–8 p.m.; Sat 10 a.m.–5 p.m.; Sun noon–5 p.m. (Closed Thanksgiving and Christmas.) Admission (suggested): $8 adults; $5 seniors, children, and students; free for children under 5. Free to all Tues.

Chicago Architecture Foundation Boat Tours

Michigan Avenue Bridge, Michigan Avenue, just north of Wacker Drive

Chicago is the first city of architecture, and the Chicago Architecture Foundation guided programs are the best way to survey the scene. Four hundred trained and enthusiastic docents lead boat tours — one docent at a time. The foundation's most popular tour is a 1½-hour "Architecture River Cruise" along the north and south branches of the Chicago River. You see 50 or so buildings, including the Gothic 1925 Tribune Tower, designed by a New York architect who won a contest, Marina City (home of Bob Newhart on *The Bob Newhart Show* if you remember back that far!), Sears Tower, and NBC Tower, built in the late 1980s and constructed in wedding-cake style in homage to the city's old zoning codes mandating that sunlight reach down to the street. For the best overview of the

Central Chicago Attractions

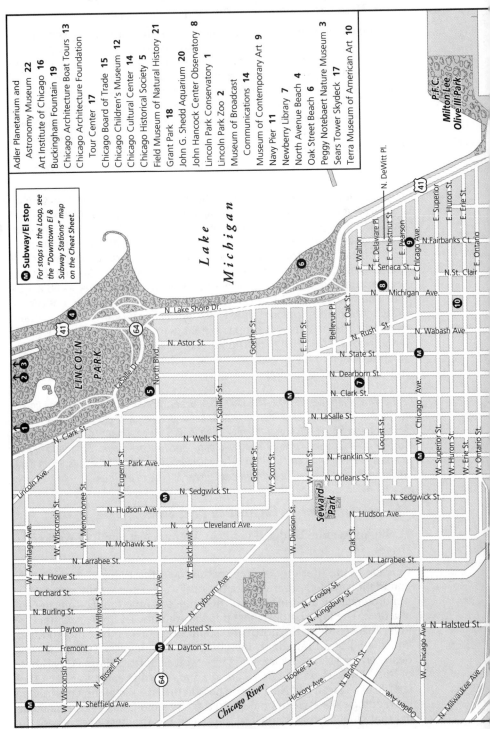

Adler Planetarium and
Astronomy Museum **22**
Art Institute of Chicago **16**
Buckingham Fountain **19**
Chicago Architecture Boat Tours **13**
Chicago Architecture Foundation
Tour Center **17**
Chicago Board of Trade **15**
Chicago Children's Museum **12**
Chicago Cultural Center **14**
Chicago Historical Society **5**
Field Museum of Natural History **21**
Grant Park **18**
John G. Shedd Aquarium **20**
John Hancock Center Observatory **8**
Lincoln Park Conservatory **1**
Lincoln Park Zoo **2**
Museum of Broadcast
Communications **14**
Museum of Contemporary Art **9**
Navy Pier **11**
Newberry Library **7**
North Avenue Beach **4**
Oak Street Beach **6**
Peggy Notebaert Nature Museum **3**
Sears Tower Skydeck **17**
Terra Museum of American Art **10**

M Subway/El stop
For stops in the Loop, see
the "Downtown El &
Subway Stations" map
on the Cheat Sheet.

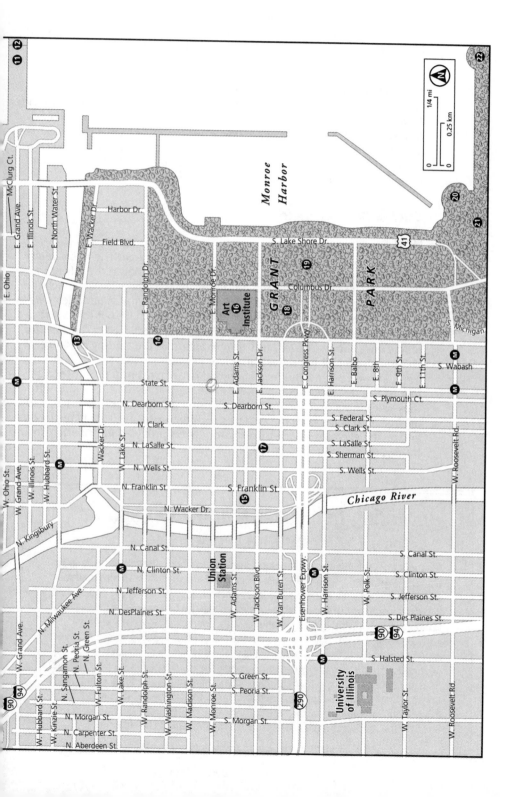

city, and a real feel for the city's personality, hop on one of these cruises and you won't be disappointed. During the busy summer season, stop by the ticket office early in the morning to secure tickets for later in the day.

224 South Michigan Ave. ☎ 312-922-4232. Boat tours from May through October, leaving from Mercury Cruise Line dock, southwest corner of the Michigan Avenue Bridge on the river level. Weekdays, 11 a.m., 1 p.m., and 3 p.m.; Saturdays and Sundays, 11 a.m., noon, 1 p.m., 2 p.m., and 3 p.m. Tickets: $21. Call Ticketmaster at ☎ 312-902-1500 (Internet:) or, to avoid the service charge, buy your tickets at one of the foundation's tour centers at 224 S. Michigan or the John Hancock Center Observatory, or from the CAF/Mercury boat launch.

Chicago Board of Trade

Loop

A statue of Ceres, the goddess of grain, watches over the *open outcry* (buying and selling by yelling and hand signals) trading in the pits at this, the world's largest options and futures exchange. And you can watch the action, too, from the fifth-floor visitor center, which has galleries overlooking the trading floors. If you ever complained that your job is stressful, watching these traders may make you feel much better. This center of Midwest commerce features frantic action in the trading pits, urgent shouting, and highly orchestrated hand signals. Action peaks at closing time (2 p.m.), when a flurry of shredded paper rises into the air then settles to the floor as these gamblers count up their chips to find out if they're winners or losers on the day. (Don't get so caught up in the trading frenzy that you miss the Art Deco architecture, especially in the lobby and on the elevator doors.) The visitor center provides information, free tours, and an enlightening 15-minute video.

Mixing fish, fossils, and outer space: Museum Campus

Museum Campus is a recent Chicago creation that brings together three great Chicago institutions — Field Museum of Natural History, John G. Shedd Aquarium, and Adler Planetarium & Astronomy Museum. Formerly divided by the northbound lanes of Lake Shore Drive, the area was much like the center grounds of the Indy 500 racetrack — without professional drivers. Today, the Drive has been moved west of Soldier Field, and you can stroll from the Field Museum to the Shedd Aquarium and the Planetarium without fear of being struck by a speeding auto. A new pedestrian underpass makes the campus a 15-minute walk east from the Roosevelt El stops or a longer but enjoyable stroll through Grant Park and along the lakefront from the Loop. If you're not up for a walk, Bus No. 146 makes the run from North Michigan Avenue and State Street in the Loop. Parking isn't bad because the museums have access to the huge lots around Soldier Field.

141 W. Jackson Blvd. ☎ *312-435-3590. CTA: Brown, orange, or purple lines to LaSalle, or blue or red lines to Jackson; Bus No. 1, 7, 60, 126, 151, or 156 to Madison and Wacker Drive. Admission: Free. Open: Weekdays 8 a.m.–2 p.m. (trading starts at 9:15).*

Chicago Cultural Center

South Michigan Avenue, near the Loop

Here's a storehouse of not-too-heavy culture and plenty of pure fun, just about all free. Built in 1897 as the city's library, the building clearly falls under the 1893 World's Columbian Exposition Beaux Arts style. But it's what's inside that will knock your socks off. Free tours guide visitors up a sweeping staircase of white Italian marble to admire what is, for my money, the most stunning interior in Chicago. You'll discover rare marble, fine hardwood, stained glass, polished brass, and mosaics of Favrile glass, colored stone, and mother-of-pearl inlaid in white marble. At the top of the grand staircase is a majestic Tiffany dome, believed to be the world's largest. It's a grand setting for an array of art exhibitions, concerts, films, lectures, and other special events, many of them free. Housed here is the free **Museum of Broadcast Communications** (see Chapter 17). The Cultural Center is one of the more underrated Chicago attractions, and I would highly recommend a stop to see an exhibit or catch a concert, especially because most everything that happens here is free.

78 E. Washington St. ☎ *312-744-6630. CTA: Brown, green, orange, or purple line El to Randolph, then walk ½ block east, or red line El to Washington/State. Bus no. 3, 4, 20, 56, 60, 127, 131, 145, 146, 147, 151, or 157 to Randolph and Michigan. Admission: Free. Open: Mon–Wed 10 a.m.–7 p.m.; Thurs 10 a.m.–9 p.m.; Fri 10 a.m.–6 p.m.; Sat 10 a.m.–5 p.m.; Sun 11 a.m.–5 p.m.*

Field Museum of Natural History

Museum Campus, South Lake Shore Drive

As a place of pure fun, the Field Museum is pretty hard to beat. Kids absolutely love the Field for its wide open spaces, giant dinos, and hands-on exhibits. Come to see Sue, the largest T Rex fossil ever unearthed, but stay to explore gleaming gems, giant stuffed elephants, mummies, and Native American artifacts. Visitors can climb into a life-size Egyptian tomb, step into the sun-drenched desert, and visit an ancient Egyptian marketplace. Take time to explore the African continent, visiting a royal Cameroon palace, witnessing some of the great savanna wildlife, and traveling across the Sahara and back to Nigeria. You can "travel" to America by ship and feel what it may have been like for Africans taken against their will and sold into slavery. The museum also has its own McDonald's on the lower level. While you're downstairs, plug a dollar bill into one of the old-fashioned wax-molding machines and watch as your very own red T Rex or green brontosaurus comes to life in front of your eyes. Kids get a real thrill out of taking home their very own Field Museum dinosaur!

RooseveltRoad and Lake Shore Drive. ☎ *312-922-9410. CTA: Bus No. 6, 10, 12, 130, or 146 to museum entrance. Admission: $7 adults, $4 seniors, children 3–17, and students. Free to all Wed. Open: Daily 9 a.m.–5 p.m.*

Frank Lloyd Wright Home and Studio

Suburban Oak Park

Controversial and brilliant, architect Frank Lloyd Wright made his first home and studio in Oak Park, a suburb just west of Chicago. Wright lived and worked here for 20 of his most productive years. His home and studio were built in 1889 as a cottage where the 22-year-old architect lived with his new bride. You can glimpse Wright's genius on a guided tour as docents show how the house became Wright's showcase and laboratory, where he experimented with and perfected what became known as the Prairie School of architecture. You may not agree with Wright's controversial lifestyle, but you have to admire a man who became the single most important influence on American architecture. While you're in Oak Park, you can check out Unity Temple, Wright's masterpiece for the Unitarian Church, and take a walking tour to view the exteriors of homes throughout the neighborhood that were built by Wright (see Chapter 21 for a complete Oak Park itinerary).

951 Chicago Ave., Oak Park (10 miles west of downtown Chicago). ☎ *708-848-1976. Internet:* www.wrightplus.org. *CTA: Green line El to Harlem; walk 4 blocks north on Harlem Avenue and 3 blocks east on Chicago Avenue. Admission: $8 adults; $6 seniors and children 7–18; free for children under 7. Combined admission for Home and Studio tour and guided or self–guided historic-district tour: $14 adults, $10 seniors and children 7–18. Admission to home and studio is by guided tour only. Guided tours: Weekdays 11 a.m., 1 p.m., 3 p.m.; Sat–Sun 11 a.m.–3:30 p.m. every 15 minutes.*

Free lunchtime entertainment under the Picasso

While you're in the Loop, stop by the Picasso sculpture in Daley Plaza at the Richard J. Daley Center any weekday at noon, where a free show awaits. It includes music, dance, and other performing arts and is a popular brown-bag-lunch spot with Loop workers. As the days grow colder, performances move indoors to the lobby. The center is between North Dearborn, North Clark, West Randolph, and West Washington streets. For "Under the Picasso" information, call ☎ 312-346-3278. To get there, take the brown, green, orange, or purple line El to Clark, walk 1 block south on Clark, and then walk ½ block east on Randolph. Or take Bus No. 22, 24, or 42 to the corner of Randolph and Clark Streets.

Grant Park

South Michigan Avenue

Festivals reign in Grant Park, Chicago's center for music and summer fun. Blues Fest, Jazz Fest, Gospel Fest, and the ever-popular Taste of Chicago food free-for-all take place here (for information on when and where festivals take place, see Chapter 2), but there are also quieter pleasures. During the summer concerts in the park series, you can sit under the stars on a blanket with a picnic dinner and hear popular musicians, such as Ray Charles and James Taylor or the stars of the Lyric Opera. (For information on the performing arts, see Chapter 23.) You can watch fireworks, and still have space to spread a picnic blanket and toss a Frisbee. (If you want to buy picnic food, go to **Corner Bakery** on the corner of Jackson Street and Michigan Avenue, across the street from the Art Institute.) This 319-acre swath of greenery wedged between South Michigan Avenue and the lakeshore is not contiguous parkland, but a patchwork of greenery dissected by city streets. Since 1994, when World Cup opening ceremonies were held at Soldier Field, the city has been undertaking an ambitious plan to spruce up the park. Chief among Grant Park's charms is **Buckingham Fountain** — twice as big as the Latona Basin at Versailles, after which it was modeled. Built in 1927 of Georgia pink marble, the baroque fountain delights park strollers with a computer-orchestrated symphony of dancing water. (If you ever watched *Married With Children* on television, you've seen the fountain spurt during the show's introduction.) After dark between Memorial Day and Labor Day, colored lights play on the splashing water.

From East Randolph Drive to East Roosevelt Road, and Michigan Avenue to Lake Michigan. ☎ *312-744-3315 for program information. CTA: All El stops in the Loop along State and Wabash; Bus No. 3, 4, 6, 60, 146, or 151 along Michigan Avenue, Randolph Street, or Roosevelt Avenue.*

John Hancock Center Observatory

Magnificent Mile

A location right on the Magnificent Mile means the John Hancock Center offers an up-close-and-personal view of the city from its observatory on the 94th floor. Okay, so it's not as popular as the Sears Tower Skydeck, but for my money, the view is more interesting (obviously the masses don't agree, because 1.52 million people went up the Sears Tower in 1996). The view up the north side is fantastic, with the curving lakefront, beaches, and high-rises that disappear in a line just up to the boundary of the northern suburbs. On a clear day, you can see 80 miles and part of three states surrounding this corner of Illinois — Michigan, Indiana, and Wisconsin. A refurbishment in 1997 added some new gadgets, such as talking telescopes. A high-speed elevator, presumably the fastest in the world, whisks passengers to the observatory in 40 seconds. The Signature Room on the 95th, a sleek restaurant with adjoining lounge, allows you to take in views with a drink in hand. (Ladies, make sure to visit the restroom — it's got the best view in the restaurant.)

94th floor of the John Hancock Center, 875 N. Michigan Ave. ☎ *888-875-VIEW or 312-751-3681. Internet: . CTA: Stops ½ block south at Delaware and Michigan. El: Red line to Chicago/State. Admission $8 adults, $6 seniors and children 5–17, free for children under 5 and military personnel in uniform or with active-duty cards. Daily 9 a.m.–midnight.*

Lakefront

Along Lake Shore Drive

Walk, run, bike, inline skate, or just sit and watch the world go by at this, Chicago's number-one free attraction. Summer in Chicago is not unlike a good Club Med vacation: beach volleyball, swimming, many tanned people, all intent on soaking up the all-too-short summer weather. A good place to start is Oak Street Beach, the city's most popular beach, located at the northern tip of the Magnificent Mile. (If you see people walking up the Magnificent Mile in flip-flops and carrying coolers, they're most likely headed here!) Pick up some picnic food from Bockwinkel's grocery store, located in the basement of Chicago Place mall, at Superior Street and Michigan Avenue. From there walk along the lakefront path six blocks north to North Avenue Beach, the beach volleyball hotspot, where the bathhouse is designed to replicate a steamship, and you can watch fitness fanatics pumping iron at the open-air gym. Walk to the lake, dig your toes into the sand, breathe in that fresh air, and gaze at sailboats on the horizon — but be forewarned about the frigid water. Even the bravest souls don't dare venture in much before July!

Between Oak Street and North Avenue on the east border of the city. CTA: El to State/Division and walk east to the lake, or Bus No. 151 along Lake Shore Drive, stops at Oak Street and North Avenue. Take the pedestrian tunnel to the beach.

Lincoln Park and Lincoln Park Zoo

Lincoln Park

Runners pound, bicyclists pedal, and walkers stroll the pathways of Chicago's famous lakefront park, which also is one of its busiest. Basketball courts, a nine-hole golf course, miniature golf, a driving range, an archery range, plus tennis and volleyball courts, pitches for horseshoes, and bocce keep sports fans happy. Playgrounds, sandboxes, a zoo, and a petting farm can engross the kids. And for relaxation you'll find placid ponds, a lagoon for fishing and crewing, and a conservatory with stunning flower shows. All this in a place that started out as a cemetery! In the 1860s, graves were moved and the park took shape (one family refused to move, and you can see the mausoleum, located behind the Chicago Historical Society). Paralleling the lakefront, the 1,212-acre park is 50 percent larger than New York's Central Park, so allow at least an afternoon to enjoy yourself here.

Lincoln Park Zoo, within the park, is convenient, compact, and charming. And what's not to love about a place that's open 365 days a year — and where admission is always free? At Christmastime, you can go carolling to the animals, and in the summer, watch a concert on the lawn and stroll among the great cats with a glass of chardonnay. But the real attraction is a major collection of gorillas, which are chief among the more than 200 species at this, the nation's oldest zoo, founded in 1868. The lowland gorillas are kept in large family groups, as they would live in the wild. The technique obviously keeps the gorillas happy, as 50 gorillas have been born at Lincoln Park Zoo since 1970, an astounding record. Seal and sea lion feeding times are always popular, as are visits to the Children's Zoo and its nursery. One of the joys of visiting the adjoining Farm-in-the-Zoo is watching urban youngsters' wonder as they wander a working farm and meet cows, pigs, horses, chicks, and goats. This lovely, small (35 acres) zoo takes two to three hours to see every exhibit.

*Lincoln Park is located between North Avenue and Ardmore Avenue, bordered by Lake Shore Drive. CTA: Purple line El to Fullerton, red line to Fullerton or North/Clybourn, or brown line to Fullerton, Armitage, or Sedgewick; Bus No. 22, 145, 146, 147, 151, or 156 along Foster Avenue and Inner Lakeshore Drive. Lincoln Park Zoo is located at 2200 N. Cannon Dr. ☎ **312-742-2000.** Internet:* www.lpzoo.com. *CTA: Bus No. 151 to zoo parking lot. Admission: Free. Open: Summer weekdays 9 a.m.–5 p.m., Sat–Sun 10 a.m.–7 p.m.; fall to spring daily 10 a.m.–5 p.m.*

Museum of Science and Industry

Hyde Park

Would you like to step aboard a captured World War II U-boat or a retired 727 United Airlines jetliner? Perhaps you'd like to travel deep into a replica of a Southern Illinois coal mine? Or concentrate on the story of space exploration at the **Henry Crown Space Center.** This huge interactive museum is so full of wonders that it is hard to know where to start. One thing is for sure — don't try to see it all in one shot. Instead, visit the museum's Web site and select the attractions that have the most appeal. Younger children (up to age ten) usually are happy to spend time at the "Idea Factory," where they can explore scientific principles. Just about everyone enjoys seeing chicks hatch in an incubator. And be sure to schedule a visit to the **Omnimax Theater.**

*57th Street and Lake Shore Drive. ☎ **800-468-6674.** Internet:* www.msichicago. org. *CTA: Bus No. 6, 10, 35, 151, or 156 to museum entrance. Open: Summer daily 9:30 a.m.–5:30 p.m.; fall through spring weekdays 9 a.m.–4 p.m., Sat–Sun 9:30 a.m.– 5:30 p.m. Admission: $9 adults, $7.50 seniors, $5 children 3–11; free to all Thurs. Museum and Omnimax Theater $15 adults, $10 seniors and children. Omnimax (Thurs only) $7 adults, $5 seniors, $6 children.*

Navy Pier

Streeterville

Jutting three-quarters of a mile into Lake Michigan, Navy Pier was built in 1916 as a shipping and recreational facility. Today, with its 50 acres of parks, gardens, shops, restaurants, and attractions, Navy Pier is Chicago's number-one tourist attraction. And rightfully so: There's no better place to stroll along, enjoying the boats, the lake, and a stunning view of the city. The downside? The crowds. The loud music. Vendors selling trinkets. Grown-ups will enjoy the outdoor cafes and bars and the periodic art shows. (One of the year's largest, Art Chicago, takes place every Mother's Day weekend. For more information, visit www.artchicago.com.) Nine restaurants and a food court are located on the Pier. **Bubba Gump Shrimp Co.** recreates the down-home atmosphere of the move *Forrest Gump* (☎ **312-595-5500**). A more elegant alternative is RIVA, specializing in fresh seafood, steaks, and pasta, where you can dine with a fabulous view of Chicago's skyline (☎ **312-644-RIVA**). Kids love the IMAX theater (☎ **312-595-0090**), mammoth Ferris wheel (sponsored by McDonald's, the cars look like red french fry boxes), and the Chicago Children's Museum. Navy Pier houses a 1,500-foot Skyline Stage (major exhibition space). It's also the spot to head for boat rides onto Lake Michigan — from speedboats to tall ships. The wonderful hands-on **Chicago Children's Museum** (☎ **312-527-1000**; see Chapter 27) makes its home here. A visit to Navy Pier can easily consume half a day, much of it spent wandering the great length. Grab a free map at the entrance to navigate.

Parking at Navy Pier is a challenge. The best bet is to hop on the free trolley service between Navy Pier and State Street along Grand Avenue and Illinois Street. Trolley hours are 10 a.m. to 9 p.m. Sunday to Thursday; 10 a.m. to 12 a.m. on Friday; and 10 a.m. to 11 p.m. on Saturday. Trolleys typically run every 20 minutes and pick-up points are indicated by "Navy Pier Trolley Stop" signs along the route.

600 East Grand Avenue (on the lakefront). ☎ *800-595-PIER or 312-595-PIER. Internet: www.navypier.com. Bus: 29, 65, 56, or 66. Admission: Free. Open: Fall (Sept–Oct): Mon–Thurs 10 a.m.–9 p.m.; Fri–Sat 10 a.m.–11 p.m.; Sun 10 a.m.–8 p.m.; Winter (Nov–May): Mon–Thurs 10 a.m.–8 p.m.; Fri–Sat 10 a.m.–10 p.m.; Sun 10 a.m.–7 p.m.; Summer (June–Aug): Sun–Thurs 10 a.m.–10 p.m.; Fri–Sat 10 a.m.–12 a.m.*

Oprah Winfrey Show

Randolph Street Market District

Are you in touch with your spirit? Reading the right books? If not, you better hightail it over to the Oprah Winfrey Show. With a little persistence, you too can be a part of the show's taping. Considered the world's largest cult by detractors, and must-see television by followers, the show is taped Tuesday through Thursday at 9 a.m. and noon. Tickets can be obtained by calling ☎ **312-591-9222** (persistence required!). Call at least four weeks in advance. Even if you don't love Oprah, watching her producers work like a well-oiled machine and seeing Oprah turn on the charm when the cameras roll can give you great insight into how television works. The studio is surprisingly small and intimate, and Oprah answers questions and talks with the audience during commercial breaks (they tape the show just as if it were airing live). After the show, head over to **Wishbone,** a Harpo Studios favorite hangout, for Southern-style cooking, and debrief about the show (see Chapter 14).

1058 W. Washington Blvd. ☎ 312-591-9222 (Mon–Fri 9 a.m.–5 p.m. CT). Internet: www.oprah.com. *$5 cab ride from the Loop. Reservations can be made generally only one month in advance. Ticket price: free. Open: Tapings take place Tues–Thurs 8 a.m. and 12 p.m. Sept–early Dec, Jan–early June.*

Sears Tower

Loop

The **Sears Tower** provides a panorama of Chicago and three neighboring states. On a clear day, you can see 50 miles and four states. You'll rocket to the top in a high-speed elevator that goes from ground to the 103rd floor in 70 seconds. Built in 1973 and long the world's tallest building, the Sears Tower has been eclipsed (but not in the mind of ever-proud Chicagoans) by a building in Malaysia with longer decorative spires. In my opinion, you'll get a better view from the John Hancock Center Observatory because it's more centrally located and surrounded by interesting architecture. The Sears Tower is somewhat isolated in the west Loop, which becomes a dead zone on weekends.

233 S. Wacker Dr. ☎ 800-SKYDECK. CTA: Bus: 1, 7, 126, 146, 151, or 156 to Jackson Avenue. El: Brown, purple, or orange line to Quincy or red or blue line to Jackson. Admission: $8.50 for adults, $6.50 for seniors, $5.50 for children 5–12. Open: daily March–Sept 9 a.m.–11 p.m., Oct–Feb 9 a.m.–10 p.m. (The last ticket is sold one half hour before closing.)

John G. Shedd Aquarium

Museum Campus, South Lake Shore Drive

The spectacular draw is the **Oceanarium,** which recreates a Pacific Northwest coastal environment. The wall of windows revealing Lake Michigan outside creates the optical illusion of an expanse of sea. You can follow a winding nature trail and watch dolphins, sea otters, and harbor seals. Most controversial are three female Beluga whales, who are remarkably cute creatures whose humped heads and natural "smiles" make them seem human. The Caribbean Coral Reef exhibit was renovated in 2000. More than 40 species have been added to the 200 already living in the 90,000-gallon circular tank in the Aquarium's central rotunda. Divers doing the feedings describe animals and their environment via underwater microphones. Watch for a hawksbill sea turtle named Hawkeye who has been here 20 years and the very scary moray eel. Don't miss the penguin colony in a separate exhibit that approximates the Falkland Islands in the southern sea off Argentina. One of the newest exhibits, "Seahorse Symphony," presents the world's largest collection of seahorses and their relatives. A new Amazon riverbank exhibit opened in 2000 and features an array of piranhas, birds, sloths, insects, snakes, catfish, stingrays, iguanas, and caimans. Allot three hours to visit the Shedd.

1200 S. Lake Shore Dr. ☎ *312-939-2438. Internet:* www.shedd.org. *CTA: Bus No. 6, 10, 12, 130, or 146 to aquarium entrance. Admission (aquarium and oceanarium): $11 adults, $9 seniors and children 3–11, free for children under 3. Admission to Aquarium galleries only, $5 adults, $4 seniors and children 3–11. Free admission on Mon, when Oceanarium admission is $6 adults, $5 children 3–11 and seniors. Oceanarium tickets are limited and available on a first-come, first-served basis. Purchase tickets in advance through Ticketmaster or by calling* ☎ *312-559-0200. Open: summer Fri–Wed 9 a.m–6 p.m., Thurs 9 a.m.–9 p.m.; fall–spring Mon–Fri 9 a.m.–5 p.m., Sat–Sun 9 a.m.–6 p.m. Last entrance into Oceanarium, 4:45 fall–spring, 5:45 in summer.*

Wrigley Field

Wrigleyville

Nothing makes you feel more optimistic than Opening Day at Wrigley Field. Sure, you may be wearing long underwear and earmuffs, but that doesn't deter Cubs fans, for whom hope springs eternal. Wrigley Field is an almost-perfect ballpark, from its ivy-covered outfield walls to the hand-operated scoreboard. And if you're one of the unlucky ones who couldn't make the game, there's a "W" or an "L" flag that is hoisted above the field after the game to announce the outcome. Attend a day game. Buy a hot dog, beer, a box of Crackerjacks, and the whole afternoon runs about $20. Because Wrigley is small, just about every seat is decent. (See Chapter 17 for more on sports venues.) Call in advance for tickets. Although the Cubs lose plenty of games every year, tickets are becoming harder to get.

1060 W. Addison St. ☎ *773--404-CUBS. Internet:. CTA: Bus 22 runs up Clark Street to Addison. El: Red line to Addison. Tickets: stop by the ticket windows at Wrigley Field, Mon–Fri 9 a.m.–6 p.m., Sat 9 a.m.–4 p.m. and on game days. Or call* ☎ *312-831-CUBS for tickets through Ticketmaster.* ☎ *800-347-CUBS outside Illinois.*

Index of Top Attractions by Neighborhood

Hyde Park
Museum of Science and Industry

Lincoln Park
Lincoln Park and Lincoln Park Zoo

Loop
Chicago Board of Trade
Chicago Cultural Center
Sears Tower

Michigan Avenue
Chicago Architecture Foundation Boat
    Tour
John Hancock Center Observatory

Oak Park
Frank Lloyd Wright Home and Studio,
    suburban Oak Park

South Michigan Avenue/ South Lakeshore
Adler Planetarium & Astronomy
    Museum
Art Institute of Chicago
Field Museum of Natural History
Grant Park
John G. Shedd Aquarium

Streeterville
Navy Pier

West Loop
Harpo Studios/The Oprah Winfrey Show

Wrigleyville
Wrigley Field

Index of Top Attractions by Type

Historic buildings and architecture
Chicago Board of Trade
Chicago Cultural Center
Frank Lloyd Wright Home and Studio,
    suburban Oak Park
John Hancock Center Observatory
Navy Pier
Sears Tower
Water Tower

Museums
Adler Planetarium & Astronomy
    Museum
Art Institute of Chicago

Field Museum of Natural History
Museum of Science and Industry
John G. Shedd Aquarium

Parks and open spaces
Chicago Architecture Foundation Boat
    Tour
Grant Park
Lakefront
Lincoln Park and Lincoln Park Zoo

Chapter 17

More Cool Things to See and Do

In This Chapter

▶ Exploring beyond the big attractions

▶ Finding sights for architecture buffs

▶ Keeping museum fanatics busy

▶ Entertaining the sports fan

So, you did the major sights, admired Chicago's best art and architecture, and made your way through the big museums. What else is there? Plenty. Do you want to sleep among dinosaurs? Climb the sheer face of Mount Chicago? Try out as a television newscaster? Walk among the butterflies at a new nature museum? You can discover it all in this chapter.

Especially for Architecture Lovers

Chicago has so much to offer that architecture buffs can go a bit crazy with the possibilities. Here are a few ideas to keep you busy.

Four free, guided architectural tours on El trains are offered on Saturday afternoons. First-come-first-served tickets are available at the **Chicago Cultural Center** (☎ **312-744-2400**). There you also can rent (for $5) a taped walking tour of the Loop, "Audio Architecture," developed by the Landmarks Preservation Council. Tours, a collaborative effort of the Office of Tourism, the CTA, and the Architecture Foundation, take 40 minutes.

Fourth Presbyterian Church

With its shaded, ivy-covered courtyard, fountain, and elaborate spire, this Gothic Revival Church would seem to be more at home in Boston than in the heart of Chicago. Built in 1914, it is a tranquil spot for quiet contemplation, a backwater just steps from the bustle of Michigan Avenue. Free lunchtime concerts take place on Fridays at 12:10 p.m. Sunday services at 8:30 a.m., 11 a.m., and 6:30 p.m. are open to the public. The Church is located on North Michigan Avenue between East Delaware Place and East Chestnut Street. To get there, take the CTA Red line El to Chicago/State. Or hop on Buses No. 3, 10, 11, 125, 145, 146, 147, or 151 to East Chestnut Street and North Michigan Avenue. The church is open daily from 9 a.m. to 5 p.m.

Marquette Building

When Chicago was still pretty much a swamp, French Jesuit explorer Pere Marquette and his party paddled the inland waterways in long "voyageur" canoes. Design elements of this 1894 Loop office building bring Marquette's adventures to life. His party endured Indian attacks, and then met successfully with Native American chiefs. Bronze panels over the doors, sculptures above the elevator doors, and a series of Tiffany mosaics in the rotunda lobby (open 24 hours a day) tell the story of early French exploration of the Mississippi Valley. The Marquette building is located at 140 S. Dearborn Street. Take the CTA purple, brown, orange, or green line El to Adams/Wabash, red line to Monroe/State, or blue line to Monroe/Dearborn; Buses No. 1, 7, 22, 24, 36, 42, 60, 62, 126, 129, or 151 can also get you to Adams and Dearborn Streets.

Water Tower

One of Chicago's best-known landmarks dominates the Magnificent Mile like a gleaming fairy-tale castle. However, one of its original pur-poses was decidedly un-fairy-tale-like. It was designed to conceal an ugly, 138-foot-high standpipe used in connection with pumping water from Lake Michigan. Many thought the structure itself even more unsightly — Oscar Wilde described it as "a castellated monstrosity with pepper boxes stuck all over it." But Chicagoans have come to be proud of their talisman, one of the few buildings to survive the Great Fire of 1871. (Its companion pumping station, across the street, was another.) The tower has been spruced up and is surrounded by lawns and park benches. It is illuminated prettily at night, and street musi-cians often play here. Located at 800 N. Michigan Ave, take the CTA Red line El to Chicago/State to get to the tower. Buses No. 125, 145, 146, 147, or 151 can take you to Michigan and Chicago Avenues.

Wicker Park

If you hit just one outlying neighborhood, Wicker Park, with its Victorian homes and 19th century buildings first built by Polish immi-grants, is the place to go. Not long ago, this was a tough neighborhood whose "mean streets" served as a model for author Nelson Algren in novels such as _The Man With the Golden Arm._ Wicker Park is now being gentrified — its many large homes are being remodeled, and restaurants and boutiques are opening. Strong evidence does remain of Wicker Park's Polish roots. Coexisting with chic coffee bars and galleries are the old shops, eateries, and churches that served the Polish immigrants.

Chicago Neighborhood Tours (☎ 800-332-3055 for information; Internet: www.ci.chi.il.us/Tourism/Neighborhood Tours) offers an excursion that explores Wicker Park. Sights include the distinctive **Flatiron Building,** 1569–79 N. Milwaukee Avenue, at North Avenue, an office building designed in 1929 by Holabird & Root that now houses galleries and artist studios. The tour also passes **Holy Trinity Russian Orthodox Cathedral,** 1121 N. Leavitt Street, designed in 1899 by Louis Sullivan and constructed with a donation from Czar Nicholas II. Many Poles still live in Wicker Park — sometimes referred to as Chicago's "Ethnic Gold Coast." The **Polish Museum of America,** 984 N. Milwaukee Avenue (☎ 773-384-3352), features an extensive exhibit about Ignacy Jan Paderewsky. The Polish Renaissance Man was a world-class pianist, composer, and Prime Minister of Poland.

Wicker Park is bordered by John F. Kennedy Expressway, Western Avenue, Chicago Avenue, and Fullerton Avenue. Take the CTA blue line El to Damen or Division; Buses No. 56, 70, or 72 take you along Milwaukee Avenue.

Especially for Movie Lovers

Those who love movies can get off the beaten path with some unusual offerings.

Chicago Cultural Center

Tuesday is the day to head for the **Chicago Cultural Center** (☎ 312-744-6630; see listing in Chapter 16) for free movies. Every Tuesday evening it screens classics, such as _Casablanca._

Oriental Institute Museum

You'll need to bring your own popcorn, but the **Oriental Institute Museum** (☎ 773-702-9507) offers free movies. Its "Sundays at the Movies" program screens the likes of _Cleopatra,_ the 1934 Cecil B. DeMille epic starring Claudette Colbert. While you're there, stop by the Suq, the museum's acclaimed gift shop. With an array of imported goods, it is like shopping at a Middle Eastern bazaar.

Second-run movie theaters

For inexpensive seats to Hollywood's more recent offerings, check out a second-run movie theater. Here are a few good ones:

- ✔ **Davis** and **Davis Art,** 4614 N. Lincoln Avenue (☎ 773-784-0893; Red or brown line El to Fullerton/Lincoln, then northbound bus 11 to the theater).
- ✔ **Village South,** 1548 N. Clark Street (☎ 312-642-2403; Bus 135 or 136 to LaSalle and North, walk 1 block east).
- ✔ **Village North,** 6746 N. Sheridan Road (☎ 312-642-2403; Bus 147 or 151 bus to the door).
- ✔ **3 Penny Cinema,** 2424 N. Lincoln Avenue (☎ 773-935-5744; Red or brown line El to Fullerton/Lincoln).

Especially for Romantics

You can always go to an expensive restaurant, but why not try some more creative ideas?

Dining at the Chicago Historical Society

An improbable dining spot — but a romantic one, at that — is the **Chicago Historical Society** (☎ 312-587-7766). The Big Shoulder Café serves an elegant Sunday brunch complete with live piano music. Incorporated into the restaurant's decor is an 1888 terra-cotta arch depicting cowboys and cattle that was removed intact from the now-defunct Union Stockyards.

Jazz at the Art Institute of Chicago

It's an unlikely spot for free jazz — as well as good quiche, wine, cheesecake, and cappuccino — but you can find it all at the McKinlock Court Garden Restaurant (☎ 312-443-3600), tucked away in the center of the **Art Institute of Chicago.** The delightful outdoor cafe surrounds the soothing Triton fountain. On Tuesday evenings during warm-weather months, jazz aficionados sit outside among the flowers and trees and listen to free live music. Museum admission is free on Tuesday, and the restaurant has an $8 per person minimum.

Especially for Fishermen

You're visiting a city on a great lake. So get out there and catch some fish!

Battling the elusive salmon

Want to do battle with a scrappy coho salmon, or tie into a tackle-testing, arm-aching 20-plus-pound Chinook? Salmon fishing has been big on Lake Michigan since Pacific species were introduced in the 1970s. Gather a group of six (to split the cost of $395 for about 5 hours' fishing), and be prepared to start at dawn. You can find a charter boat through the **Chicago Sportfishing Association** (☎ 312-922-1100).

Catching the lazy lake perch

Lake perch won't give you the fight that salmon do, but they're fun to catch and good to eat. Jumbo perch weigh in at around one pound and are caught with ultralight spinning tackle or hand lines rigged with multiple hooks. Check sporting goods stores for equipment and bait. The local anglers' favorite spot is Montrose Harbor Pier, east of Lake Shore Drive at Wilson Avenue. Don't ask me what to do with the fish after you catch it if you're staying in a hotel. Maybe you can donate it to your fellow fishermen and fisherwomen. To find out more, call **Chicago Park District** harbor information (☎ 312-747-7527).

Especially for Sports Fans

Chicago is a great sports town — one whose teams, paradoxically, struggle just to break even. Fans of Chicago's professional sports franchises are fanatically devoted, fiercely loyal, and, in general, pitifully long-suffering.

Chicago's pro-sports teams tend to be underachievers. The **Cubs** (for information on Wrigley Field, see Chapter 16) haven't played in a World Series since 1945, and the **White Sox** have been excluded from baseball's fall classic since 1959. Not since the glory days of 1961 have the **Blackhawks** hoisted hockey's Stanley Cup. The **Bears** won their one and only Super Bowl after the 1985–86 season. The **Bulls** were the exception. During the Jordan years, they took six NBA championships. But with Michael gone, the Bulls are mired at the bottom of the league.

The general lack of success doesn't deter hard-core fans, but it does keep away fair-weather followers. That means tickets are generally available through the teams' box office, through agencies such as TicketMaster, and over the Internet. Cubs and Bears tickets are a little tougher than the others, especially for key match-ups and marquee visitors.

Comiskey Park

The South Side baseball club, the White Sox, has a reputation for attracting "blue-collar" fans (compared to the Cubs' "white-collar" supporters). *The* toughest ticket in town is Sox–Cubs. **New Comiskey Park** (☎ 312-674-1000; Red line El to Sox/35th Street), a modern baseball-only facility that opened in 1991, is located at 333 W. 35th Street.

Soldier Field

Soldier Field (☎ 847-295-6600; Bus 146), home of the Chicago Bears, is another storied stadium. Although the "Monsters of the Midway" no longer scare their opponents, both still must deal with winds, snow, and fog off Lake Michigan. It's located at 425 E. McFetridge Drive (Lake Shore Drive at 16th Street).

United Center

The Bulls and Blackhawks share the state-of-the-art **United Center** (☎ 312-455-4000; Bus 20), built in 1994. The life-size bronze statue of Michael Jordan out front pretty much sums up the recent success of pro sports in Chicago. The arena is located at 1901 W. Madison Street.

Especially for Serious Museum Buffs

Even if you hit the main museum campus, many more treasures lie ahead of you.

Chicago Historical Society

In a state that dubs itself "the Land of Lincoln," you'd expect to see a wealth of memorabilia relating to the 16th president. This museum doesn't disappoint. The powerful exhibit "A House Divided: America in the Age of Lincoln" uses video, audio, and memorabilia to capture the era and its problems, including slavery and the destruction created by the Civil War. Displays include Lincoln's deathbed and the table at which generals Robert E. Lee and Ulysses S. Grant signed the surrender at Appomattox. Other exhibits deal with pioneer life, the Great Chicago Fire, and the city's ethnicity. Family groups enjoy the "Hands-On History Gallery," full of interactive displays, where they can visit a fur-trading post, play old-time radio sound effects, and view the contents of early mail-order catalogs.

The Chicago Historical Society is located at 1601 N. Clark Street (at North Avenue). Call ☎ 312-642-4600 for more information or visit their

Web site at www.chicagohs.org. The CTA Buses 11, 22, 36, 72, 151, or 156 can take you to Inner Lakeshore Drive and North Avenue. The museum is open from Monday through Saturday, 9:30 a.m. to 4:30 p.m., and on Sunday from noon to 5 p.m. Admission is $5 for adults, $3 for seniors and students age 13 to 22, and $1 for children 6 to 12 years. Your best bet is to visit on Mondays, however, when admission is free to all.

DuSable Museum of African-American History

The pride and the pain of African-Americans is chronicled in the museum named for Jean Baptiste Point du Sable, born of a French father and a black mother. The affluent, well-educated DuSable became Chicago's first permanent settler when he established a trading post in 1779. Exhibits portray the degradations and cruelty of slavery and the hope of the civil rights movement. Offering a mix of art and history, the museum displays significant work by African-American artists and celebrates African-Americans' exploits in the armed forces — as well as documenting lynchings, Ku Klux Klan activities, and demeaning products, such as *Little Black Sambo* books. The DuSable Museum is located in Washington Park, at 740 E. 56th Place. Call ☎ **773-947-0600** for more information or visit their Web site at www.dusablemuseum.org. To get there, take the CTA red line El to 55th or 63rd Streets. If you prefer taking the bus, No. 3, 4, or 55 can get you to 55th Street and Cottage Grove. The museum is open Monday through Saturday from 10 a.m. to 5 p.m. and on Sunday from noon to 5 p.m. Although admission is free on Sunday, the rest of the week it's $3 for adults, $2 for seniors and students, and $1 for children, ages 6 to 13.

Museum of Broadcast Communications

Live out your news-anchor fantasy at the Museum of Broadcast Communications. You slip into an MBC blazer, clip on a mic, and spend 15 minutes at an anchor desk (solo, or with a co-anchor). You read the news from a teleprompter as news footage rolls, covering everything from fires and floods to weather and sports. For $19.95, you receive a 15-minute tape, complete with actual news footage, your voice-over, and even commercials. Phone ahead to reserve a time slot at the anchor desk. The museum itself, a storehouse of radio and television memorabilia, is also fun and interesting. You can even borrow a copy of a favorite TV episode and screen it in a private booth.

You'll meet Mortimer Snerd and Charlie McCarthy at the Museum of Broadcast Communications. Don't know who they are? Edgar Bergen, actress Candice Bergen's father, was a ventriloquist and an old-time radio star. Mortimer and Charlie were his famous dummies.

The museum is located within the Chicago Cultural Center, 78 E. Washington Street, at North Michigan Avenue (☎ 312-629-6000; Internet: www.mbcnet.org). Take the CTA red line El to Washington/State, and then walk 2 blocks east, or take the brown, green, orange, or purple line El to Randolph and then walk ½ block east. Buses No. 3, 4, 60, 145, 147, and 151 also go to Randolph and North Michigan. The museum is open Monday through Saturday from 10 a.m. to 4:30 p.m., and on Sunday from noon to 5 p.m. The admission is free.

Museum of Contemporary Art

The nation's largest contemporary art museum opened in 1996 to mixed reviews. Set between the lake and Water Tower on a piece of prime real estate, the building feels a bit inaccessible, with a daunting set of stairs leading to the entrance. The museum highlights works dating back to 1945, including work by Alexander Calder, Sol LeWitt, Donald Judd, and Bruce Nauman. In the last couple years, the museum hosted retrospectives of Cindy Sherman and Chuck Close. You may want to take the free daily tour or rent an audio tour because these works of art are a challenge.

The Museum of Contemporary Art is located at 220 E. Chicago Avenue, just east of Michigan Avenue (☎ 312-280-2660; Internet: www.mcachicago.org). Take the CTA Bus No. 3, 10, 11, 66, 125, 145, 146, or 152. The red line goes to Chicago/State. The museum hours are Tuesday and Thursday through Sunday from 10 a.m. to 5 p.m. On Wednesday, closing time is 8 p.m. Admission costs $6.50 for adults, $4 for seniors and students with ID, and free for children under 12. Admission is free to all on the first Tuesday of the month.

Oriental Institute Museum

Don't be misled by the name — it predates the term *Middle East.* Here you'll find mummies, Persian kings' gold jewelry, a fragment of the Dead Sea Scrolls, and Tutankhamen's tomb. This user-friendly, free museum contains a world-class collection of Middle Eastern antiquities, including a massive statue of the boy-king, Tutankhamen. If you're interested in ancient Egypt, Syria, Palestine, Iran, Iraq, Turkey, and other Mideastern countries, this is where you can find out about them from such artifacts as a 40-ton Assyrian winged bull. The museum schedules lots of entertaining children's programs, such as "Food and Fun from Long Ago."

The museum is located at 1155 E. 58th Street (☎ 773-702-9521; Internet: www-oi.uchicago.edu). Take the CTA Bus No. 55 to 55th Street and Cottage Grove. Hours are Tuesday and Thursday through Saturday from 10 a.m. to 4 p.m., and on Wednesday the museum closes at 8:30 p.m. On Sunday, the museum is open from noon to 4 p.m.

Terra Museum of American Art

This tiny gem of a museum is tucked away amid the glittery shops of the Magnificent Mile. Its permanent collection of 19th- and 20th-century American paintings includes works by Sargent, Stella, Whistler, and Wyeth. The museum is especially strong on impressionist paintings. Compact, with each level connected by a winding walkway, this is a manageable museum — perfect for taking an hour or two off from shopping. The museum is located at 664 N. Michigan Avenue (**☎ 312-664-3939**; Internet: www.terramuseum.org). Take the CTA red line El to Grand or Chicago/State; Bus No. 3, 11, 125, 145, 146, 147, or 151 can get you to Michigan Avenue and Erie Street. On Tuesday, the museum's hours are from 10 a.m. to 8 p.m. On Wednesday through Saturday, it's open from 10 a.m. to 6 p.m., and on Sunday from noon to 5 p.m. Admission is $5 for adults, $2.50 for seniors, and it's free for children under 14.

Especially for Book Lovers

Bibliophiles find plenty to keep them entertained in Chicago.

Harold Washington Library Center

Chicago's first African-American mayor was a charismatic leader, and this handsome library — the world's largest — is a fitting tribute. The ten-story building is decorated with the work of African-American artists. It contains a permanent exhibition that chronicles the life of the popular mayor, who died in 1987, during his second term. The political memorabilia includes a button collection (one reads "Honkies for Harold," symbolizing his universal appeal). The ninth-floor winter garden is a sun-dappled public space for study and contemplation. Off the atrium is the stylish **Beyond Words Café.** A children's library offers puppet shows and other activities. On the ground floor, **Second Hand Prose** sells (for pennies) books retired from circulation.

The library offers free one-hour guided tours of its art and architecture. Tours (Monday through Saturday at noon and 2 p.m.) view the work of African-American artists and visit the winter garden.

The library center is located at 400 S. State Street (**☎ 312-747-4200**; Internet: www.chipublib.org). Take the CTA purple, brown, or orange line El to the library; Buses No. 2, 6, 10, 11, 29, 36, 44, 62, 99, 146, or 164 can get you to the library entrance. The center is open on Monday, Wednesday, Friday, and Saturday from 9 a.m. to 5 p.m., and on Tuesday and Thursday from 11 a.m. to 7 p.m. Sunday hours are 1 p.m. to 5 p.m.

Newberry Library

This attractive five-story granite building houses a noncirculating research library with rare books and manuscripts (including Shakespeare's first folio and Jefferson's copy of *The Federalist Papers*). The library is a major destination for genealogists and those holdings are available to the public free if you are over age 16 with a photo ID. Public exhibitions display many of the library's books and maps. There are concerts, lectures, and children's story hours. The Newberry Library is located at 60 W. Walton Street at Dearborn Parkway (☎ **312-943-9090** or 312-255-3700 for programs; Internet: www.newberry.org). Take the CTA buses No. 22, 36, 125, 145, 146, or 151 red line to Chicago/State. The library's reading room is open on Tuesday and Thursday from 10 a.m. to 6 p.m., and on Friday from 9 a.m. to 5 p.m. The library's gallery is open on Monday and Friday from 8:15 a.m. to 5:30 p.m., and Tuesday through Thursday from 8:15 a.m. to 7:30 p.m. The bookstore hours are Tuesday through Thursday from 10 a.m. to 6 p.m., and on Friday and Saturday from 9 a.m. to 5 p.m. Free one-hour tours are available on Thursday at 3 p.m. and on Saturday at 10:30 a.m. Admission is free.

Especially for Kids

Here are some unusual suggestions for new or off-the-beaten track activities for kids. For more, check Chapter 27 for a listing of what is best to do with kids here.

Peggy Notebaert Nature Museum

Chicago's newest museum (also known as the Nature Museum of the Chicago Academy of Sciences) focuses on human activities and the environment. Interactive exhibits include the *Children's Gallery,* where kids can check out a beaver lodge from the inside or climb around in a model ground squirrel town. **Butterfly Haven** lets 25 Midwestern species of butterflies and moths carry on their life cycles in a greenhouse environment. **Water Lab** is a model river system that shows a waterway making its way from rural to urban environments, and some of the uses and abuses it sustains along the way.

The museum is located at Fullerton Parkway and Cannon Drive (☎ **773-871-2668;** Internet: www.chias.org). Take the CTA 151 or 146 bus. The museum is open from fall through spring on Monday, Tuesday, and Thursday through Sunday from 10 a.m. to 6 p.m. On Wednesday, the museum closes at 8 p.m. The museum is also closed on Thanksgiving, Christmas, and New Year's Day. Admission is $5 for adults; $3 for seniors, students, and children ages 3 to 14; children under 3 get in free. On Tuesday, admission is free.

Ride the ducks

Yes, I said "ducks." There was a time when you had to travel to Wisconsin Dells to ride a retired World War II "duck" on land and water. Now **Chicago Duck Tours** (☎ **312-461-1133**) offers Windy City tours using the amphibious landing craft. Board at the Rock-N-Roll McDonald's parking lot at Ontario and Clark Streets. After a narrated tour of downtown Chicago, you take the plunge at Burnham Harbor for a 35-minute ride on Lake Michigan. Tickets are $20 for adults, $10 for children under 12. Reservations are strongly recommended and can be made up to two days in advance.

Speeding on a Seadog

Seadog (☎ **312-822-7200**) combines sightseeing and thrills. Expect to get wet as the distinctive yellow speedboat knifes through the waters of Lake Michigan and kicks up a 15-foot-high spray. The 149-seat *Seadog* can reach speeds of more than 50 knots and offers exciting 30-minute rides along the lakefront. Adults pay $13 on weekdays, $14 on weekends; children ages 3 to 12 pay $8 on weekdays, $9 on weekends. Board at Navy Pier.

Sleeping among the dinosaurs

How about bedding down for the night among the dinosaurs at the **Field Museum of Natural History** (☎ **312-922-9410**)? A special program held six or more times a year allows up to 300 kids and parents to spend the night in the museum. Included are flashlight tours of Ancient Egypt, natural science workshops, and storytelling. Participants bring sleeping bags and are provided with snacks and breakfast. The "Family Overnight" program, which usually runs from Saturday evening to Sunday morning, costs $40 per participant.

Brookfield Zoo

Chicago's largest zoo is spread over 216 acres with 2,700 animals in residence. Observe giraffes, snow leopards, Siberian tigers, green sea turtles, baboons, and more. Habitat Africa! is a multiple ecosystem exhibit, which will ultimately grow to 30 acres in size. All the animals live in naturalistic environments that allow them to live side-by-side with other inhabitants of their regions. The Seven Seas show featuring dolphins is a perennial hit with kids. If you plan to visit on a weekend, make sure to buy tickets to the dolphin show several hours in advance, as it always sells out.

The zoo is located at First Avenue and 31st Street in Brookfield (☎ **708-485-0263;** Internet: www.brookfieldzoo.org). Take the CTA Bus No. 304 or 311. The zoo is open daily in the summer from 9:30 a.m. to 5:30 p.m. In the fall through spring the zoo is open daily from 10 a.m. to 4:30 p.m. Parking is $4. Take the Stevenson (I-55) and Eisenhower (I-290) Expressways 14 miles west of the Loop. Admission is $6 for adults, $3 for seniors and children age 3 to 11, and free for children under 3. On Tuesday and Thursday, from April through September, admission charges change to $4 for adults and $1.50 for seniors and children age 3 to 11. Admission is free on Tuesday and Thursday from October through March.

Especially for Teens

From biking to climbing to skating, Chicago presents loads of adventure for teens.

Bike Chicago

Bike Chicago (☎ **800-915-BIKE**) at Navy Pier can fix you up with a rental so you can explore Chicago's 18 miles of lakefront bike paths. If you make a reservation and show up before 1:30 p.m., you can join a free two-hour, six-mile bicycle lakefront sightseeing tour led by Chris Dunstatter. An actor-comedian leads the self-styled "Slightly Aloof Bike Chicago Tour Guide" at night, and a tour guide takes the lead during the day. Bike rental costs $8 an hour, $30 a day. Other Bike Chicago locations are at Oak Street Beach, the Lincoln Park Zoo, and Buckingham Fountain.

Climbing "Mount Chicago"

Teens might enjoy hanging by their fingertips on the sheer face of "Mount Chicago." Waiting to challenge climbers at the **Athletic Club** (☎ **312-616-9000**) is what is billed as the "world's highest indoor climbing wall." Rising 110 dizzying feet, the man-made wall offers a climbing adventure even to those who lack previous experience. There's an orientation and safety class and a protective body harness. The club is private, open to guests of any hotel for $18 a day and to guests at the Fairmont Hotel and the Hyatt Regency Chicago for $15 a day. It's located at 211 N. Stetson, one block east of North Michigan Avenue, at Lake Street. Buses serving many routes stop along North Michigan Avenue.

Illinois Center Golf

The Illinois Center Golf Course and Driving Range (☎ 312-616-1146) has a sporty little nine-hole course among the skyscrapers east of Michigan Avenue. It even has an island green like those you find in Florida (minus the alligators). The center has a clubhouse, pro shop, and 40-slot, double-decker driving range that's lighted for night play. Tee times may be reserved through the concierge desk of the adjacent Swissotel. The center is at 221 N. Columbus Drive, south of Wacker Drive. Many bus routes stop along North Michigan Avenue, two blocks west.

Morton Arboretum

Let teens burn off excess energy by cruising through 1,700 acres of flora from around the world, plus a wildlife refuge for foxes, beavers, and birds. Some 30,000 different tree specimens grow at this spectacular arboretum in west suburban Lisle, founded in 1922 by Morton Salt Company founder Joy Morton. You can drive through, but the best way to see it is a walk along the more than 25 miles of pathways. Check out landscapes from prairies to dense woods and waterways. A one-hour tram ride offers an overview and runs twice daily and costs $2. If you're in need of refreshment, check out the Gingko Tea Room, an absolutely charming spot for a light lunch, which sits on the bank of a scenic pond.

The arboretum is on Route 53, just north of the East-West Tollway (I-88), in Lisle (☎ **630-968-0074**; Internet: www.mortonarb.org). The Morton Arboretum opens at 7 a.m. and closes at 7 p.m. daily from early April to late October. The rest of the year, the arboretum closes at 5 p.m. Admission is $7 per car ($3 per car on Wednesday).

Skate on State

Whether you're a graceful glider or merely a stumbler, you can ice skate (weather permitting) in the heart of Chicago's Loop. **Skate on State** (☎ 312-744-3315) is a 20,000-square-foot ice rink that's open from late November through March. Admission is free. Skate rental is $3 for adults, $2 for children. There are free lessons on Saturdays from 9 to 11 a.m., and "IceBreaker" performances by local skaters every Monday, Wednesday, and Friday at 11:30 a.m. For the holidays, the rink is decorated with trees representing each of Chicago's 20 sister cities. Skate on State is west of State Street, between Madison and Washington Streets. Buses serving many routes stop along State Street.

Chapter 18

And on Your Left, Lake Michigan: Seeing Chicago by Guided Tour

In This Chapter

▶ Orienting yourself with a sightseeing tour

▶ Sailing smoothly on boat tours

▶ Exploring far-flung neighborhoods by tour

▶ Investigating special-interest tours

*W*hile you already have a friend to show you around Chicago (that's this book!), I won't be offended if you want an in-person guided tour. A good guide can escort you around the city and its neighborhoods, pointing out the sights and giving you special insights.

Sampling the City with Orientation Tours

Take a tour as soon as you arrive. You can take a basic sightseeing tour on a motor coach, van, double-decker bus, open trolley, or boat. Even if you did your homework and have read this book cover to cover, there's nothing like seeing the city firsthand. Suddenly, the geography you tried to fix in your mind makes sense. Attractions and sights you read about come to life. It's like the difference between viewing a movie in black-and-white and in color.

One popular spot for picking up a land or water tour is at the Michigan Avenue Bridge (over the Chicago River at East Wacker Drive). Other land tours take off from the intersection of Pearson Street and Michigan Avenue (near the Water Tower).

One word of caution about guided tours. Don't regard everything you hear as fact. Narrators are known to take liberties with the truth and are apt to spread a rumor or two. They also read from a script that is usually memorized — the 10,000th repetition may be dull. Treat these tours for what they are: They provide basic sightseeing and orientation — here's the Water Tower, here's Daley Plaza, there's the Sears Tower, there's Lake Michigan. Here's a list of some reliable companies to check out:

✔ **American Sightseeing Tours (☎ 312-251-3100).** This company offers ten different bus excursions that include basic orientation, neighborhood, nightlife, and architectural tours. Tours run two to five hours and cost $15 to $32.

✔ **Chicago Duck Tours (☎ 312-461-1133;** Internet: www.chicago-ducks.com). These bright yellow amphibious transports go on land and water — although originally they were designed to bring troops and supplies ashore during World War II. You'll start with a 45-minute land tour of the Loop, Michigan Avenue, Grant Park, and the museum campus. There, your duck rolls into the water and transports you on a 35-minute tour of Chicago from the lake. Tickets are $20 for adults, $10 for children 11 and under.

✔ **Chicago Trolley Company (☎ 312-663-0260).** Breezy trolleys provide narrated tours of the major sites and also offer all-day on-and-off privileges. Trolleys run every 15 to 20 minutes. The fare is $15 for adults, $12 for seniors, $8 for children 3 to 11.

✔ **Gray Line Tours (☎ 312-251-3107).** You'll find the granddaddy of tour companies in every major city. It offers a range of bus excursions, including three-hour *Inside Chicago* tour packages, which cost $24 for adults, $12 for children.

Water, Water Everywhere: Boat Tours

A variety of excursion boats travel the Lake Michigan shoreline and three branches of the Chicago River. They offer sightseeing by day, dining and dancing at night. Primary boarding spots are along the Chicago River between North Michigan and Wabash Avenues; Ogden Slip, at the east end of East Illinois Street next to River East Plaza; and Navy Pier.

You may be surprised at this advice from an off-the-beaten-path aficionado, but here goes: Get thee on that boat. Chicagoans know the absolute best way to get the lay of the land is by water. You save oodles of time. Instead of wandering around (like a tourist, I must add), you can maneuver with something resembling confidence and get a taste of Chicago's beautiful lakefront from a unique perspective.

For most sightseeing boats, the season runs from early May through late October. Tours typically last 90 minutes, but shorter and longer trips are available. Most operate on a set schedule, and reservations are advisable during prime times, such as weekends and holidays in the middle of summer. At other times it is possible to walk on. The following tour companies offer great ways to see the city from the water:

- ✔ **Wendella Sightseeing Boats** (☎ 312-337-1446; Internet: www.wendellaboats.com) has operated cruises on the Chicago River and onto Lake Michigan since 1935. Guides identify the skyscrapers spiking above the distinctive shoreline, which are brilliantly lighted at night. Guided lake and river tours run one, one-and-a-half, and two hours. Tickets for adults run $11 to $15, for seniors $10 to $14, and for children 3 to 11, $6 to $8.

- ✔ **Mercury Chicago's Skyline Cruiseline** (☎ 312-332-1353) also offers river and lake cruises. Day-long weekend excursions along the National Heritage Corridor, the river route connecting Chicago and the Mississippi River, cost $49. For kids, Mercury runs the popular "Wacky Pirate Cruise," combining buccaneer capers and sing-alongs with pain-free history and geography. The fare is $14 for adults, $7 for children.

- ✔ **Spirit of Chicago** (☎ 312-836-7899; Internet: www.spiritcruises) and **Odyssey II** (☎ 630-990-0800; Internet: www.odyssey-cruises.com), a pair of sleek motor yachts, offer luxury cruises. They include lunch, brunch, or dinner, and there's a romantic moonlight cruise with bubbly and dancing. The 600-passenger *Spirit of Chicago* and the 800-passenger *Odyssey II* depart from Navy Pier. Tickets run $53 to $83.

- ✔ **uglyduck Cruises** (☎ 888-289-8833 or 312-396-9007; Internet: www.uglyduckcruises.com) offers a dinner cruise. You know by the name and its bright yellow color that this boat isn't going to be stuffy. An emcee involves (sometimes reluctant) guests in contests, TV monitors play music videos, and dancing is spirited. This is where you're likely to run into a bachelor or bachelorette party. Food is served buffet-style. The fare is $15 to $40, depending on the time of day and the meal they serve.

- ✔ The **Windy** (☎ 312-595-5555) is for those who enjoy listening to the slap of sails as they plow through the waves of Lake Michigan. The 148-foot, four-masted schooner offers 90-minute daytime and evening cruises. Passengers help raise and trim sails and take turns at the ship's wheel. Adults ride for $25, seniors and children under 13 for $15.

Bricks and Mortar, Steel and Glass: Architectural Tours

Chicago is a living textbook of architectural styles, and the high-quality tours offered by the Chicago Architecture Foundation (☎ **312-922-3432** or 312-922-TOUR; Internet: www.architecture.org) provide an excellent introduction. More than 50 tours are offered — by bus, train, boat, and bicycle, and on foot. (For more on their most popular tour, the Architecture River Cruise along the north and south branches of the Chicago River, see Chapter 16.) Other perennial favorite tours are the "Rise of the Skyscraper," "On and About North Michigan Avenue," and the "Chicago Architecture Highlights by Bus" trip. The bus tour covers a number of high-impact historical districts. It departs at 9:30 a.m. on Saturday, lasts over three hours, and costs $25.

Cultivating International Appreciation: Neighborhood Tours

Chicago Neighborhood Tours (☎ **312-742-1190**; Internet: www.chgocitytours.com) offers half-day narrated weekly bus excursions. The tours visit different neighborhoods each week, accompanied by local greeters. This series takes visitors to landmarks, cultural centers, and museums. Tours also explore shopping centers and allow you to taste local cuisine. For example, the Chinatown/Pilsen tour includes a guided walking tour of Chinatown led by Chinese American Service League representatives, with a stop for refreshments at a Chinese bakery. Then there's a visit, reception, and shopping at the Mexican Fine Arts Center Museum, and a guided bus tour of the Pilsen neighborhood that takes in murals by local artists. Other tours include Bronzeville on the south side, a tour of Chicago's Jewish neighborhoods. They depart from the Chicago Cultural Center, 77 E. Randolph Street, at 10 a.m. on Saturdays and last approximately four hours. Call first, because the tours don't run on major holidays and generally close during the month of January. The fare for adults is $30, and for seniors and children 8 to 18 years of age, it's $27.

Want to take a ride on the giant Ferris wheel at Navy Pier, and then perhaps head to River North to grab a burger at Rock-N-Roll McDonald's or Rainforest Café? Take advantage of the free trolley shuttle that operates along the Illinois Street–Grand Avenue corridor between Navy Pier and State Street. It runs every 10 to 20 minutes from 10 a.m. to 10 p.m., daily, year-round. It makes about a dozen stops along the way. It's designed to relieve parking congestion at Navy Pier.

Gangsters and Ghosts: Specialty Tours

Untouchable Tours (☎ 773-881-1195 — ask for Bugsy; Internet: www. gangstertour.com) are led by Da Boys and their molls. Suitably costumed guides — the men in snap-brimmed fedoras, the women in flapper outfits — brandish machine guns and pistols. Two-hour tours visit Prohibition-era gangster hangouts and hit spots (such as the Biograph Theatre, where John Dillinger met his end, and the site of the St. Valentine's Day massacre). The fare for adults is $22, for children $16.

Another company offers tours that are perfect for *X-Files* fans. Focusing on the supernatural and paranormal, **Tour of Haunted and Legendary Places** (☎ 708-499-0300) visits graveyards, haunted houses, and other ghostly places. A five-hour narrated bus tour costs $30 per person; a two-hour supernatural boat excursion is $20 per person.

Read all about it

Want to see how a newspaper is "put to bed" and printed? If you're visiting Chicago after January 2002, call the **Chicago Tribune** (☎ 312-222-3232). (Tours are currently suspended due to construction.) Tours are free but offered only if you call ahead for a reservation.

Chapter 19

A Shopper's Guide to Chicago

• •

In This Chapter

▶ Scouting out the best shopping neighborhoods

▶ Checking out the big department stores

▶ Finding the right place for what you want

• •

Chicago is a shopping mecca. Why do you think the Magnificent Mile is called "magnificent?" Not because of the sightseeing, believe me. On Michigan Avenue, the stores are the thing.

You can find most anything you want around Michigan Avenue. Finding the department stores and four high-rise shopping malls is no problem. For those who want to discover Chicago's boutiques and specialty stores, in this chapter I point you in the right direction. (Even within the downtown mall complexes, you may miss some of the smaller shops that make Chicago a great shopping destination.) I also explore other neighborhoods that offer great boutique shopping.

Stores traditionally stay open later on Thursday night, until 8 p.m. or so. Department stores stay open until about 7 p.m. all other nights except Sundays, when they open around 11 a.m. and close around 6 p.m. Smaller stores close by 5 p.m. or 6 p.m. The biggest sales of the year take place in January when retailers slash prices on winter clothing to make room for spring offerings. Great shopping — if you didn't blow all your bucks over the holidays! You'll want to hit sales, especially because our tax is high — 8.75 percent. Ouch.

Buying from the Big Department Stores

Chicago's homegrown department store is Marshall Field's (yes, the Field Museum is named after the merchant). Trademarks are the dark green shopping bags, Frango mints, and of course, the storefront windows of the State Street store. But more on Marshall Field's later. Many, many more department stores await you:

✔ **Bloomingdale's,** 900 N. Michigan Avenue (☎ 312-440-4460). New York City's beloved Bloomie's opened its first Midwestern outpost in Chicago. The six-level store includes a section devoted to store logo merchandise.

✔ **Carson Pirie Scott,** 1 S. State Street (☎ 312-641-7000). Stunning architecture by Louis Sullivan (one of Frank Lloyd Wright's mentors) makes this century-old department store easy on the eyes. The exterior incorporates intricate ornamental iron filigree. The store is easier on your pocketbook than nearby Marshall Field's and carries slightly lower-end merchandise as well.

✔ **Lord & Taylor,** 835 N. Michigan Avenue (☎ 312-787-7400). The multi-level department store anchors Water Tower Place (along with a Marshall Field's branch). Known for conservative, "all-American" style.

✔ **Marshall Field's,** 111 N. State Street (☎ 312-781-1000). Chicago traditions include meeting under the Field's clock and viewing the animated holiday window displays at the 1852-built store. Another custom is afternoon tea in the gracious Walnut Room (which, during the holidays, is home to a giant Christmas tree and another tradition, "breakfast with Santa"). The chain's flagship store also offers 73 acres of shopping. A smaller branch is located in Water Tower Place (☎ 312-335-7700).

✔ **Neiman Marcus,** 737 N. Michigan Avenue (☎ 312-642-5900). Texas' favorite department store has top merchandise and prices to match. If you're in town in late January, the "Last Call" sale is one of the city's best. The fourth-floor epicure shop specializes in pâté, caviar, and other delicacies.

✔ **Nordstrom's,** The Shops at North Bridge, 520 N. Michigan Avenue (☎ 312-464-1515). Opened in fall 2000, Nordstrom's anchors a new mall that has attracted traffic to the south end of Michigan Avenue. Why go to Nordstrom's? Shoes. On the weekends, you'll have to take a number, as an employee with a microphone walks around the huge department calling numbers. Service is renowned.

✔ **Saks Fifth Avenue,** Chicago Place, 700 N. Michigan Avenue (☎ 312-944-6500). High-priced designer fashions are what this seven-story department store is all about. Beautiful jewelry department on the first floor, as well as make-up and the city's best selection of Jo Malone scents, lotions, and other beauty products.

Shopping: Prime Hunting Grounds

In this section you find the very best of Chicago's shopping broken down by neighborhood.

Magnificent Mile Shopping

Active Endeavors **37**
Agnes b. **12**
American Girl Place **23**
Ann Taylor **28**
Anthropologie **1**
Aveda **18**
Banana Republic **25**
Barney's New York **9**
Bloomingdale's **15**
Borders Books & Music **21**
Brooks Brothers **29**
Burberry's Ltd. **35**
Cartier **32**
Chalet Wine &
   Cheese Shop **16**
Chicago Place **28**
Crate & Barrel **33**
Diesel **16**
The Drake **14**
Eddie Bauer **36**
Elements **6**
FAO Schwartz **20**
Filene's Basement **21**
Georg Jensen **14**
Hello Chicago **28**
Hermes **7**
Jil Sander **10**
John Hancock Center **18**
Kate Spade **13**
L'Appetito **18**
Linens 'n' Things **28**
Lord & Taylor **19**

Marshall's **28**
Material Possessions **17**
Neiman Marcus **30**
Niketown **30**
900 North Michigan Avenue **15**
Nordstrom's **39**
Original Levi's Store **28**
Polo Ralph Lauren **24**
Pottery Barn **25**
Prada **2**
Saks Fifth Avenue **28**
Salvatore Ferragamo **34**

Shabby Chic **22**
Shops at North Bridge **39**
Sony **31**
Sugar Magnolia **3**
Sulka **5**
Tiffany & Co. **26**
Timberland **38**
Ultimo **7**
Urban Outfitters **11**
Virgin Megastore **37**
Water Tower Place **19**
Wolford **8**

Magnificent Mile and environs

This high-priced stretch of real estate on Michigan Avenue reaches from Oak Street south to the Chicago River (see map of "Magnificent Mile Shopping" in this chapter). You find high-visibility names, from Cartier to Kenneth Cole, Filene's Basement to Ralph Lauren, Gucci to Nike.

- ✔ **Active Endeavors,** 45 E. Grand Avenue (☎ 312-822-0600). Gear for outdoor pursuits, from hiking to biking to skiing. Fun casual clothes too.

- ✔ **Agnes B.,** 46 E. Walton Street (☎ 312-642-7483). Simple and ultra-stylish, this French clothing line's shop has minimalist decor and clothes that for some reason always remind me of what Audrey Hepburn would be wearing if she were in her 20s or 30s today.

- ✔ **American Girl Place,** 111 E. Chicago Avenue (☎ 887-AG-PLACE). The "in" place for the pre-teen set. You can never collect enough American dolls . . . and then you need to add to their extensive wardrobe and accessories. Call ahead to book lunch in the chic cafe or to catch a performance of "The American Girls Revue," performed five days a week in a 150-seat theater.

- ✔ **Ann Taylor,** 600 N. Michigan Avenue (☎ 312-587-8301). The Chicago flagship store for this seller of women's casual and career clothing, accessories, and shoes, including petite and regular sizes. An **Ann Taylor Loft** (☎ 312-329-1639) is located on the second level of The Shops at North Bridge mall, 520 N. Michigan Avenue, and offers casual clothing at less expensive prices.

- ✔ **Anthropologie,** 1120 N. State Street (☎ 312-255-1848). Ethereal and funky clothing combine with household decorating items in this really beautiful store. Great for gifts.

- ✔ **Aveda,** 875 N. Michigan Avenue, in the plaza of the John Hancock Center Observatory (☎ 312-664-0417). The Minnesota company creates all-natural scents, lotions, hair care products, and make-up. Come here and breathe in the aromatherapy.

- ✔ **Banana Republic,** 744 N. Michigan Avenue (☎ 312-642-0020). The Gap's stylish sibling has a mega-store on Michigan Avenue and a smaller shop in the Water Tower mall. This store has great going-out clothes and clothing to blend in with the city folk.

- ✔ **Borders Books & Music,** 830 N. Michigan Avenue (☎ 312-573-0564). This enormously popular and well-trafficked bookstore has a cafe that overlooks Michigan Avenue as well as the standard assortment of books, CDs, and videos. On the main floor is a section of books on Chicago. Downstairs, you'll find a colorful selection of writing accessories, including notebooks and pens.

- ✔ **Brooks Brothers,** 713 N. Michigan Avenue (☎ 312-915-0060). The East Coast preppy haven is still *the* place for men's shirts. (They look good on women, too.)

✔ **Burberry's Ltd.,** 633 N. Michigan Avenue (☎ **312-787-2500**). Formerly traditional, newly hip. This is the place to pick up that kilt you wanted for years.

✔ **Cartier,** 630 N. Michigan Avenue (☎ **312-255-7440**). Jewels, jewels, jewels. Need we say more? The window displays alone cause sidewalk traffic jams.

✔ **Chalet Wine & Cheese Shop,** 40 E. Delaware Place. (☎ **312-787-8555**). Wine, liquor, beer, a wonderful cheese counter, pâté, crackers, and anything else to make a romantic picnic or party with friends.

✔ **Crate & Barrel,** 646 N. Michigan Avenue (☎ **312-787-5900**). Stylish home furnishings and housewares in a three-floor store that's fun to browse. Another large store has opened in Lincoln Park at 850 W. North Avenue (☎ 312-573-9800).

✔ **Diesel,** 923 N. Rush Street (☎ **312-255-0157**). Cutting-edge industrial-style fashion. Great jeans. Connected to Zoom Kitchen, a hip lunch spot.

✔ **Eddie Bauer,** 600 N. Michigan Avenue (☎ **312-951-5888**). The preppy East Coast clothier has great casual styles and is offering dress casual clothing, too. Furniture and household furnishings are upstairs.

✔ **FAO Schwarz,** 840 N. Michigan Avenue (☎ **312-587-5000**). Boxing kangaroos, a life-sized gorilla, a perpetual-motion machine, and thousands of toys make this three-level store irresistible. Outside, you find friendly guys dressed like toy soldiers, trying out new toys on passers-by.

✔ **Filene's Basement,** 830 N. Michigan Avenue (☎ **312-482-8918**). This bargain "basement" with name-brand clothing for less occupies the upper floors of a flashy Mag Mile building. There's another store at 1 N. State Street (☎ 312-553-1055).

✔ **Georg Jensen,** 959 N. Michigan Avenue (☎ **312-642-9160**). Scandinavian design in jewelry, silver, and other household items. Housed in The Drake hotel.

✔ **Hello Chicago,** 700 N. Michigan Avenue (☎ **312-787-0838**). Local memorabilia and sports merchandise.

✔ **L'Appetito,** 875 N. Michigan Avenue (☎ **312-337-0691**). An Italian grocery located in the lower level of the John Hancock Center Observatory that carries a wide selection of cheeses, sausages, and cold cuts.

✔ **Linens 'n' Things,** 600 N. Michigan Avenue (☎ **312-787-0462**). Wide selection of bed and bath apparel and cookware at good prices.

✔ **Marshall's,** 600 N. Michigan Avenue (☎ **312-280-7506**). A key Mag Mile spot for finding heavily discounted designer labels.

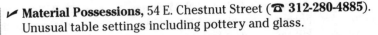

✔ **Material Possessions,** 54 E. Chestnut Street (☎ 312-280-4885). Unusual table settings including pottery and glass.

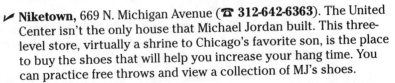

✔ **Niketown,** 669 N. Michigan Avenue (☎ 312-642-6363). The United Center isn't the only house that Michael Jordan built. This three-level store, virtually a shrine to Chicago's favorite son, is the place to buy the shoes that will help you increase your hang time. You can practice free throws and view a collection of MJ's shoes.

✔ **Original Levi's Store,** 600 N. Michigan Avenue (☎ 312-642-9613). If you can't find a pair of jeans here, you won't find a pair anywhere. Or, let them measure you and send you a pair of custom-made jeans.

✔ **Polo Ralph Lauren,** 750 N. Michigan Avenue (☎ 312-280-1655). Ralph Lauren has built a giant Polo palace where you can revel in his look. A small Italian restaurant named, appropriately, RL (and decorated in Ralph's style, of course), is attached to the palace on Chicago Avenue.

✔ **Pottery Barn,** 734 N. Michigan Avenue (☎ 312-587-9602). Everything to decorate your home, plus furniture.

✔ **Salvatore Ferragamo,** 645 N. Michigan Avenue (☎ 312-397-0464). Upscale Italian fashions ranging from shoes and handbags to tailored suits for men and women.

✔ **Shabby Chic,** 46 E. Superior Street (☎ 312-649-0080). The famous decorating look is for sale in this furniture store.

✔ **Sony Gallery of Consumer Electronics,** 663 N. Michigan Avenue (☎ 312-943-3334). Stop to surf the Net or try out electronic games as you explore three floors of the latest high-tech products.

✔ **Tiffany & Co.,** 730 N. Michigan Avenue (☎ 312-944-7500). Home of the little blue box, you can get your engagement ring on the first floor and register for wedding gifts upstairs. Affordable silver jewelry can be had for under $100.

✔ **Timberland,** 545 N. Michigan Avenue (☎ 312-494-0171). Boots and clothing for treks to the north woods (or to Starbucks).

✔ **Urban Outfitters,** 933 N. Rush Street (☎ 312-640-1919). Fun, funky, and offbeat clothing and accessories, from beanbag chairs to trendy clothing and glittery nail polish.

Magnificent Mile Malls

North Michigan Avenue's three shopping malls are also places for a fast snack, a good meal, or a movie. Your journey takes you from north to south.

900 North Michigan Avenue

This indoor mall doesn't have a name, but most locals call it the "Bloomingdale's Building," after the anchor store. Along with about 75 shops are some good restaurants on the fifth and sixth floors, including **Typhoon** (pan-Asian) and **Tucci Bennuch** (Tuscan). On the main floor of the marble-clad atrium, a branch of the celebrated **Corner Bakery** sells coffee, crusty bread, rolls, and pastries; on the lower level is a movie theater and Mario Tricoci Salon and Day Spa (highly recommended). The Four Seasons Hotel is also in this building (to get there through the mall, go to the sixth floor and walk west to the Four Seasons elevator bank). Stores include

- ✔ **Cashmere Cashmere** (☎ 312-337-6558). Top-of-the-line cashmere, straight from Scotland.

- ✔ **Club Monaco** (☎ 312-787-8757). Minimalist fashions at affordable prices for the young crowd.

- ✔ **Coach Store** (☎ 312-440-1777). Everything leather, from handbags to luggage.

- ✔ **Gucci** (☎ 312-664-5504). From loafers and leather goods, to leading edge fashion, Gucci sets the styles.

- ✔ **J. Crew** (☎ 312-751-2739). Sweaters, slacks, hats, belts, and other clothing featuring the scrubbed-clean look.

- ✔ **Mark Shale** (☎ 312-440-0720). Chicago's own upscale clothing store has a fine selection of men's and women's casual and dress clothing. Especially good for men. Service is excellent and the clothing is unique.

- ✔ **Museum Shop of the Art Institute of Chicago** (☎ 312-482-8275). Jewelry, posters, knick-knacks, and other gifts.

- ✔ **Specttica Fashion Opticians** (☎ 312-944-2050). Glasses as a fashion accessory reign here.

- ✔ **Williams-Sonoma** (☎ 312-587-8080). Chefs love this store offering the latest in kitchen gadgets and high-quality cookware.

Water Tower Place, 835 North Michigan Avenue

Chicago's showcase mall, with cascading fountains and waterfalls and glass-cage elevators, contains more than 100 stores spread over seven floors. Marshall Field's and Lord & Taylor are the anchors. The innovative **Foodlife** food court (see Chapter 15) contains more than a dozen stations, from burgers and pizza to Mexican and Moroccan, plus the **Mity Nice Grill**, a faux-1940s diner. Two movie complexes contain eight screens. Shops include

- ✔ **Warner Bros. Studio Store** (☎ 312-664-9440). Bugs Bunny? Elmer Fudd? That's not all, folks.

- ✔ **Michael Jordan Golf** (☎ 312-944-4545). Clothing, clubs, balls, and almost everything you want and need before hitting the links.

- ✔ **Accent Chicago** (☎ 312-944-1354). T-shirts, pizza pans, logo sports gear, and other souvenirs that say "Chicago."

- ✔ **WTTW Store of Knowledge** (☎ 312-642-6826). Educational games, videos, and other intellectually stimulating merchandise.

Chicago Place, 700 North Michigan Avenue

This eight-floor, 50-store mall has **Saks Fifth Avenue** as its anchor and a small supermarket called **Bockwinkel's** (☎ 312-482-9900) in its lower level, which is a good spot for made-to-order sandwiches and daily soup selections, and has a small dining area. Skip the food court on the eighth level. It's depressing and smells greasy. But if you need a watch battery, there's a little shop on that floor that will replace yours while you wait. Stores include

- ✔ **Ann Taylor** (☎ 312-335-0117). Clothing and accessories for women.

- ✔ **The Body Shop** (☎ 312-482-8301). All-natural shampoos and lotions.

- ✔ **Room & Board** (☎ 312-266-0656). This Minnesota-based furniture company has contemporary furniture and a sister store, **Retrospect** (☎ 312-440-1270), in the same mall, offering more traditional furniture.

- ✔ **Talbot's** (☎ 312-944-6059). Conservative, classic women's clothing in a wide range of sizes. A **Talbot's Kids** is also located here (☎ 312-943-0255).

- ✔ **Williams-Sonoma** (☎ 312-787-8991). Stylish cookware and epicurean foodstuffs.

The Shops at North Bridge, 520 North Michigan Avenue

Chicago's newest high-rise mall features popular urban men's and women's clothing, jewelry, and specialty items. The third level is dedicated to children's fashions, accessories, and toys (kids love the oversized Lego models on this floor!). The fourth floor is Chicago's "Magnificent Meal," an upscale food court. Shops include

- ✔ **A/X Armani Exchange** (☎ 312-467-5702). Urban wear for the hip among us at reasonable prices.

- ✔ **The LEGO Store** (☎ 312-494-0760). All things red, yellow, and blue are built out of the little colored building blocks. Kids can spend an hour here.

✔ **Sephora** (☎ 312-494-9598). Make-up mecca. You can find many of the small, chic make-up companies' products here.

✔ **Vosges Haut-Chocolat** (☎ 312-644-9450). Truffles to die for in pretty packaging.

Oak Street

If you want sophistication and high fashion and are prepared to pay for them, you'll be in heaven along the short stretch of Oak Street between Michigan Avenue and Rush Street. In one block you can find more than 40 stores in converted brownstone mansions. Included are

✔ **Barneys New York,** 25 E. Oak Street (☎ 312-587-1700). A mini-version of New York's Barneys, the store has the latest, from make-up to shoes, bags, and clothes. If you want top-of-the-line men's suits, this is the place. Not for those who faint at high prices. Excellent for spotting trends and people-watching.

✔ **Elements,** 102 E. Oak Street (☎ 312-642-6574). High-end, high-design gifts and home decorating items.

✔ **Hermes of Paris,** 110 E. Oak Street (☎ 312-787-8175). Hermes makes the world's most sought-after scarves and ties. Don't be intimidated: Walk in and take a look at the displays of color and design that make these silk scarves and ties stunning, season after season.

✔ **Jil Sander,** 48 E. Oak St.(☎ 312-335-0006). Ultra modern clothing and shoes.

✔ **Kate Spade,** 101 E. Oak Street (☎ 312-604-0808). The handbag designer's newest and largest store opened in 2001. From plaid to gingham and basic black, Kate Spade does bags. Her shoes are adorable, too.

✔ **Sugar Magnolia,** 34 E. Oak Street (☎ 312-944-0885). Women's clothing boutique also has small gifts, jewelry, and handbags. Casual clothes for relaxing, sexy clothes for going out.

✔ **Prada,** 30 E. Oak Street (☎ 312-951-1113). So chic it's almost painful. The ultimate spot for buying the designer's signature bags.

✔ **Sulka,** 55 E. Oak Street (☎ 312-951-9500). Tailored suits for men, plus furnishings.

✔ **Ultimo,** 114 E. Oak Street (☎ 312-787-0906). Chicago's best-known upscale clothier offers men's and women's clothing by big-time labels such as Isaac Mizrahi and John Galliano.

✔ **Wolford,** 54 E. Oak Street (☎ 312-642-8787). Bodysuits and hosiery.

State Street/Loop Shopping

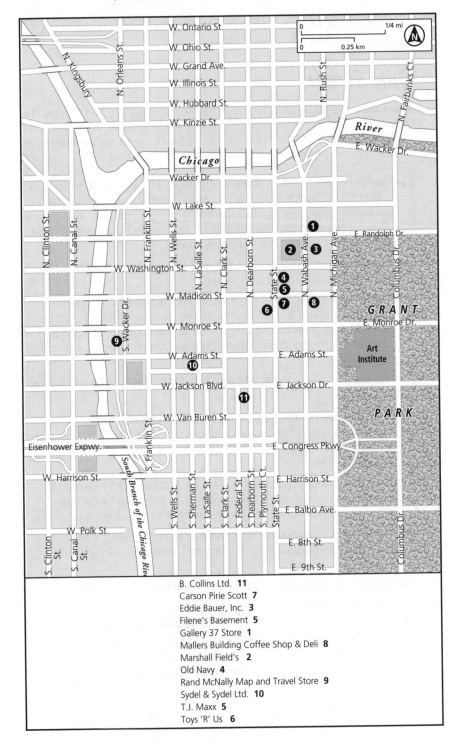

B. Collins Ltd. **11**
Carson Pirie Scott **7**
Eddie Bauer, Inc. **3**
Filene's Basement **5**
Gallery 37 Store **1**
Mallers Building Coffee Shop & Deli **8**
Marshall Field's **2**
Old Navy **4**
Rand McNally Map and Travel Store **9**
Sydel & Sydel Ltd. **10**
T.J. Maxx **5**
Toys 'R' Us **6**

State Street and the Loop

Before falling on hard times, State Street wore the shopping mantle that now belongs to the Mag Mile. But "that great street" — in the heart of the Loop — is reversing its fortunes and luring back shoppers.

State Street — that great street . . .

Although a number of department stores closed or fled to the 'burbs, Marshall Field's and Carson Pirie Scott stuck it out. They now lead the renaissance along State Street. Shops include

- ✔ **Toys 'R' Us,** 10 S. State Street (☎ 312-857-0669). This mostly suburban toy chain went urban when it took a chance on State Street with this three-level store.

- ✔ **Filene's Basement,** 1 N. State Street (☎ 312-553-1055). The East Coast discount department store chain's first Chicago branch.

- ✔ **Old Navy,** 35 N. State Street (☎ 312-551-0522). Casual wear at low, low prices.

- ✔ **T.J. Maxx,** 1 N. State Street (☎ 312-553-0515). As the ads say, get the max for the minimum price. Bargain-hunter heaven with stock that changes constantly.

Shopping for a watch, ring, or piece of jewelry? Chicago's best selection is in the **Mallers Building,** 5 S. Wabash Avenue, a Loop office building that dates from 1911. Tiny jeweler's shops are crammed into 16 of the building's 21 floors. Stop for breakfast or lunch at the **Mallers Building Coffee Shop & Deli** (☎ 312-263-7696), a time-warp diner on the third floor.

Elsewhere in the Loop

As State Street becomes revitalized, its environs are taking on a new shine, too. New hotels, restaurants (see Chapter 8 for hotels and Chapter 14 for restaurants), and theaters attract crowds to the area even on weekends. Shops include

- ✔ **Rand McNally Map and Travel Store,** 150 S. Wacker Drive (☎ 312-332-2009). Chock-full of maps, globes, and other travel aids. Also at 444 N. Michigan Avenue (☎ 312-321-1751).

- ✔ **Sydel & Sydel Ltd.,** 208 S. LaSalle Street (☎ 312-332-4653). Beautiful high-quality jewelry.

Tired of buying "local" souvenirs made in Malaysia or the Republic of China? Check out the **Gallery 37 Store,** 66 E. Randolph Street (☎ 312-251-0371; Internet: www.gallery37.org). Paintings, jewelry, ceramics, decorated furniture, textiles, and sculptures are all made by Chicago young people ages 14 to 21 who are part of Gallery 37, a not-for-profit arts training program. These young artists are mentored by experienced artists, and proceeds from the sales benefit the program.

- ✔ **Eddie Bauer, Inc.,** 123 N. Wabash (☎ **312-263-6005**). Preppyland, with casual indoor and outdoor wear. (A larger store is located at 600 N. Michigan Avenue; ☎ **312-951-5888**).

- ✔ **B. Collins Ltd.,** 318 S. Dearborn (☎ **312-431-1888**). Charming pen and stationery shop.

Lincoln Park

Yuppie heaven must include shopping, right? You'll find some of Chicago's best boutique shopping near Lincoln Park's tree-lined residential streets.

Starting at the intersection of Halsted Avenue and going west, Armitage Avenue in Lincoln Park is a string of charming boutiques, from shoes to designer clothing, tableware, and decorations for the home. Going north on Halsted from Armitage Avenue, you find more shops, including chain stores such as The Gap, Banana Republic, Ann Taylor, and more boutiques and restaurants. Shops include

- ✔ **Cynthia Rowley,** 808 W. Armitage Avenue (☎ **773-528-6160**). Feminine (but not too girlie) styles from the designer who's originally from Chicago.

- ✔ **Endo-Exo Apothecary,** 2034 N. Halsted Avenue (☎ **773-525-0500**). Colorful, fun make-up store. Let the aspiring make-up artists who work there try some of the store's latest products on you.

- ✔ **Findables,** 907 W. Armitage Avenue (☎ **773-348-0674**). Out-of-the-ordinary home and kitchen accessories.

- ✔ **Lori's Designer Shoes,** 824 W. Armitage Avenue (☎ **773-281-5655**). Shoe mecca. Discounted shoes from major designers. On the weekend, the store is swarming. Happy hunting!

- ✔ **MOSAIC (My Own Little Shop on Armitage),** 843 W. Armitage Avenue (☎ **773-935-1131**). A very hip clothing boutique.

- ✔ **Tabula Tua,** 1015 W. Armitage. (☎ **773-525-3500**). Everything you need to set the perfect table.

Bucktown/Wicker Park

Fun, funky, and off-the-beaten path purchases are best found in Bucktown and Wicker Park, Chicago's artist enclaves. Shops include

- ✔ **Pagoda Red,** 1714 N. Damen Avenue, second floor (☎ **773-235-1188**). Imported antique furniture and art objects from China, Tibet, and Burma.

- **Phoebe 45,** 1643 N. Damen Avenue (☎ 773-862-4523). A cool little boutique that has received acclaim from East Coast fashion editors. Women's and men's clothing by young designers.

Old Town

One of my favorite shopping strips is North Wells Street in Old Town. Take a jaunt down one of the side streets and you'll be able to admire the neighborhood's restored brownstones. Shops include

- **A New Leaf,** 1818 N. Wells Street (☎ 312-642-8553). One of Chicago's top florists has a breathtaking storefront with a carriage house in the back, all packed with flowers, plants, pots, candles, glassware, and more.
- **Fleet Feet Sports,** 210 W. North Avenue, in Piper's Alley (☎ 312-587-3338). Runner's heaven. They'll videotape you running on the treadmill and give you the verdict on shoes that work best for you.
- **Handle With Care,** 1706 N. Wells Street (☎ 312-751-2929). Located on a little strip of shops on Wells Street north of North Avenue, you'll find little gifts and colorful clothing.

River North

Furniture, art, and objects are found in abundance in the River North gallery area. Shops include

- **Mig & Tig,** 549 N. Wells Street (☎ 312-644-8277). Monumental furniture that's very charming.
- **Paper Source,** 232 W. Chicago Avenue (☎ 312-337-0798). Find out how to make your own scrapbook, buy cards and small gifts, choose among reams of exotic papers, and add to your collection of rubber stamps.
- **Primitive Art Works,** 706 N. Wells Street (☎ 312-943-3770). The owner of this store packs a brownstone with furniture, rugs, jewelry, beads, and objects from his world travels. One day you may find a giant Buddha head rescued from a Korean temple that was being destroyed, another an exquisite embroidered rug from Turkmenistan.
- **Sawbridge Studios,** 153 W. Ohio Street (☎ 312-828-0055). Stunningly crafted furniture with stunning prices to boot. Some of the most beautiful woodworking I've ever seen.

Southport Avenue

This recently gentrified area retains some of its funkier past with eclectic boutiques for clothing and home accessories. Shops include

- ✔ **Pink,** 3338 N. Southport Avenue (☎ 773-755-7488). Clothes, purses, and make-up for the trendy set. The owners also run **Whimsy** (see later in this list).

- ✔ **P.O.S.H.,** 3729 N. Southport Avenue (☎ 773-529-7674). Tableware, including never-used vintage silver and commercial-grade China from European and American hotels, restaurants, and cruise ships.

- ✔ **She One,** 3402 N. Southport Avenue (☎ 773-549-9698). New boutique for chic yet inexpensive women's clothing.

- ✔ **Whimsy,** 3234 N. Southport Avenue (☎ 773-665-1760). Handmade items for the home, plus bath products and other gifts.

West Lakeview

The West Lakeview neighborhood, between 1100 and 2400 West, is known as "antique row." More than 20 shops offer a mind-boggling range of antiques and collectibles, from books and furniture to Depression glass and dolls. Destinations include

- ✔ **Father Time Antiques,** 2108 W. Belmont Avenue (☎ 773-880-5599), which sells antique timepieces.

- ✔ **Richard M. Weisz Antiques,** 1741 W. Belmont Avenue (☎ 773-871-4242), which carries items from the 12th century through the Art Deco era.

- ✔ **Olde Chicago Ltd. Antiques,** 3100 N. Kedzie Avenue (☎ 773-935-1200), which stocks European and American furniture.

- ✔ **The Antiquarians Building,** 159 W. Kinzie Street (☎ 312-527-0533). Fine antiques for big bucks.

- ✔ **Armitage Antique Gallery,** 1529 W. Armitage Avenue (☎ 773-227-7727). Four floors of merchandise.

- ✔ **The International Antique Center,** 2300 W. Diversey (☎ 773-227-2400). Antiques from across the planet.

- ✔ **Wrigleyville Antique Mall,** 6131 N. Broadway (☎ 773-868-0285). Two floors of funky, fun, somewhat pricey antiques and collectibles.

Chapter 20

Four Great Chicago Itineraries

In This Chapter

▶ Four itineraries for kids, shoppers, and more

▶ Getting tips from a native on how to enjoy Chicago

▶ Discovering how to pace yourself every day

*L*et's say Picassos bore you. Perhaps bargain-hunting is more your thing. Or you're a parent with kids in tow. You came to the right chapter. If you're a shopaholic or a parent, I take you through itineraries for each, plus show you how to hit Chicago's high notes, whether you're in town for a short stint or a longer stay.

Many of the sightseeing stops I recommend are described in more detail elsewhere in this book, especially in Chapters 16 and 17, which list Chicago's top attractions. Restaurant reviews appear in Chapter 14. Where appropriate, I cross-reference the listings.

Chicago in Three Days

This section covers the best that Chicago has to offer if you have a limited amount of time to spend in the city.

Day One

Experiencing Chicago's neighborhoods is an essential part of any stay. An early-morning walk or jog is a great way to discover the lay of the land. If you stay downtown, you may want to explore nearby Streeterville on foot. Lake Michigan borders the neighborhood on the east, and the Chicago River borders Streeterville on the south, so plenty of recreational opportunities exist.

Head for the intersection of **Oak Street and Michigan Avenue** and cross to the **lakefront.** (If it's daytime and busy in the area, use the pedestrian tunnel. This is not recommended at night or very early in the morning.) After you're on the lakefront-jogging path, head south. You'll go around a bend and see a set of four stunning glass apartment buildings designed by Mies Van Der Rohe. Keep heading south. You may see swimmers (in wetsuits during much of the year) who are training for triathlons swimming alongside you. After you reach the end of the path and can see **Navy Pier,** head east. Run out along the pier, circle around the end, admire the sculptures, and head down the backside of Navy Pier. Return home on the same route. Navy Pier is ¾ mile in length. The run (or walk) from Oak Street adds just over two miles. If you like what you see at Navy Pier, head back during the day to explore further.

Streeterville residents take advantage of two neighborhood freebies. The **Museum of Contemporary Art** waives admission on the first Tuesday of every month. On Thursday evenings, admission to the **Chicago Children's Museum** at Navy Pier is free. (For more on free days at Chicago museums, see Chapter 16.)

On your first day, you may want to see a few of the gems that make Chicago an architectural crown jewel. My number-one recommendation to newcomers to the city is the Architectural River Cruise (see Chapters 16 and 18). You'll see Chicago's glorious architecture from a spectacular, watery point of view.

After you're back on land, see the architecture up close. Visit the **Tribune Tower,** 435 N. Michigan Avenue, built in 1922 after a worldwide design competition. The walls are studded with pieces of stone from world-famous buildings such as the Taj Mahal, Westminster Abbey, and the Parthenon. Wander around and admire them. WGN radio occasionally broadcasts live from a showcase window studio. Stop and stare at the DJs. Sometimes they'll come out onto the street and interview passers-by. Go into the lobby and read inspiring quotes engraved in the marble above the rotunda about journalism and the First Amendment. At street level is a Chicago sports and trivia store and Hammacher Schlemmer, a fascinating store of gadgetry.

Continue your architectural explorations a few blocks south from the Tribune Tower. Even if you're not staying at the luxurious **Hotel Inter-Continental,** 505 N. Michigan Avenue, take a free self-guided tour. Ask to borrow a portable tape player and explore the eight floors, a living textbook of classical design (see Chapter 8).

Treat yourself to a big night out. You may mix and mingle with Chicago natives at **The Saloon,** 200 E. Chestnut Street at Mies Van Der Rohe Way, ☎ 312-280-5454. Start with a drink and the calamari or crab cakes in the bar. After you're in the main dining room, dig into a steak (the largest is a 24-ounce porterhouse), pork chops, or fresh fish. Don't miss the bacon-scallion mashed potatoes and key lime pie with a peanut butter–graham cracker crust.

Day Two

Set aside this day to visit Chicago's **Museum Campus,** the most beautiful collection of museums in any city in the United States. See Chapter 16 for information.

Finish your museum day with something completely different: live, down-and-dirty Chicago blues. My personal favorite venue is **Buddy Guy's Legends,** 754 S. Wabash Avenue (☎ **312-427-0333;** Internet: www.buddyguy.com). Decorated with blues memorabilia, Chicago's premiere blues nightclub features a Creole/Cajun menu. The club has become an icon of the Chicago music scene — but if jazz or rock are more your speed, the city has ample venues. See Chapter 24 for more.

Chicago natives love local bluesman Lonnie Brooks and his son Wayne Baker Brooks. Both play the Chicago area frequently. Lonnie, who was discovered in Louisiana and came north decades ago, plays classic Chicago-style blues, while Wayne's style is blues-rock. They are also co-authors, with the late Cub Koda, of *Blues For Dummies* (Hungry Minds, Inc.). For more information, visit their Web sites, www.lonniebrooks.com and www.WayneBakerBrooks.com; Alligator Records has Lonnie Brooks' tour schedule online at www.alligatorrecords.com.

Day Three

If the weather is good, toss a Frisbee or watch a volleyball game (and the attending "volley girls") at **Oak Street Beach** (located at Oak Street and Lake Shore Drive). Tucked inside a curve of Lake Shore Drive, the popular beach attracts Chicago's young, single crowd.

Take a ride to the 94th-floor observatory of the **John Hancock Center,** 875 N. Michigan Avenue, for a bird's-eye view of the sights and sounds of Chicago (see Chapter 16).

Even without plenty of time, you can easily do justice to the compact **Terra Museum of American Art,** 666 N. Michigan Avenue, in just over an hour. One of the few cultural sites on Michigan Avenue, the museum has a stellar collection of American art, including works of Whistler and Wyeth. Admission is free on Tuesday.

Check out the historic **Water Tower** and **Pumping Station,** facing each other across Michigan Avenue, between Pearson Street and Chicago Avenue. Built two years before the Great Fire of 1871, they were among the few buildings to survive it. Along with the Picasso sculpture in Daley Plaza in the Loop, these castle-like sandstone buildings are Chicago's most recognizable landmarks.

Chicago in Five Days

In addition to all of the activities suggested in "Chicago in Three Days," check out these favorite Chicago activities.

Day Four

Having a couple of extra days allows for some strolling and down time. The best place to stroll in Chicago? Lincoln Park. A beautiful oasis of trees, shrubs, and grassland stretching alongside Lake Michigan, the park is located in the heart of the city. Here you'll find some of Chicago's finest attractions — a great many are free. Head due north from the Magnificent Mile (or ride Bus No. 151) and begin by exploring Chicago's compact lakefront zoo.

Lincoln Park Zoo, 2200 N. Cannon Drive at Fullerton Parkway (☎ **312-742-2000**), is open 365 days a year, and offers free admission. The Zoo covers 3.5 acres and has a collection of more than 1,200 reptiles, birds, and other animals. Check out the small mammal and reptile house that re-creates the climates and conditions of four continents and has more than 200 species. The zoo's large gorilla collection, seal exhibit (with an underwater viewing area), koala bear "condo," and a premier collection of big cats are worth seeing. The Children's Zoo, with its nursery and a chance to handle animals, is perennially popular.

If you visit Chicago in early December, you can join Chicagoans in crooning to the camels, serenading the seals, and singing to the swans at Lincoln Park Zoo's annual "Caroling to the Animals." Free songbooks, local choral groups, hot cider, and cookies accompany the holiday tradition. It begins at the Sea Lion Pool with Santa giving seals their holiday treat — a bag of fish. Also check out the Zoo Lights Festival, which runs from late November through New Year's.

The Lincoln Park Conservatory is north of the zoo. Follow the curving walking paths north from the Zoo and check out the four massive Victorian-era greenhouses, where tropical and desert environments are reproduced to create an exotic assortment of trees, plants, and shrubs from around the world. Seasonal flower shows featuring holiday poinsettias, Easter blooms, and fall chrysanthemums draw big crowds. Admission is free.

Anglers love to fish in the lagoons of Lincoln Park, but kids are often content to pedal a paddleboat around South Pond. Boats hold up to four people; rentals cost $9 per half-hour, $15 per hour.

At lunchtime, head for **Café Brauer,** located just north of the boat rentals. The cafe is a good choice for a light lunch or indulging in ice cream. Built in 1908 in the Prairie School style, the building has been painstakingly restored and is listed on the National Register of Historic

Places. If what you want is a real meal, then head for **R.J. Grunt's,** 2056 Lincoln Park W. (☎ 773-929-5363), where the salad bar was first invented.

Oz Park, three blocks west of the zoo, is named for *The Wonderful Wizard of Oz.* Its author, L. Frank Baum, lived and worked in Chicago and wrote his first Oz book in the city. The park contains a statue of the Tin Man, a Yellow Brick Road of bricks that are sold to raise money for the park, and "Dorothy's Playground." The park is a favorite spot for Chicago's unique 16-inch softball games. After such a relaxing day, you'll want to shake things up at night. Head for Wicker Park/Bucktown for dinner. You can't go wrong at Pacific-Northwest–inspired **Meritage** (for restaurant listings, see Chapter 14). Hit the music scene afterwards at Wicker Park fixture **Double Door** or **Empty Bottle,** the place to see local and national indie-rock and jazz acts (for nightlife, see Chapter 24).

Day Five

On your fifth day, broaden your horizons a bit by exploring the River North Gallery District.

Start at the banks of the Chicago River at Wells Street, site of the Merchandise Mart. (You can't miss it — it's the monolithic building that dwarfs everything around it.) Occupying two city blocks, the **Merchandise Mart** (☎ 312-527-7600) is the world's largest wholesale buying center. Behind-the-scenes tours depart from the concierge desk in the south lobby at noon on weekdays. Outside, flanking the Chicago River, is a salute to the barons of business. Mounted on massive pillars are bronze busts, four times life-size, of eight merchandising giants. Marshall Field and Montgomery Ward are there, as are Frank Winfield Woolworth and Edward A. Filene.

Located just east of the Merchandise Mart is the **Chicago Sun-Times** plant, which hugs the north bank of the Chicago River. The daily is written, produced, and printed in this building. Even if you don't take a plant tour, stroll through the ground-floor corridor, with a window running its length that lets you gaze down on the giant presses. You can usually see an exhibit — sometimes of prize-winning newspaper photography.

Explore Chicago's gallery district, River North. More than 70 galleries are scattered throughout the area roughly reaching from Huron and Wells west to Orleans Street, and north to Chicago Avenue. This area has been dubbed *Su-Hu* for Superior and Huron streets. My favorite? **Primitive Art Works,** featuring a gallery with authentic tribal and ethnic art, textiles, and unique home furnishings from around the world (for more information, see Chapter 19).

It's your last night in the city. Take in a show in the Loop's revitalized theater district (for more on Chicago theater, see Chapter 22). Start with dinner at funky **Atwood Café** (1 W. Washington; ☎ **312-368-1900**) in the Hotel Burnham. (Don't miss the garlicky mussels in tomato sauce served with grilled bread brushed with olive oil . . . yum!)

Chicago for Shopaholics

What could be more magnificent than strolling Michigan Avenue, admiring the shops and people watching? You won't need refined navigational skills to enjoy Chicago as a shopaholic. It's a straight shot north and south along Michigan Avenue from the Michigan Avenue Bridge, moving north to Oak Street.

Do breakfast like a Chicagoan: grab the newspaper and head for **Corner Bakery,** 676 N. St. Clair Street, at Erie Street (☎ **312-266-2570**). You'll find dozens of breads, from olive chiabatta to walnut and raisin rolls, and an array of pastries. Egg frittatas, scrambled eggs, breakfast potatoes, and oatmeal studded with dried cranberries, almonds, and brown sugar are all excellent choices.

Traveling Michigan Avenue, shopaholics run into loads of temptation in the form of Virgin Records, Burberry's Ltd., Crate & Barrel, Sony, Nike, Tiffany & Co., Pottery Barn, Banana Republic, Borders Books & Music, FAO Schwarz, and Chanel. You can also find major department stores: Nordstrom's, Saks Fifth Avenue, Neiman Marcus, Marshall Field's, Lord & Taylor, and Bloomingdale's. You will also find three big malls: North Bridge, Chicago Place, and Water Tower Place, plus the building anchored by Bloomingdale's at 900 N. Michigan Avenue. For a complete listing of Chicago's best shops, see Chapter 19.

Chicago Magazine is now publishing an annual shopping guide. For more information, check out the magazine's Web site at www. chicagomag.com.

This itinerary isn't recommended during the holidays or on most Saturdays. Magnificent Mile has become a major shopping destination and is packed to the gills during those times. Follow the cues of real Chicagoans and shop on a weekday to avoid the jostling crowds.

Shopaholics want to grab a bite, rest their feet a bit, and head back out into the fray quickly. For lunch, head to **L'Appetito,** an Italian grocery store in the plaza of the John Hancock Center Observatory. Order a sandwich to go and head across the street to the courtyard of the ivy-clad **Fourth Presbyterian Church,** between East Delaware Place and East Chestnut Street. Sit by the fountain and have a mini-picnic. The church is known for its occasional lunchtime and Sunday afternoon concerts. After lunch, check out the sanctuary, the setting for the wedding scene in Julia Roberts' movie, *My Best Friend's Wedding.*

Treat yourself to a haircut at **Mario Tricoci Salon & Day Spa** (☎ 312-415-0960), on the lower level of the Bloomie's building, 900 North Michigan Avenue. (If it's a cut you want, ask for Griselda. For color, Marisa is the expert.)

If you're still near Michigan Avenue at dinnertime, you may want a special dinner — so you can get decked out in all your new finery purchased that day. Head to **Iron Mike's Grille** on Chestnut Street, just west of Michigan Avenue, and soak in the sports memorabilia. After dinner, head to **Cru,** 888 N. Wabash Avenue at Delaware Street (☎ 312-337-4078), a European wine bar that's decorated with a zebra-wood bar, gold-tone paint accents, and chandeliers. Get a sofa next to a fireplace, watch the stylish crowd, and relax.

Chicago for Kids

River North is a pop-culture paradise, a popular venue with kids during the day and with club-goers at night.

Baseball fans should head for **Harry Caray's,** 33 W. Kinzie Street (☎ 312-828-0966), where the steaks and basic Italian dishes are excellent and showcases display uniforms, helmets, bats, and other memorabilia relating to the Cubbies and other not-so-favorite teams. Outside, look for the huge baseball bat and the "Holy Cow" sign memorializing the charismatic announcer's favorite exclamation.

When it comes to popularity, only the Golden Arches in Moscow claims to be busier than **Rock-N-Roll McDonald's,** 600 N. Clark Street at Ohio Street, ☎ 312-664-7940). Stop in for a soft drink or coffee and check out the unique ambience. Along with Big Macs, shakes, and fries, you'll find a storehouse of memorabilia and other 1950s and 1960s stuff, including a restored Corvette parked in the dining room and a collection of Beatles mementos.

Hands up

Are your hands big enough to hold a football without fumbling? Match them against those of former Bears superstar Walter Payton. The handprints of dozens of Chicago sports celebrities are captured in cement on the exterior walls of the SportMart store at 620 N. LaSalle, at West Ontario Street, in River North.

Not for those afraid of heights

Navy Pier's 148-foot-high Ferris wheel, opened in 1995, quickly became a Chicago landmark. It was modeled after the very first Ferris wheel, which was built for Chicago's 1893 World Columbian Exposition. Only weeks after the new Ferris wheel opened, a couple who had met on the Internet were married during a ride. A seven-and-a-half-minute ride costs $3 (bride or groom not included), and the views are spectacular.

Despite newer competition, the **Hard Rock Café,** 63 W. Ontario Street at Clark Street (☎ **312-943-2252**), with guitars, gold records, and a photo gallery of rockers, remains a draw to visiting teens and their "cool" parents. Recently redecorated, the restaurant is loud and bustling, as may befit a musical shrine; the burgers and shakes are okay, and the chili is pretty good. If you have teens, you may be stopping here to pick up a souvenir.

Leaving River North for Lincoln Park, children delight in the cows, pigs, and horses at **Farm-in-the-Zoo,** located next to the Lincoln Park Zoo, 2200 N. Cannon Drive at Fullerton Parkway, ☎ **312-742-2000.** Kids can watch chicks hatching and goats being milked at this replica of a Midwestern-working farm. Admission is free.

Head out to Navy Pier to visit **Chicago Children's Museum** (☎ **312-527-1000;** Internet: www.chichildrensmuseum.org). This hands-on museum offers three floors of attractions. Included is an interactive art studio, a three-story climbing schooner fashioned after those that once sailed Lake Michigan, exhibitions on inventions, water, and garbage, and an information technology arcade. It's open Tuesday through Sunday from 10 a.m. to 5 p.m., and admission is $6. The museum store is filled with educational and multicultural books, science toys, videos, music, and art supplies. You'll find plenty of activities to keep kids entertained while at **Navy Pier.** Attend a free concert or an art fair. Linger at Magic Masters, where staff members demonstrate sleight-of-hand to passers-by. Tour the studio of National Public Radio affiliate WBEZ 91.5 FM, which broadcasts live from Navy Pier every day. Spend time at Crystal Gardens, a one-acre indoor botanical oasis. Full-size palm trees, Chinese evergreens, a bounty of blooming lilies, and other seasonal flowers fill the six-story glass atrium.

Hungry? Kids love stopping for a juice or smoothie at **Foodlife,** located on the mezzanine of Water Tower Place at Michigan Avenue and Chestnut Streets. Pizza, burgers, Chinese food, and more await you in the giant food court.

Chapter 21

Exploring Beyond Chicago:
Five Great Trips

. . . .

In This Chapter

▶ Hitting the road in search of adventure

▶ Scoping out the 'burbs

▶ Checking out Hemingway, Burroughs, and Wright

. . . .

*E*ven with all the city has to offer, if you're in town for more than a few days (or if you're staying with friends and relatives in the suburbs), you may want to explore beyond the city limits. In this chapter, I let you in on the best attractions and day trips to the Chicago suburbs.

Getting to Know Oak Park's Native Sons

Two fiercely independent men — both innovators with controversial personal lives who are considered flawed geniuses — left their marks on this quiet, leafy suburb. Frank Lloyd Wright perfected his Prairie School of architecture here, designing 25 homes. Ernest Hemingway was born in Oak Park and lived there into his late teens (see the "Oak Park Attractions" map in this chapter).

Getting to Oak Park

Suburban Oak Park is ten miles west of downtown Chicago. You can take the green line El to Harlem, about a 25-minute ride from downtown. To reach the **Oak Park Visitor Center,** get off the train at Harlem and walk two blocks north to Lake Street. Take a right onto Lake, and then walk to Forest Avenue, where you make a left. The Visitor Center is located at 158 Forest Avenue (☎ **708-848-1500**), and is open daily from 10 a.m. to 5 p.m. April to October, and from 10 a.m. to 4 p.m. from November to March. Pick up maps and guidebooks at the center, located only a few blocks from the heart of the historic district and the Frank Lloyd Wright home and studio.

Oak Park Attractions

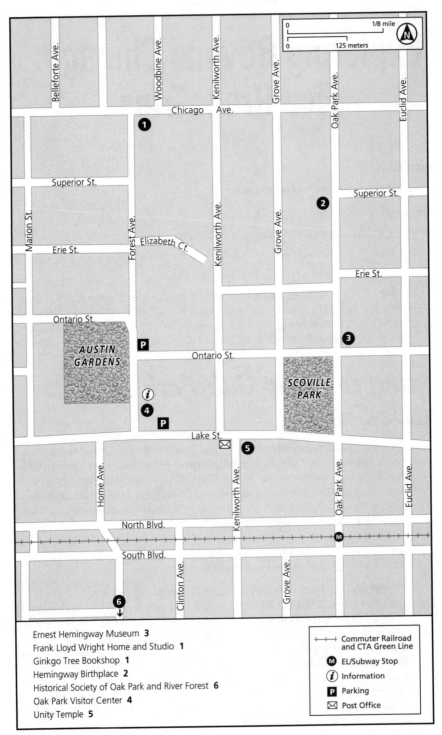

Ernest Hemingway Museum **3**
Frank Lloyd Wright Home and Studio **1**
Ginkgo Tree Bookshop **1**
Hemingway Birthplace **2**
Historical Society of Oak Park and River Forest **6**
Oak Park Visitor Center **4**
Unity Temple **5**

├──┤ Commuter Railroad and CTA Green Line
Ⓜ EL/Subway Stop
ⓘ Information
🄿 Parking
⊠ Post Office

Wide lawns, narrow minds

At one time, the Oak Park city fathers shunned one of their most famous sons, Nobel laureate Ernest Hemingway. They apparently took umbrage at his supposed description of Oak Park as a town of "wide lawns and narrow minds." Today, all seems to be forgiven — the community welcomes visitors to a Hemingway museum, to tours of the Hemingway birthplace, and to an annual festival that includes readings, a "Papa" look-alike contest, and other shenanigans.

By car, take the Eisenhower Expressway (I-290) west to Harlem Avenue (Ill. 43) and exit north (about ten miles from downtown). Continue on Harlem north to Lake Street. Take a right on Lake and continue to Forest Avenue. Turn left. Immediately on the right, you see the Oak Park Visitor Center.

Touring Oak Park

You can tour the **Frank Lloyd Wright Home and Studio** (see listing in Chapter 16) or **Unity Temple** (☎ **708-383-8873**; tours on weekends only). Or take a **Guided Walking Tour,** an extensive tour of the neighborhood around the Home and Studio. The tour leaves the Ginkgo Tree Bookshop, 951 Chicago Avenue, on weekends from 10:30 a.m. to 4 p.m. The tour lasts one hour and costs $8 for adults and $6 for seniors and children 7 to 18, and is free for children under 7. You can also follow a self-guided map and audiocassette tour of the historic district, available at the Ginkgo Tree Bookshop, from 10 a.m. to 3:30 p.m. The cost is $8 for adults and $6 for seniors and children. You'll see Wright's work, as well as the charming Victorian homes that Wright hated so intensely.

Next you may want to visit the restored **Hemingway Birthplace,** 339 N. Oak Park Avenue (☎ **708-848-2222**), and just down the block, the **Ernest Hemingway Museum,** 200 N. Oak Park Avenue (☎ **708-848-2222**). The museum traces the author's life — from his first job out of high school as a young reporter with the *Kansas City Star* to his work as a war correspondent in Europe during World War II (and his "liberation" of the Ritz Bar in Paris). Screenings of videos of 15 films made from his work, from *A Farewell to Arms* (1921) to *Islands in the Stream* (1977) are shown.

Oak Park has a third famous son, though less so than Lloyd Wright and Hemingway. Edgar Rice Burroughs, best known as the creator of Tarzan, wrote a total of 67 books, which sold 36 million copies and were translated into 30 languages. The author was born in Oak Park and lived there between 1910 and 1919. After gaining fame, Burroughs moved to Los Angeles — amazingly, he never set foot in Africa. Visitors can view a display commemorating Burroughs at the **Historical Society of Oak Park and River Forest,** 217 Home Avenue, Oak Park (☎ **708-848-6755**).

Dining in Oak Park

If you need to get refueled between walking tours, many restaurants, cafes, and ice cream shops are located on and around Oak Park Avenue, near Unity Temple. My favorite is the **Avenue Ale House** 825 S. Oak Park Ave. (☎ 708-848-2801), a tavern that specializes in steaks, chops, hearty sandwiches, homemade French onion soup, and giant salads. Eight beers are offered on tap, plus 50 more available in the bottle. An outdoor dining area is open in summertime.

Shopping in the Historic Village of Long Grove

Nestled among the northwest suburbs is Long Grove Village. Settled in the 1840s by German immigrants, Long Grove has preserved its old-fashioned character and makes a fine day trip for those looking for relief from big-city noise and commotion. You feel like you stepped into a rural village, circa 1900. Set amongst 500 acres of oak and hickory-tree groves, Long Grove is a browsers' and shoppers' mecca. More than 100 specialty shops, galleries, and restaurants are housed in historic buildings. For additional information on shops and events, visit the village Web site at www.longgrove.net.

Getting to Long Grove

Long Grove is about 30 miles northwest of Chicago. From the Loop, take the I-94 tollway north until it separates at I-90, another tollway that travels northwesterly. Follow I-90 until you reach Route 53, and drive north on 53 until it dead-ends at Lake Cook Road. Take the west exit off 53 and follow Lake Cook Road to Hicks Road. Turn right on Hicks Road and then left on Old McHenry Road, which takes you into the center of town.

What to do in Long Grove

For updates on coming events and general information, call Long Grove's **information center** (☎ 847-634-0888). Be sure to pick up a map listing all the shops and their locations — many of the streets are small and winding, and addresses alone won't be of much help.

Two shops not to miss: **Long Grove Confectionery,** 220 Robert Parker Coffin Road (☎ 847-634-0080), where you can eat hand-dipped chocolate-covered strawberries in the summer and gigantic caramel apples in the fall. The **Pine Cone Christmas Shop,** 210 Robert Parker Coffin Road (☎ 847-634-0890), is a wonder of decorated trees and Charles Dickens villages, year-round.

The village hosts several cultural and entertainment events, festivals, and art fairs during the year. The annual **Strawberry Festival** is the biggest, held during the last weekend in June. An Apple Festival is held in September.

Dining in Long Grove

For lunch, stop at **Village Tavern,** Old McHenry Road (Route 22) at Country Lane (☎ **847-634-3117**), a Long Grove institution offering soups, sandwiches, and other comfort food.

Exploring Evanston's Suburban, Urban Charm

Northwestern University contributes to the liberal, intellectual culture of Evanston. Chicago's oldest suburb, Evanston is also one of the most scenic. Evanston manages to combine the peaceful feeling and green space of a suburb, with the culture and lively atmosphere that you expect of an urban center. From downtown Chicago, the drive to Evanston on Lake Shore Drive and Sheridan Road takes about 25 minutes.

Getting to Evanston

From the Loop, drive north on Lake Shore Drive to Sheridan Road. Continue north on Sheridan. As you enter Evanston, Northwestern University is on your left.

For public transport, take the Metra North train line from Northwestern Station in the Loop to the Davis Street stop, and walk west on Davis Street into the heart of downtown Evanston. The ride takes about 20 minutes.

What to see and do in Evanston

Relive college life at **Northwestern University,** 633 Clark Street (☎ **847-491-3741;** Internet: www.nwu.edu). The lakefront campus is worth wandering around for a couple of hours. Check out the stained-glass windows at Alice Millar Chapel and the art at Mary and Leigh Block Gallery.

The former mansion of Charles Gates Dawes, 225 Greenwood, now houses the **Evanston Historical Society** (☎ **847-475-3410**), which gives free tours of this century-old national landmark. Dawes, a wealthy financier, served as vice president under Calvin Coolidge and won the Nobel Peace Prize in 1925 for his smooth handling of German reparations on behalf of the League of Nations following World War I. At Central Street and Sheridan Road in Evanston, you'll find **Lighthouse Park,** 2601 Sheridan Road (☎ 847-328-6961), site of a lighthouse built in 1873 after the wreck of the *Lady Elgin*. Nature-center tours, a wildlife trail, a little museum, and an experimental greenhouse are all part of the park. A replica of a 16th-century manor houses an art center. Tours of the lighthouse start at 2, 3, and 4 p.m. on weekends. Admission is $4 for adults, $2 for seniors and students.

Dining in Evanston

To experience Evanston's Bohemian side, grab a cup of coffee or enjoy breakfast or lunch at **Blind Faith Café,** 525 Dempster Street (☎ 847-328-6875), where organic and vegetarian specialties include scrambled tofu, huevos rancheros, granola, and pancakes. Stop in, soak in the atmosphere, and feel healthier by the minute.

Ambling Up the North Shore

A long string of suburbs runs along the lake going north from Chicago — many of them are among the nation's wealthiest zip codes.

Getting to the North Shore

If you're driving, you can make your way up Sheridan Road from the city on Lake Shore Drive, which turns into Sheridan Road. Sheridan winds through the campus of Northwestern University in Evanston and into the upper-crust North Shore suburbs of Wilmette, Kenilworth, and Winnetka (you'll recognize them by the multimillion-dollar homes that flank the road).

As you drive north on Sheridan Road, turn left onto Central Street (at Evanston Hospital). Go west to Green Bay Road. Turn right on Green Bay Road and drive ¼ mile to **Kohl Children's Museum,** 165 Green Bay Road, Wilmette (☎ 847-251-7781). This museum is a hands-on, dress-up-and-pretend, blow-bubbles sort of place where kids amuse themselves for hours. They shop at a "supermarket," take a simulated voyage on a Phoenician sailing ship, and join in puppet shows and sing-alongs. The museum is open Monday through Saturday from 9 a.m. to 5 p.m., on Sunday from noon to 5 p.m. Admission is $5 per person, $4 for seniors, free for children under age one.

Farther north in Wilmette is the dazzling white **Baha'i House of Worship,** 100 Linden Avenue at Sheridan Road (☎ 847-853-2300). The domed temple has nine identical sides and is ornately decorated with intricate filigree, scrollwork, and bas-relief. It is so distinctive that it is easily spotted from airliners on the O'Hare flight path. It's open daily from 10 a.m. to 10 p.m., and admission is free.

General's road

Sheridan Road, named for Civil War General Philip Sheridan, was a pleasure drive in Evanston in 1892. The road was only extended north later, in 1900, when federal authority was granted to allow a right-of-way through Fort Sheridan and to pay for construction on the Fort's grounds. Today, the road winds through genteel Evanston, Glencoe, and Winnetka, as well as army-leave town Highwood.

Dining in Wilmette

Next door to the Kohl Children's Museum, **Walker Bros. Original Pancake House,** 153 Green Bay Road (☎ **847-251-6000**), is a favorite North Shore breakfast spot. Expect a huge wait on weekends. Top choices are apple pancakes, German pancakes served with fruit, and oven-baked omelets. The restaurant serves lunch and dinner too and is a favorite with kids.

Hanging Out in Hyde Park

Anchoring the Hyde Park neighborhood is the Museum of Science and Industry, a perennial favorite with kids and one of Chicago's most popular tourist attractions. What many visitors don't know is that the museum is located in a leafy neighborhood that is also the home of the sprawling 175-acre campus of the University of Chicago. Many fine attractions sit amid the gothic architecture and tree-lined streets of the university campus (see the map of "Hyde Park Attractions" in this chapter).

Getting to Hyde Park

By car, take Lake Shore Drive south to 59th Street. Follow 59th Street west (you'll pass the Museum of Science and Industry) into the heart of the University of Chicago campus (59th Street and Ellis Avenue). The drives takes about 20 minutes from downtown.

The Metra Electric train takes about 15 minutes to reach Hyde Park from downtown. Trains run at least every hour, Mondays to Saturdays from 5:15 a.m. to 12:50 a.m., and Sundays and holidays from 5 a.m. to 12:55 a.m. Pick up the train at Randolph and Michigan, Van Buren and Michigan, or Roosevelt Road and Michigan. The 55th-56th-57th Street Station is nearest the Museum of Science and Industry; the 59th Street Station is nearest the University of Chicago campus. Fare is about $1.95.

Hyde Park Attractions

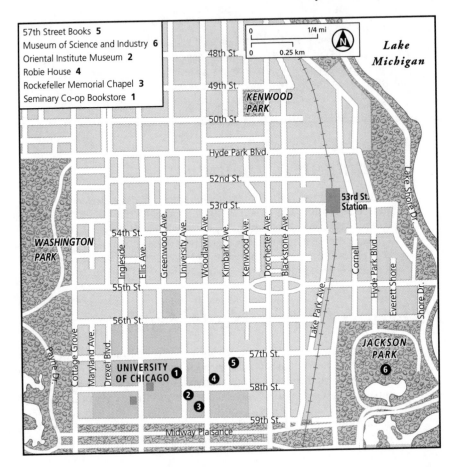

57th Street Books **5**
Museum of Science and Industry **6**
Oriental Institute Museum **2**
Robie House **4**
Rockefeller Memorial Chapel **3**
Seminary Co-op Bookstore **1**

From the Loop, bus No. 6 Jeffrey Express takes about 30 minutes. Pick up the bus on Wacker Drive on weekdays from 5:30 a.m. to 10:30 p.m., and on weekends and holidays from 7:30 a.m. to 7 p.m. Another way to go is local bus No. 1, which originates at Union Station on Jackson Boulevard and Canal Street.

Taxi fare to Hyde Park is about $13.

Exploring Hyde Park

Because the **Museum of Science and Industry** is so huge, tackling the museum in small bites is a good strategy. On this trip, maybe you'll walk the "hangar deck" of an aircraft carrier or board a retired United Airlines 727 for a seven-minute simulated flight from San Francisco to Chicago. Buy advance tickets for an Omnimax performance and return toward the end of the day for a big-screen movie. For more on the museum, see Chapter 16.

About 10 blocks west of the Museum of Science and Industry on the campus of the University of Chicago is the stunning **Rockefeller Memorial Chapel,** 5850 S. Woodlawn Avenue (☎ 773-702-2100). The gothic chapel, built in 1928, has a carillon tower and holds hour-long **carillon concerts** on Sunday evenings during the summer. (During the school year, they're at 6 p.m. on weekdays, noon on Sunday.) Simply find a spot on the lawn — the grassy area at the corner of 58th Street and South Woodlawn Avenue is ideal. Plan to arrive a half-hour early for a tour by the carillonneur.

Also on the campus of the University of Chicago is the **Oriental Institute Museum,** where you'll find mummies, gold jewelry, and other treasures of ancient Egypt, Syria, Iran, and other Mideastern countries. Admission is free. The world-class museum is one of Chicago's best-kept secrets. A good shopping stop, the museum gift store is packed with high-quality reproductions and imported jewelry, fabrics, artwork, and crafts. For more on the Oriental Institute, see Chapter 17.

Although Nobel-prize-winning novelist Saul Bellow has left Chicago, he occasionally returns to the neighborhood he wrote about in novels such as *Herzog.* One of his favorite stops is the **Seminary Co-Op Bookstore,** 5757 S. University (☎ 773-752-4381) and its sister bookstore, **57th Street Books,** 1301 E. 57th Street (☎ 773-684-1300). These rambling bookstores have an amazing array of titles.

Fans of Frank Lloyd Wright's Prairie School architecture will find one of the most successful examples in the 1909 **Robie House,** 5727 S. Woodlawn Avenue (☎ 773-834-1847). One-hour tours start at 11 a.m., 1 p.m., and 3 p.m. on weekdays. Admission is $8 for adults, $6 for seniors and students. The former garage houses a gift shop well stocked with Wright items.

Dining in Hyde Park

For lunch, travel north to **Mellow Yellow,** 1508 E. 53rd Street (☎ 773-667-2000), where you can get a bowl of Cincinnati-style, five-way chili. University of Chicago students and faculty members go to this Hyde Park institution for potent chili (including a vegetarian version) and to linger over coffee and dessert. Quiche and hamburgers are reliable choices.

Part VI

Living It Up After the Sun Goes Down: Chicago Nightlife

The 5th Wave   By Rich Tennant

"That's the third time tonight that's happened. They start out playing the blues, but by the end, everyone's playing a polka. I blame the new bass player from Milwaukee."

In this part . . .

Chicago after dark means world-class performances by the Chicago Symphony Orchestra and the Lyric Opera of Chicago. It's comedy at Second City, or a drama at the Steppenwolf or Goodman Theaters. Chicago's theater district is booming in the North Loop, with shows on their way to Broadway — or touring after a successful Broadway run.

Or, going out in Chicago can be as simple as a game of pool at a neighborhood pub or a glass of wine in front of the fireplace at a wine bar.

Chicago has a thriving music scene, including first-rate jazz joints and some of the planet's best blues clubs. Of course, the Windy City also has its quota of noisy, raucous meat-market bars and clubs. And it has its touristy nightlife spots, concentrated in places such as River North. Chicago offers culture hounds options that stack up favorably against anything you'll find anywhere else in the world.

With so many interesting places to go after dark, the sights and sounds of nighttime Chicago that are covered in this part will fill your evenings. Chapter 22 runs the gamut of information on Chicago's live theater, Chapter 23 brings you the performing arts scene (including symphony, opera, and dance), and Chicago's best bars and clubs are discussed in Chapter 24.

Chapter 22

The Play's the Thing: The Chicago Theater Scene

In This Chapter

▶ Finding out what's going on while you're in town

▶ Surveying the Chicago theater scene

▶ Minding your manners: Theater protocol

▶ Eating out or enjoying a nightcap in the theater district

▶ Getting to the performance via public transit

*C*hicago's theater scene is changing faster than you can shout "Bravo!" You can see the boom times for Chicago's theater scene in the renaissance of the North Loop. Not so long ago, the Loop was comatose after hours. No more. Lively bars and bistros, splashy hotels, and a number of thriving theaters are pumping new life into the Loop.

The biggest theater news involves the **Goodman Theater.** In the fall of 2000, the Goodman inaugurated an attractive new home on Randolph and Dearborn Streets, a total-gut rehab of the historic Harris and Selwyn Theaters. The focal point is the 830-seat mainstage theater, a brand-new limestone-and-glass structure in the center of the block. Completing the complex is a 400-seat studio theater, two restaurants, and retail space.

Another new addition is the **Palace Theatre,** 151 W. Randolph Street (☎ **312-902-1500** for TicketMaster orders). Connected to the hip Hotel Allegro, the theater is a refurbished, 1926 vaudeville house that offers 2,400 seats and stages first-run and touring Broadway musicals.

Visitors to touristy Navy Pier will find that the play's the thing there, where **Shakespeare Repertory** has a new home — an intimate 550-seat theater patterned after the Swan Theatre at Stratford-upon-Avon in England.

Theatergoers will also find a robust contingent of long-running staples such as *Shear Madness, Forever Plaid,* and *Tony and Tina's Wedding.* **Shear Madness** plays at the Mayfair Theatre, 636 S. Michigan Avenue (☎ **312-786-9120**). Tickets are $28 to $32. **Forever Plaid** goes up at the Royal George Theatre Center, 1641 N. Halsted (☎ **312-988-9000**). Tickets are $29.50 to $39.50. And **Tony and Tina's Wedding** unfolds at Piper's Alley, 210 W. North Avenue (☎ **312-664-8844**). Tickets are $47 to $60.

Finding Out What's Happening

Chicago's vibrant theater scene is in a constant state of flux, with openings, closings, revivals, and extensions. The best tools to help you scope out a show are the *Chicago Tribune, Chicago Sun-Times,* and *Daily Herald,* which offer comprehensive weekly listings in their Friday entertainment pull-out sections. The papers also run reviews of larger shows around town (for older reviews, check their Web sites). Other reliable sources of reviews and commentary are *Chicago* and *North Shore* magazines. To find out about out-of-the-mainstream performances, pick up the *Chicago Reader* and *New City,* the leading free alternative newspapers. These tabloids cover nearly every upcoming production, from traveling Broadway musicals to avant-garde performance art.

Getting Tickets

Nothing can ruin an evening at the theater like not getting tickets, so unless you really prefer watching HBO in your hotel room, check out these helpful tips.

Timesavers

If you're surfing the Web, do as Chicagoans do and check out the following sites, which bring the Chicago theater world to your fingertips:

- www.metromix.com, supported by the Chicago Tribune.
- www.centerstage.net-chicago, run by a group of Northwestern alumni in association with MediaOne.
- www.enteract.com, run by 21st Century Telecom.

Availing yourself of cheap tickets

Hot Tix, operated by the League of Chicago Theatres, sells same-day half-price tickets for about 125 city and suburban theaters. Same-day, half-price tickets are sold Tuesday through Thursday and on Sunday; on Friday, tickets for weekend and Monday shows become available (they become available at 5 p.m. Thursday at the State Street location). Because the selection changes continuously, a personal visit to a Hot Tix location or a logon to www.hottix.org (the Web site is updated Tuesday through Friday at 10 a.m. and 2 p.m.) is required (fee for the call is $1 a minute — the average call is three minutes) to determine what's available. However, no tickets are sold by phone. Credit cards are accepted everywhere but at the Tower Records stores, which are cash-only. Hot Tix locations also offer full-price tickets for Ticketmaster events (cash only). For all purchases, there are no exchanges and no refunds and a service charge that varies with ticket price is included. Hot Tix booth hours are from 10 a.m. to 6 p.m. Tuesday through Saturday; noon to 5 p.m. Sunday; closed Monday.

Getting the best seat available

After you decide on a production and show time, make your life easier by ordering tickets in advance over the phone or the Internet. Sources include **TicketMaster** arts line (☎ **312-902-1500**; Internet: www.ticketmaster.com) and the **Ticket Exchange** (☎ **800-666-0779**). If you're unable to land the tickets you want, try contacting the concierge at your Chicago hotel. If all else fails, arrive at the box office at around noon the day of the show and try your luck at getting cancellation seats.

Getting the lowest prices

You can find the best deals if you wait until the day of the show to buy tickets. **Hot Tix** (☎ **312-977-1755**) is a service that offers half-price, same-day tickets for many Chicago theaters. They must be purchased in person, with cash only, and there's a $3 to $5.50 service charge. Tickets are available, starting at 10 a.m. Tuesday through Saturday and 11 a.m. Sunday, at a number of center-city locations (including **Tower Records,** 214 S. Wabash Avenue). And **Steppenwolf's box office** (see later in this chapter) usually has a limited number of half-price same-day seats.

The **League of Chicago Theaters** (☎ **900-225-2225;** Internet: www.theaterchicago.org) has a daily listing of discounted shows, as well as information about upcoming shows and a current theater guide. The call costs $1 per minute, with calls lasting an average of three minutes.

Many theaters offer discounts for full-time students and senior citizens on off-peak days during the week. If you're unsure, call the theaters. These specials aren't always well advertised, so many low-cost seats go unclaimed.

Understanding Chicago Theater 101

Want to see an over-the-top musical spectacle? Hate musicals but love drama? Here's what you'll find.

The Loop: An awakening theatrical giant

Chicago's Loop imports the best and biggest of Broadway's musicals and dramas (see the "Loop After Dark" map in Chapter 24). The largest theaters often play host to extended runs of popular shows, filling out their schedules with special events and one-night-only performances by big-name artists. Major Loop theaters include

- **Auditorium Theatre,** 50 E. Congress Parkway at Michigan (☎ 312-902-1500).
- **Chicago Theatre,** 175 N. State Street at Lake (☎ 312-443-1130).
- **Ford Center for the Performing Arts-Oriental Theater,** 24 W. Randolph Street (☎ 312-902-1500).
- **Goodman Theatre,** Randolph and Dearborn Streets (☎ 312-443-3800).
- **Palace Theater,** 151 W. Randolph Street (☎ 312-902-1500).
- **Shubert Theatre,** 22 W. Monroe Street at State (☎ 312-902-1500).

Lincoln Park: The cutting edge

Theaters in Lincoln Park leave the glitzy Broadway shows to larger venues and focus on original, edgy drama (see the "Lincoln Park and Wrigleyville After Dark" map in Chapter 24). Count on cutting-edge, first-run productions from the Lookingglass Company, a local fixture co-founded by "Friends" star David Schwimmer. Steppenwolf Theater on Halsted Street launched the careers of Joan Allen, John Malkovich, and Gary Sinise, who often return to direct and act. In 2001, Victory Gardens Theater became the third Chicago theater (after Steppenwolf and the Goodman) to win a Tony for sustained excellence by a resident theater. Other Lincoln Park theaters offer popular performances by traveling troupes such as Blue Man Group. Catch these acts and others at

- **Briar Street Theatre,** 3133 N. Halsted Street at Briar (☎ **773-348-4000**).

- **Ivanhoe Theater,** 750 Wellington Street at Halsted (☎ **773-975-7171**).

- **Lookingglass Theatre Company,** Ruth Page Theater, 1016 N. Dearborn Street (☎ **312-642-2273**; Internet: www.lookingglass.org).

- **Royal George Theatre Center,** 1641 N. Halsted Street, at North (☎ **312-988-9000**).

- **Steppenwolf Theatre Company,** 1650 N. Halsted Street at North (☎ **312-335-1650**; Internet: www.steppenwolf.org).

- **Victory Gardens Theater,** 2257 N. Lincoln Avenue at Belden (☎ **773-871-3000**).

Other notables

As the demand for theatrical production grows, new venues continue to pop up. Two of the most significant additions are

- **Rosemont Theatre,** 5400 N. River Road, Rosemont (☎ **847-671-5100**).

- **Shakespeare Repertory Theater,** 800 E. Grand Avenue (at Navy Pier) (☎ **312-642-2273**).

Oriental Theater's reversal of fortune

Among the success stories in the Loop theater revival is the Ford Center for the Performing Arts-Oriental Theater. But the road to success was long and winding.

- **1903:** On December 30, fire sweeps through the Iroquois Theater killing 603 people during a Christmas show.

- **1926:** On the site of the Iroquois, the Oriental Theatre opens — one of the first movie palaces to feature Far East-inspired decor, including turbaned ushers. The theater quickly becomes Chicago's top spot to see first-run films and elaborate stage shows. Bob Hope, Judy Garland, the Three Stooges, and Danny Kaye are among those who tread its boards.

- **1970s:** The theater falls into disrepair and is shuttered, the terrain of theatrical ghosts and rodents.

- **1998:** After a makeover, the theater reopens as the Ford Center for the Performing Arts with a lavish production of the smash Broadway hit Ragtime.

> ## Steppenwolf style
>
> What is the Steppenwolf style? It's vital, cutting-edge, creative, experimental — difficult to pin down. Or perhaps not. Say authors Sherry Kent and Mary Szpur in *Sweet Home Chicago:* "Imagine Mick Jagger as Hamlet and you come close to the Steppenwolf style."

Taking Note of Theater Etiquette

So you negotiated the hard stuff — deciding what to see and where to see it, and reserving your seats — now you're wondering about those pesky details like what to wear, whether to tip, and what happens if you're late. Not to mention what to do about the kids. Relax! I've got it covered. Some general tips:

- ✔ Don't use cameras or camcorders in theaters. Not only is it rude, it is prohibited by law. Plus, you could even endanger the actors.

- ✔ Don't talk during a performance. It's rude and distracting. (You're not at home in front of your television.)

- ✔ Do shut off all beepers and cell phones. (When was the last time you were at a performance where one didn't go off?)

Deciding what to wear

Chicago is a relaxed Midwestern city. Patrons of the theater and of theater district restaurants dress relatively informally. In most cases, a sweater and slacks or jeans, perhaps with a light jacket, works for men. For women, similarly low-key attire is appropriate — pants and shirt or skirt and blouse.

For most theatergoers, the bottom line is how comfortable they feel about the appropriateness of what they're wearing. They're likely to dress up for a hot-ticket blockbuster musical and dress down for storefront repertory. Most prefer the safety of the middle ground to feeling self-conscious about being over- or underdressed.

Tipping tips

Happy news: Ushers in Chicago theaters don't expect tips. Acknowledging their help with a thank-you or a pleasant nod or smile is all it takes. However, if you battle your way to the bar during intermission, the beleaguered bartender appreciates your tip.

Arriving late

The show must go on — and on time. Chicago-area theaters tend to be punctual, and tardy patrons usually must wait to be seated until the conclusion of the scene or musical number in progress. Arriving late for the opera can be especially troublesome. With acts lasting for over an hour, you'll be sitting outside watching the performance on a television. Not the experience you hoped for — so get there on time!

Enjoying the theater with kids

Some Chicago theaters have specially designed performances (usually on weekdays, or weekend matinees) that cater to families. These shows often offer discounted children's tickets or special discounts for large groups. You can find out about these performances in the papers (see "Finding Out What's Happening" earlier in this chapter).

The annual "Take Your Child to the Theater" day offers free admission to children accompanied by a parent for one day during the fall. You can get details from the **League of Chicago Theaters** (☎ **900-225-2225;** Internet: www.theaterchicago.org).

Dining: Before or After?

I prefer dining before a show, because sitting in a theater with a growling stomach for two hours is no fun. (I wind up thinking about food more than the entertainment in front of me!) Whether you choose to dine before or after the show, I have recommendations for you.

Eating before the show

A number of quality restaurants lie within walking distance of the large Loop theaters and in the Lincoln Park theater district. For specific suggestions, see Chapter 14. Many establishments cater to the theater crowd and are accustomed to getting diners in and out quickly.

Remember, the opening curtain rises whether your party arrives on time or not. Make dinner reservations early enough so you aren't gulping your drinks and inhaling your dinner, which can lead to indigestion during a long show. Make your reservation for two to two-and-a-half hours before curtain to make sure you arrive on time.

Waiting until after the show

If you're more comfortable eating after the show, Chicago has plenty of restaurants whose kitchens stay open late. If you crave more entertainment, nightclubs (see Chapter 24) usually are just getting up to speed around the time the curtain falls. Some late-night clubs also provide good food late at night. Two notable examples are **Green Dolphin Street,** 2200 N. Ashland Avenue, at Webster (☎ **773-395-0066**), and **56 West,** 56 W. Illinois Street at Dearborn Street (☎ **312-527-5600**).

Get Me to the Theater on Time

Public transportation options for popular entertainment venues

✔ **Chicago Theatre:** Purple, brown, green, or orange line El to State-Lake, or State Street bus (No. 2, 6, 10, 11, 29, 36, 44, 62, or 146) to corner of Lake and State.

✔ **Shubert Theatre:** Red line El to Monroe, or State Street bus (see the preceding list of bus numbers) to corner of Monroe and State.

✔ **Ford Center for the Performing Arts:** Green, purple, orange, or brown line El to Randolph, or State Street bus (see the preceding listing) to corner of Randolph and State.

✔ **Goodman Theatre:** Green, purple, orange, or brown line El to Adams, or Michigan Avenue bus (No. 3, 4, 60, 145, 147, or 151) to corner of Michigan and Monroe.

✔ **Steppenwolf Theatre Company:** Red line El to North-Clybourne, or bus No. 33 or 41 to corner of North and Halsted.

Chapter 23

The Performing Arts

In This Chapter

▶ Scoping out the classical music, opera, and dance scene

▶ Finding out about performances

▶ Getting tickets and getting there

C ulture is alive and accessible in Chicago. The performing arts scene — symphony, opera, and dance — keeps things hopping just about every night, making Chicago a city that certainly doesn't sleep *much*. With such Chicago fixtures as the Lyric Opera, Joffrey Ballet, Hubbard Street Dance Chicago, and Chicago Symphony Orchestra (CSO), the question is not so much, "Should we see a performance?" as, "How many of these fabulous performances can we see?"

Deciding When to See a Show

In addition to the many performances that are scheduled throughout the year, events, too, are part of the performing arts annual cycle. Check out the performing arts calendar in advance for Dance Chicago (the Chicago Dance Coalition's Spring Festival), summer performances by the Grant Park Symphony and Chorus, and the Ravinia Festival, the summer home of the Chicago Symphony Orchestra, plus big-name entertainers.

Finding out what's on

Getting connected to the Chicago fine arts scene requires only a phone call. The **Chicago Dance Coalition** (☎ 312-419-8383) and **Chicago Music Alliance** (☎ 312-987-1123) offer listings of upcoming events. Local newspapers and magazines run listings, especially the Friday editions of the two dailies, *Chicago Tribune* and *Chicago Sun-Times*. *Daily Herald* is the major suburban newspaper and also has a Friday events section. Chicago *Reader* and *New City* are free, alternative papers that run listings. *Chicago Magazine* is a glossy magazine with extensive listings.

Bach in the 'burbs

In summertime, music lovers pack their picnic hampers and spread their blankets on the lawns at the **Ravinia Festival** (☎ **847-266-5100**). Located in suburban Highland Park, the festival runs from mid-June through Labor Day weekend. Ravinia is the unofficial summer home of the Chicago Symphony Orchestra; the symphony plays most weekends beginning at the end of June. The festival has featured performances by both the Joffrey Ballet and Hubbard Street Dance Chicago. You can also catch pop performers such as Tony Bennett, Lyle Lovett, and many more. A program of Saturday afternoon performances is geared toward kids. Tickets for the lawn run $8 to $10; for pavilion seating, $25 to $50. For big names, call well in advance. To get there, take the Metra commuter train from the Loop to Ravinia.

Going with the flow: Cultural seasons

Fine arts in the Windy City pick up when the leaves start to fall. The Chicago Symphony Orchestra and the Lyric Opera begin their seasons in September. The opera concludes its schedule in March; the symphony continues into June. Area dance troupes are active all year. Highlights include performances at the Ravinia Festival and Dance Chicago in late summer and early autumn, Joffrey Ballet's *Nutcracker* over the holidays, and Hubbard Street Dance Chicago's spring engagement.

The arts don't exactly take the summer off, either. One Chicago summer tradition is concerts by the Grant Park Symphony and Chorus in Grant Park (in the Loop between Michigan Avenue and Lake Michigan). Grant Park is also the venue for such major music festivals as the Blues Festival, Gospel Festival, and Jazz Festival (see Chapter 2).

Picking Your Pleasure

Do you love the string section? Is your secret dream to become a professional dancer or to belt out "La Donna e Mobile" with the likes of Luciano Pavarotti? Symphony, dance, and opera lovers will find plenty to love in Chicago.

Striking up the . . . orchestra

Tickets to the world-renowned **Chicago Symphony Orchestra** are always in high demand. (We're talking about the third-best orchestra in the world, so what do you expect?) Still, good seats are often available on the day of the performance. Performances are held at the **Symphony Center,** 220 S. Michigan Avenue, at Jackson (☎ 312-294-3000; Internet: www.cso.org). A $105 million renovation has connected the original Orchestra Hall to the surrounding buildings, expanding the stage and seating area and creating an on-premises restaurant and education center. Music director Daniel Barenboim, who was brought in from the Orchestre de Paris after the death of Sir Georg Solti, Chicago Symphony Orchestra's previous director, in 1997, is introducing more modern works by 20th-century composers. Of course, you find classical music's greatest hits by Beethoven, Brahms, and Mozart in the repertoire too.

Now entering its second century, the symphony reserves most seats for season subscribers — but don't fear. You can call in advance for a limited number of tickets or order tickets over the Web site.

The **Chicago Cultural Center,** 78 E. Washington Street (☎ 312-744-6630) books a number of ensembles throughout the year, including the Chicago Chamber Musicians. Many performances are free. For schedules, call the **Chicago Music Alliance** (☎ 312-987-1123).

Music on the half-shell

Grant Park, a popular spot with picnickers trying to catch a breeze off Lake Michigan, plays host to free outdoor classical music concerts from late June through August. The Grant Park Symphony and Chorus perform Wednesday through Sunday at the Petrillo Music Shell, at the corner of Jackson Boulevard and Columbus Drive (☎ 312-742-4763). Bring a blanket and sit on the lawn, or wait until empty seats in the band shell are released 15 minutes before the performances.

Civic duty

The Civic Opera House has played host to scores of famous operas, and when it comes to staging great plays, the adjoining Civic Theatre is no slouch. Perhaps best known for the 1944 premiere of Tennessee Williams' classic *The Glass Menagerie*, the Civic Theatre continues to put on plays, dance performances, and films. The theater (☎ 312-419-0033) is now part of the Civic Opera House.

Solti's story

If you try to conjure up the names of multiple Grammy winners, what performers spring to mind? Perhaps The Beatles, Whitney Houston, or Tony Bennett? How about the late, great Georg Solti? As the long-time director of the Chicago Symphony Orchestra, Sir Georg Solti won many honors during his illustrious career. His 32 Grammy Awards make Solti the most decorated musician in both classical and popular music.

Taking in the tenors, sopranos, and more

The **Lyric Opera of Chicago** (☎ 312-332-2244; Internet: www. lyricopera.org) is one of the world's premier opera companies and performs at the Civic Opera House, West Madison Street and North Wacker Drive. The Art Deco building is the country's second-largest opera house, with 3,563 seats. After a $100 million renovation completed in 1996, patrons have a setting that's pleasing to the eye *and* the ear. The Lyric offers English supertitles, and you can always count on a spectacular set and outstanding music. The season sells out far in advance, but you can usually get turn-back tickets just before the performance.

Less highbrow than the Lyric Opera, **Chicago Opera Theater** (☎ 773-292-7578; Internet: www.chicagooperatheater.org) appeals to a broader audience that appreciates its emphasis on English-language productions, lower prices, and abundance of available seats. Performances take place at the Merle Reskin Theater, 60 E. Balboa Drive at Wabash.

Being one with the dance

Chicago's hometown dance troupes are highly portable. Without a major dance venue for many years, they perform at the Auditorium, the Schubert, and other Loop venues. But all that will change in 2001 when Lakefront Millenium Park (the cultural and recreational center under construction in Grant Park) opens. A state-of-the-art, 1,500-seat music and dance theater will provide a home for a dozen performing arts groups. Meanwhile, you can find performances of Chicago's leading troupes, Joffrey Ballet of Chicago and Hubbard Street Dance Chicago, by calling or checking their Web sites.

Founded in 1956 in New York and transplanted to Chicago, the **Joffrey Ballet of Chicago** (☎ 312-739-0120; Internet: www.joffrey.com) performs in a variety of venues, including the suburban Rosemont Theatre (☎ 847-671-5100) and several large halls in the Loop. The Joffrey's focus on classic works of the 20th century and experiments with contemporary music by pop stars have made this troupe popular with a wide range of audiences.

Dance lovers have flocked to contemporary dance performances by **Hubbard Street Dance Chicago** (☎ **312-850-9744;** Internet: www. hubbardstreetdance.com) since 1978. The 22-member ensemble blurs the lines separating traditional forms and comes up with a truly American and original style. You see elements of jazz, modern, ballet, and theater dance in their performances. In 2001, Hubbard Street becomes the flagship resident of Millenium Park's new theater.

Tactics for Obtaining Tough Tickets

Getting tickets to symphony, opera, ballet, and theater performances is largely a function of what's hot and what's not. Try TicketMaster — if tickets are readily available, you can get them there. Another tactic is to wait until you get to town and show up at the venue around lunchtime on the day of the performance and ask for turn-back tickets, you may luck out.

If all else fails, try a licensed ticket agency. Brokers include **Gold Coast Tickets** (☎ **800-889-9100** or 773-244-1222) and **Union Tysen Entertainment Ticket Service** (☎ **800-372-7344** or 312-726-3486). Here, too, supply and demand rules. You could end up paying double or triple face value (or even more) for those coveted tickets.

Getting to the Show on Time

Here's a list of transportation directions to major venues:

- ✔ **Lyric Opera:** Metra train to Near Northwestern station, or take the green, purple, brown, or orange line El to Washington. Take the Madison Street bus No. 14, 20, 56, 131, or 157 to the corner of Madison and Wacker.

- ✔ **Symphony Center:** Purple, green, orange, or brown line El to Adams. Michigan Avenue bus No. 3, 4, 60, 145, 147, or 151 to the corner of Michigan and Jackson.

- ✔ **Petrillo Music Shell:** Purple, green, orange, or brown line El to Adams. Michigan Avenue bus No. 3, 4, 60, 145, 147, or 151 to the corner of Michigan and Jackson.

- ✔ **Allstate Arena (formerly Rosemont Horizon):** Bus No. 221 from the Rosemont El station to the parking lot. By car, take I-90 to the Mannheim Road north exit.

Chapter 24

Hitting the Clubs and Bars

. . . .

In This Chapter

▶ Hanging at Chicago's best bars

▶ Scoping out the music and club scene

▶ Yukking it up on the comedy circuit

▶ Checking out gay and lesbian bars and clubs

. . . .

*I*s your perfect night out spent in a seedy but exceedingly hip bar in an up-and-coming part of town, or nestled into a sofa in a wine bar? Do you want to dance the night away, or laugh until you cry at a comedy club? Maybe you'd like to experience the quintessential Chicago hangout — the neighborhood Irish bar, with patrons quaffing pints of stout as folk singers perform soulful ballads. Chicago has whatever gets you going after dark.

 The legal drinking age is 21, and bars and clubs in the Lincoln Park area are especially tough on checking IDs. Some require patrons to be 23 — a policy aimed at circumventing the use of fake IDs. So if you're blessed with a baby face, don't forget your driver's license!

Prime areas for clubs and bars include River North; the Clybourn Corridor (along Clybourn Avenue north of West North Avenue); Lincoln Park, especially along Lincoln Avenue and Halsted Street; Bucktown and Wicker Park; plus the Randolph Street Market District west of the Loop.

Upscale bars and piano bars lie along the Magnificent Mile and adjoining streets (especially in hotels such as The Drake, Raphael, and Hotel Inter-Continental). Then there is the gay and lesbian scene, which plays out in clubs and bars in the Lakeview neighborhood (especially along Belmont Avenue) and along North Halsted Avenue, also known as Boys' Town. In this chapter, I'll help you find just the right spot as you explore Chicago after dark.

Clubs generally open late and close in the early morning, so it's best to travel to and from them by cab. Most bars stay open until 1 a.m. or 2 a.m., while clubs stay open until 4 a.m. Depending upon the area, you could take public transportation to pubs and bars — but consider returning to your hotel by cab. Leave your rental car in the garage unless you have a designated driver.

Hanging Out at Chicago's Best Bars

A huge beer selection and a dance floor in the back for cutting a rug later in the evening brings the crowds into the **Artful Dodger,** 1734 Wabansia Street, Bucktown/Wicker Park (☎ 773-227-6859). The 20- and 30-something crowd makes this a good singles and group scene, and the indie rock music really gets going after midnight.

The popular neighborhood pub **Brehon's,** 731 N. Wells Street, at Superior, River North (☎ 312-642-1071), is a good place to shoot the breeze with the locals. Irish and Chicago memorabilia hangs on the walls. Order a pint, get to talking, and you may find that the fellow on the barstool next to you is a Chicago politician. There's no cover.

Celtic Crossings, 751 N. Clark Street, near Chicago, River North (☎ 312-337-1005), is a warm, dark, friendly pub with two fireplaces and no TV. A diverse crowd of the young and the old, the corporate and the artistically minded gathers for quiet conversation over pints of Guinness and Harp. Go on Sunday evening for the traditional Irish music jam and you're sure to meet some natives of the Emerald Isle.

Baseball fans vent before or after games at **Cubby Bear,** 1059 W. Addison Street, across from Wrigley Field, Wrigleyville (☎ 773-327-1662). Pool tables, darts, and TV screens are the focus. At night, the club is one of Chicago's premier rock venues, generally drawing a youngish crowd by booking popular bands. There's no cover during the day or after games; otherwise, tickets run $10 to $30. Music really begins to rock after 10 p.m. **Gamekeepers,** 345 W. Armitage Avenue at Lincoln, Lincoln Park (☎ 773-549-0400), appeals to a young, sports-minded crowd intent on watching the game on big-screen TVs. There's no cover.

Cullen's Bar and Grill, 3741 N. Southport Avenue, Lakeview (☎ 773-975-0600), is a classic Irish bar with great food, including grilled shrimp appetizers, huge Caesar salads, mashed potatoes, and the requisite Irish dishes such as shepherd's pie. Combined with a movie at the old-time **Music Box Theatre** next door, (☎ 773-871-6604), you have a perfect evening. Sunday nights are among the liveliest here. **Fado,** 100 W. Grand Avenue, at Clark, River North (☎ 312-836-0066), is a reproduction of a Dublin pub. Traditional Irish music plays nonstop and you can order up authentic Irish food and drink, plus standard pub grub, including many sandwiches, burgers, fries, and salads. There's no

Loop After Dark

W. Ontario St.
W. Ohio St.
W. Grand Ave.
W. Illinois St.
W. Hubbard St.
W. Kinzie St.

N. Kingsbury
N. Orleans St.
N. Rush St.
N. Fairbanks Ct.

Chicago River

E. Wacker Dr.

Wacker Dr.

W. Lake St.

N. Clinton St.
N. Canal St.
N. Franklin St.
N. Wells St.
N. LaSalle St.
N. Clark St.
N. Dearborn St.
State St.
N. Wabash Ave.
N. Michigan Ave.
E. Randolph Dr.
Columbus Dr.

W. Washington St.

S. Wacker Dr.

W. Madison St.

W. Monroe St.

GRANT
E. Monroe Dr.

W. Adams St.
E. Adams St.

Art Institute

W. Jackson Blvd.
E. Jackson Dr.

W. Van Buren St.

PARK

Eisenhower Expwy.

S. Franklin St.

South Branch of the Chicago River

E. Congress Pkwy.

W. Harrison St.
E. Harrison St.

S. Wells St.
S. Sherman St.
S. LaSalle St.
S. Clark St.
S. Federal St.
S. Dearborn St.
S. Plymouth Ct.
State St.

E. Balbo Ave.

W. Polk St.

S. Clinton St.
S. Canal St.

E. 8th St.

E. 9th St.

Columbus Dr.

Auditorium Theatre **10**
Buddy Guy's Legends **12**
Chicago Cultural Center **5**
Chicago Theatre **3**
Civic Opera House **6**
Ford Center for the Performing Arts/
  Oriental Theater **2**

Goodman Theatre **1**
Kitty O'Shea's **13**
Merle Reskin Theater **11**
Palace Theater **4**
Petrillo Music Shell **8**
Shubert Theatre **7**
Symphony Center **9**

Go, Cubs, Go

Although Chicago is renowned for blues and jazz, it was also home to talented folk musician Steve Goodman. Goodman wrote "The City of New Orleans" (a hit for Arlo Guthrie); "Go, Cubs, Go," which became the North Siders' unofficial theme song; and the dark, droll "A Dying Cub Fan's Last Request." He died of leukemia in 1984 at 36.

cover except on holidays. At **Kitty O'Shea's,** in the Chicago Hilton and Towers, 720 S. Michigan Avenue, between Balbo and 8th Streets, the Loop (☎ 312-922-4400), the brogues are as authentic as the Guinness and Jameson's beer on tap — most of the wait staff is hired through an Irish government work-permit program. You'll find live Irish entertainment, a jukebox stacked with favorite Gaelic tunes, a collection of shillelaghs, and Irish pub food such as lamb stew. There's no cover. At all these, main courses range from about $8 to $15.

Delilah's, 2771 N. Lincoln Avenue, Lincoln Park (☎ 773-472-2771), is a punk rock bar ironically situated smack dab in the middle of yuppie Lincoln Park. Showcasing the best whiskey selection in town and arguably the most rocking jukebox as well, Delilah's is home to hardcore punk rockers, plus neighborhood regulars.

Located near the heart of Wicker Park, **Holiday Club,** 1471 N. Milwaukee Avenue (☎ 773-486-0686), is home to Chicago's most diverse jukebox, offering Englebert Humperdink, Social Distortion, Naked Raygun, and Ray Charles! Holiday not only shakes out gallons of martinis and manhattans a night, but also has a decent beer selection. Groups of singles and couples in their 20s and 30s hang out here.

Jake's Pub, 2932 N. Clark Street, Lincoln Park (☎ 773-248-3318) is a classic Chicago neighborhood bar nestled on busy Clark Street. More than just a regular haunt for the local bar flies, Jake's hops on Friday and Saturday nights with an eclectic mix of neighborhood regulars, college kids, and people looking for an alternative to the sports-bar scene. Imported beers, a nicely stocked jukebox, and a pool table in the back make Jake's a great hangout. **Lemmings,** 1850 N. Damen Avenue, Bucktown/Wicker Park (☎ 773-862-1688), is the Bucktown version of Jake's Pub. Lemmings exemplifies the laid-back atmosphere of Bucktown. It's the perfect place to escape the craziness of other over-populated Bucktown bars.

Lava Lounge, 859 N. Damen Avenue, Bucktown/Wicker Park (☎ 773-772-3355), doesn't look like much from the entrance, where there's a pretty standard bar, but in the back you'll discover a bunch of rooms offering occupants some privacy. Bring a group and take over a back room. Lava is definitely a late-night place — great as your last stop on a tour of Bucktown and Wicker Park. The crowd is young and hip, but not trendy.

Matilda's, 3101 N. Sheffield, Lincoln Park (☎ 773-883-4400), is a 23-and-older bar. Low-key Matilda's is a hipster (but not hip), meet-market (but not meat-market) bar. Filling two large rooms with ample seating, Matilda's serves food and a wide selection of beers. The jukebox is piled high with "college radio" material. Matilda's attracts a twenty- and thirty-something crowd. The menu boasts the famed one-pound "Heartstopper" burger, plus sandwiches, salads, and appetizers. The bar offers 30 types of martinis, plus 26 beers on tap — with a heavy emphasis on Chicago microbrews.

North Beach, 1551 N. Sheffield Avenue at North Avenue, Lincoln Park (☎ 312-266-7842), is a cavernous bar and entertainment complex that provides outdoor sports indoors. Sand volleyball, basketball, bowling, table tennis, and miniature golf entertain a youngish, corporate crowd. There's a $3 cover on Saturday only.

You'll find a cozy atmosphere of booths and tables, as well as an inviting bar that caters to the hipsters of Chicago at the **Rainbo Club,** 1150 N. Damen Avenue, Bucktown/Wicker Park (☎ 773-489-5999). Packed to the gills with a mix of "scensters" and young professionals on the weekends, you may have a better experience if you go on a weekday night. Be sure to take some photos in the antiquated photo booth!

Tickling the ivories: Piano bars

An evening spent hanging in a piano bar is a relaxing escape from the bustle of the city, whether you choose to sit near the piano and exchange small talk with the piano stylist or decide to crawl into a cozy booth.

Coq d'Or, in The Drake Hotel, 140 E. Walton Street at Michigan, Magnificent Mile (☎ 312-787-2200), showcases gravelly-voiced, pianist-vocalist Buddy Charles, who has a large and loyal following. No cover.

The most striking element of the **Zebra Lounge,** 1220 N. State Parkway, between Division and Goethe, Gold Coast (☎ 312-542-5140), is its decor. The walls are covered with zebra-skin rugs and pictures of tropical wildlife. Go late and be sure to stay for the nightly sing-along led by the piano stylist. No cover.

Rush Street is home to **Jilly's,** 1007 N. Rush Street at Oak Street, Gold Coast (☎ 312-664-1001). The cover charge is $5. Piano stylists play this dark room, named after Frank Sinatra's manager. Photos of the Rat Pack decorate the walls. It's a lively place with a 30s to 50s aged crowd. In the basement, Jilly's Retro, a dance club, spins tunes from the 1970s ($10 cover).

The upscale **Pump Room,** in the Ambassador East Hotel, 1301 N. State Pkwy., at Goethe, Gold Coast (☎ 312-266-0360), attracts an older crowd. Piano stylists and trios play smooth, soft standards. Jackets are required for men. There's no cover, but reservations are strongly recommended. Come right after dinner.

Lincoln Park and Wrigleyville After Dark

Berlin **11**
B.L.U.E.S. **24**
Briar Street Theater **31**
Circus **38**
Closet **10**
Club 950 **21**
Cubby Bear **7**
Cullen's **2**
Delilah's **22**
Duke of Perth **18**
Elbo Room **19**
Gamekeepers **29**
Glow Nightclub **36**
Green Dolphin Street **27**
Green Mill **61**
Improv Olympic **5**
Ivanhoe Theater **17**
Jake's Pub **20**
Kingston Mines **23**
Manhole **9**
Matilda's **14**
Metro/Smart Bar **4**
North Beach **37**
Old Town Ale House **32**
Park West **30**
Pops for Champagne **16**
Royal George Theater **34**
Schuba's Tavern **34**
Second City **31**
Steppenwolf Theater Company **35**
Theatre on the Lake **25**
Uncommon Grounds **3**
Vic Theater **32**
Victory Gardens Theater **28**
Webster's Wine Bar **26**
Wild Hare **6**
Zanie's Comedy Club **33**

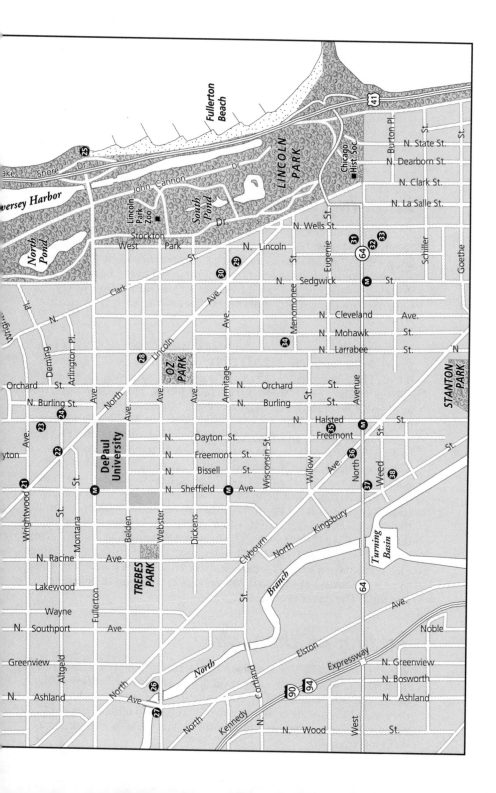

Searching Out Your Kind of Music

Chicago is home to the world's most popular and widely heard style of blues and an important venue for jazz. The city offers just about anything you're looking for, including music for listening, dancing, and damaging your hearing (not recommended!). You can find comfortable piano bars and wild clubs with wilder people. Many music venues don't get hopping until after 11 p.m., but arrive between 9 p.m. and 10 p.m. to allow time to get seats in the club, have a drink, and relax before the show.

Catching the blues

If Chicago is the body and soul of blues music, then **Buddy Guy's Legends,** 754 S. Wabash Avenue, between Balbo and 8th Streets, South Loop (☎ 312-427-0333), is its heart. Everyone from Eric Clapton to Muddy Waters has stopped in to jam and listen to the best in blues at this club owned and operated by blues legend Buddy Guy. Every January, Guy plays a series of shows that sell out early. The cover charge is $6 to $8.

Celebrate the women of blues at **Blue Chicago,** 736 and 536 N. Clark Street, River North (☎ 312-642-6261), which showcases top female talent. The cover charge ($5 to $8) is good for both locations. Keep an eye out for Jake and Elwood at **House of Blues,** 329 N. Dearborn Street at Kinzie, River North (☎ 312-923-2000). The hotel, restaurant, bar, and concert venue (Dan Aykroyd, aka Elwood, is an owner) books a wide variety of acts and stages a popular Sunday gospel brunch ($29 to $32). Cover for shows varies from about $8 to $50 for a big name. **Kingston Mines,** 2548 N. Halsted Street, between Wrightwood and Fullerton, Lincoln Park (☎ 773-477-4646), has two stages' worth of blues greats. It may not be up to par with Buddy Guy's, but it is certain to satisfy your craving for down-home blues. Performances last until the wee hours (4 a.m.) on Saturdays. The cover charge is $8 to $12. **B.L.U.E.S.,** 2519 N. Halsted Street, between Wrightwood and Fullerton, Lincoln Park (☎ 773-528-1012), satisfies the most ardent fans with live music 365 days a year. The dark, narrow club places patrons up close to performers. As at Kingston Mines, expect to spend the evening standing. The cover is $4 to $12.

Jazzing up the night

Velvet Lounge, 2128½ S. Indiana Avenue, South Loop (☎ 312-791-9050), is an ultra-cool jazz club. I warn you, if you are not cool entering this place, you will be by the time you leave! The scene is so underground, they didn't even start charging patrons admission until a couple of years ago. Dark, smoky, and filled with hipsters, this is everything a jazz club should be.

Live jazz is performed virtually around the clock, mostly by nationally known musicians, at **Andy's Jazz Club,** 11 E. Hubbard Street, between State and Wabash, River North (☎ 312-642-6805). This loud, grungy hangout for serious jazz fans offers three-hour sets at lunch on weekdays and music throughout the evening all week. The kitchen stays open late; pizza and burgers are decent. The cover charge before 5 p.m. is $3 on weekdays, $5 Saturday; after 5 p.m., $5 Sunday through Thursday, $7 and up Friday and Saturday. Joe Segal, founder of **Jazz Showcase,** 59 W. Grand Street, at Clark, River North (☎ 312-670-BIRD), has created a family-friendly venue that books some of the hottest names in the business. With two performances each night (open to audiences of all ages) and a 4 p.m. Sunday matinee, this club is ushering in the next generation of fans. The cover charge usually is $15 or more.

If you're in the mood for bubbly, **Pops for Champagne,** 2934 N. Sheffield Avenue, at Oakdale, Lincoln Park (☎ 773-472-1000), offers more than 100 labels, plus live jazz combos. The cover is $9. **Green Dolphin Street,** 2200 N. Ashland Avenue at Webster, Lincoln Park (☎ 773-395-0066), is a retro supper club that's slick — and pricey. Stylish patrons in their 30s to 50s enjoy seafood and contemporary American cuisine from a celebrated kitchen, and then head to an adjacent room that accommodates 200 people for live jazz. The music ranges from headliners, such as Wynton Marsalis, to experimental artists, plus Latin jazz and big band music. The cover is $10. Main courses range from $20 to $30.

Known for great jazz in a historical setting, **Green Mill,** 4802 N. Broadway at Lawrence, near Andersonville (☎ 773-878-5552), was established in 1907 and was frequented by infamous mobster Al Capone. You'll hear Latin jazz, big band jazz, jazz piano, and more. On Tuesday and Thursday nights, jitterbugging hipsters swarm to the club for Prohibition-era swing and big band music. On Sunday, the club hosts Chicago's best-known poetry slam. The cover costs $4 to $7.

Rocking to the latest in live music

A Wicker Park fixture, **Double Door,** 1572 N. Milwaukee Avenue at North Avenue (☎ 773-489-3160), attracts a broad audience by inviting edgy new groups to its stage nightly. The cover is $5 to $12. **Empty Bottle,** 1035 N. Western Avenue, Bucktown/Wicker Park (☎ 773-276-3600), is the place to see local and national indie-rock and jazz acts. Located on the west side of Chicago, the Empty Bottle has been a bastion of ultra-cool for quite some time. The bar also features pool tables and pinball machines, as well as Pabst Blue Ribbon (in a bottle) for $1.50. The annual Polyester Fest (each fall) is the best time to catch the interesting mix of local artists along with some national acts. The cover is $3 to $8. Tiny **Fireside Bowl,** 2646 W. Fullerton Avenue, between California and Western, Bucktown/Wicker Park (☎ 773-486-2700), draws tattooed rockers and their ilk to its out-of-the-way location. The cover charge is $3 to $10.

Chicago's big music venues

The roar of jet engines from nearby O'Hare greets visitors to the **Allstate Arena** (formerly the Rosemont Horizon), 6920 N. Mannheim Road, Rosemont (☎ **847-635-6601**; Internet: www.rosemont.com). The hockey arena doubles as a concert hall where big-name artists, from Fleetwood Mac to the Beastie Boys, take the stage. Two levels of seating in the round arena, and acoustics more appropriate to a monster truck show (an annual event, incidentally), leave many fans with an obstructed view, pained eardrums, or both. Ticket prices vary, but usually start at $25.

The **Riviera Theater**, 4746 N. Racine Avenue at Lawrence (☎ 773-275-6800), is a moderately large theater that usually books new acts of the MTV variety. It's a classy venue that attracts a head-bobbing, standing-room-only crowd.

Just down the street from the Riviera, the **Aragon**, 1106 W. Lawrence Avenue (☎ 773-561-9500), caters to guitar-heavy rockers and rapping MCs. With an open floor and festival seating, this venue is not for the faint of heart.

Elbo Room, 2871 N. Lincoln Avenue at George, Lincoln Park (☎ 773-549-5549), defies classification. The eclectic acts range from hip-hop to Goth to rockabilly, and the crowds are equally diverse. The cover charge is $3 to $12. One of Chicago's most famous concert venues, **Metro,** 3730 Clark Street at Racine, Wrigleyville (☎ 773-549-0203), packs in a capacity crowd of about 1,100 people for local and national acts. (If you're going to see a popular act, be sure to get tickets in advance to avoid getting stuck outside.) The best bet is to hit the late-night, 18-and-over shows, when the crowd is subdued and into the music on stage. Admission varies, but is usually $6 to $16. **Schuba's Tavern,** 3159 N. Southport Avenue at Belmont, Lincoln Park (☎ 773-525-2508), is best known for folk singers and songwriters and attracts rock and country-western acts as well. **Harmony,** the tavern's restaurant, has a capable kitchen that offers inexpensive (some dishes under $10) late-night dining including the usual bar appetizers, hearty sandwiches, thin-crust pizzas, and a small but eclectic selection of entrees, ranging from Southern-style fried chicken to a large Mexican salad called the "Galexico." The cover is $6 to $15.

The **Vic Theater,** 3145 N. Sheffield Avenue at Belmont, Lincoln Park (☎ 773-472-0366), stages a variety of acts as well as the popular **Brew 'n View,** whose patrons enjoy second-run movies and an open bar.

Staying Up Late: The Club Scene

Among the newest of Chicago's superclubs, **Circus,** 901 W. Weed Street, Lincoln Park (☎ 312-266-1200), boasts an enormous dance floor and more than 120 feet of bars. Sword swallowers, fire breathers, and contortionists entertain waiting patrons. The cover charge is usually $10. For a taste of post-apocalyptic decor in an industrial neighborhood, head for **Crobar,** 1543 N. Kingsbury Street, south of North Avenue, Lincoln Park (☎ 312-413-7000). Young, hip patrons wag their tails to trip-hop, techno, and old-school beats in one of Chicago's largest dance halls. You can view the action from the upstairs booths. The cover is $4 to $5 Wednesday and Sunday, $10 to $15 Friday and Saturday. **Glow Nightclub,** 1615 N. Clybourn Avenue, Lincoln Park (☎ 312-587-8469) greets patrons with an all-out assault on their senses — a woman dressed as a mermaid hangs from the ceiling, confetti falls from the heavens, and chest-pounding music throbs from the speakers. If you want to mingle with the club "scenesters" long into the following morning, this is your place. Very fun, if you feel like having a 100-mile-per-hour evening. The music is throbbing music and the dancing is bump-and-grind at the long-established **Club 950,** 950 Wrightwood Avenue, at Lincoln, Lincoln Park (☎ 773-929-8955). It's open Wednesday through Sunday; there's no cover before 10 p.m., but it's $5 after. Merengue, mambo, and cha-cha are among the pulsating dance rhythms at **Club 720,** 720 N. Wells Street, at Superior, River North (☎ 312-397-0600). This multilevel dance hall offers different styles of Latin music on each floor. **Club Inta's,** 157 W. Ontario Street, River North (☎ 312-663-6595), caters to a diverse professional crowd whose musical tastes vary from smooth R&B to steamy Latin rhythms. The crowd is aged 25-plus and knows how to do some serious dirty dancing. On Saturdays at 7 p.m., the club offers free salsa and merengue lessons. No sneakers, hats, or jeans on every night except Sundays and Mondays. The cover is $5 to $10. **Equator Club,** 4715 N. Broadway, between Lawrence and Wilson, North Side (☎ 773-728-2411), is a truly international destination. It offers everything from calypso to soukous to live West African bands. The cover varies, but it's usually $5.

The **Clique,** 2347 S. Michigan Avenue at 23rd Street, South Side (☎ 312-326-0274), attracts a largely African-American crowd to its basement-level comedy club and upstairs discotheque.

Roll out the barrel

Attention, polka fans! Slug down your slivovitz and roll out to polka at the **Baby Doll Polka Club,** 6102 S. Central Avenue (☎ 773-582-9706). The accordion reigns supreme and Frankie Yankovich is a folk hero at this unique club, which offers swirling patrons live bands every weekend. It's at its liveliest on Sundays.

Pulsing house music greets you as you approach **Red Dog,** 1958 W. North Avenue at Milwaukee, Bucktown/Wicker Park (☎ 773-278-1009), an out-of-the-way techno club in Wicker Park. People-watchers find the trek worthwhile for such events as the Boom-Boom Room (Monday), where an outrageous collection of drag queens and cage dancers meets and mingles. It's open Friday, Saturday, and Monday, with a $10 cover on weekends, $5 on Monday.

Smart Bar, 3730 N. Clark Street, Wrigleyville (☎ 773-549-4140), is in the basement of the Metro (see the "Rocking to the latest in live music" section earlier in this chapter) and is one of the coolest clubs in Chicago. Most of the time patrons of late-night shows often head here after the show to gulp a couple of cocktails and listen to a DJ do some serious spinning. Every night features a different style of music, so ask before you enter. Dreadlocks and Red Stripe beer abound at the **Wild Hare and Singing Armadillo Frog Sanctuary,** 3530 N. Clark Street, between Addison and Roscoe, Wrigleyville (☎ 773-327-4273). Chicago's premier reggae bar has been host to such notables as the Wailers and Yellowman. There's no cover until 9:30 p.m. (and none at all on some nights); afterward it's $8 to $12.

Laughing Until Your Stomach Hurts

Dan Ackroyd, Alan Alda, Alan Arkin, Ed Asner, John Belushi, John Candy, Don Castellaneta (also known as "Homer Simpson"), Chris Farley, Shelley Long, Elaine May, Tim Meadows, Bill Murray, Brian Doyle-Murray, Mike Nichols, Gilda Radner, Joan Rivers, Martin Short, George Wendt . . . whew! The list goes on and on, but you get the point: The alumni of Second City — Chicago's comic breeding ground — reads like a laundry list of great American comedic talent. Some of them hail from the Toronto branch, but they are all part of the improv factory, one of the most prolific training grounds in American theater history. The few who make it through are truly gifted in the art of ensemble comedy, and you rarely see a bad show. Tickets are easy to get, and shows change frequently — and no doubt you'll be seeing at least one rising star. **Second City,** 1616 N. Wells Street, at North Avenue (☎ 312-337-3992; Internet: www.secondcity.com), packs a comic punch line. You can choose between two sketch comedy productions on the main stage and ETC (et cetera), a smaller venue. The cover charge runs $6 to $16.

A block away at **Zanies Comedy Club,** 1548 N. Wells Street, between North and Schiller (☎ 312-337-4027), high-caliber comedians treat sold-out houses to the best in stand-up. The cover charge is $14, with a two-drink minimum. **Improv Olympics,** 3541 N. Clark Street at Addison (☎ 773-880-0199), engages the audience as the talented cast solicits suggestions and creates original performances. It's free to get in on Wednesday; otherwise you pay a $3 to $8 cover charge.

Discovering the Gay and Lesbian Scene

At **Berlin,** 954 W. Belmont Avenue at Sheffield (☎ 773-348-4975), the party doesn't start until midnight. The dance club showcases male dancers twice a week and holds bragging rights to the longest-running disco party in Chicago (held the last week of every month). It's open nightly; there's no cover except after 11 p.m. on Friday and Saturday, when it's $5.

A leather-and-whips joint, **Manhole,** 3458 N. Halsted Street at Newport Avenue (☎ 773-975-9244), is decorated á la sewer. Admission to the back bar and dance floor is granted only if you remove your shirt, slip into some leather, or both.

Big Chicks, 5024 N. Sheridan Road, between Argyle and Foster (☎ 773-728-5511), appeals to the culture-hungry. The club generally attracts gay men and a few lesbians interested in checking out the artwork displayed on the bar and bathroom walls. There's no cover.

A bank of television monitors, cycling through music videos and sporting events, greets visitors to the **Closet,** 3325 N. Broadway at Buckingham (☎ 773-477-8533). The bar attracts mostly lesbian regulars. There's no cover. **Roscoe's,** 3356 N. Halsted Street at Roscoe (☎ 773-281-3355), has a dance floor and antique decor. The $3 cover applies only after 9 p.m. on Saturday. Across the street, **Sidetrack,** 3349 N. Halsted Street (☎ 773-477-9189), draws a diverse gay crowd with its snappy video bar. The patio holds outdoor seating in the summer. There's no cover.

Part VII
The Part of Tens

The 5th Wave   By Rich Tennant

I enjoyed yelling out improvisational situations at Second City last night too. But this is the Chicago Ballet...

In this part . . .

In this part, lists of information are provided to make your vacation perfect — from the top ten Chicago experiences to kid-friendly activities and ten creative ideas for days when the weather isn't cooperating. Most importantly, you'll discover indispensable tips for experiencing Chicago as the locals do.

Chapter 25

Top Ten Chicago Experiences

In This Chapter

▶ Experiencing the best Chicago has to offer

▶ Discovering favorite activities of real, live Chicagoans

▶ Going beyond the typical tourist activities

In this living, vibrant, diverse city, you will be faced with a serious dilemma: one human being can't possibly see and do everything. (Particularly on summer weekends, when festivals, the beach, and Lincoln Park all beckon at once, I'd love to be able to clone myself!) So here's a list to get you started on what I consider the quintessential Chicago experiences.

Strolling the Lakefront

Chicagoans use the lakefront in every possible way: walking, rollerblading, biking, running, swimming, picnicking, and playing volleyball. Whatever you do, be sure not to miss Chicago's endless blue inland sea. The lake is a year-round destination. Summers can get a little crowded, but that's part of the fun. Even in winter, you can see hardy souls out for a run while waves crash onto the shoreline. Most activity takes place around Oak Street Beach (just north of the Magnificent Mile) and North Avenue Beach (several blocks north of Oak Street). (See Chapter 1 for more on the lakefront.)

Sightseeing on the Chicago River and Lake Michigan

By far the best way to scope out the city is a boat tour. My favorite is the Chicago Architecture Foundation's "Architecture River Cruise," which travels up and down the north and south branches of the Chicago River. Getting onto the water gives you a fresh perspective on a city that grew up around a lake and a river. Nothing beats being on the water on a warm day with the sun glinting off Chicago's glorious skyscrapers and a cool breeze at your back. Choose from dinner cruises, the "ducks" (amphibian land/water transports), speedboats, and tall ships. To find a boat trip, see Chapter 18 for more information, or head for the Michigan Avenue bridge (Michigan Avenue and the Chicago River), where most tours start.

Shopping on Michigan Avenue

Tourists aren't the only ones crowding Michigan Avenue on the week-ends: Chicagoans love to shop. Whether you're browsing, buying, or people watching, hit Michigan Avenue. And try, just try, to resist its temptations, from Niketown to Nordstrom's, Burberry's to Blooming-dale's. Don't get so caught up in retail frenzy that you miss the charming points of the avenue: Fourth Presbyterian Church, the plaza of the John Hancock Center, Water Tower (the actual tower, not the mall of the same name), and the Terra Museum of American Art. And do not (I repeat, *do not*) miss the best view of the city from the Michigan Avenue Bridge, looking up and down the Chicago River at the architectural gems lining the banks. (See Chapter 19 for more on shopping.) Go at night when the colored lights shine on the river and the Wrigley Building, and I guarantee you will fall in love with Chicago.

Visiting Marshall Field's around the Holidays

Marshall Field's State Street store puts on a real show during the holi-days. The unveiling of the windows is a much-anticipated event, and having breakfast or lunch around the gigantic Christmas tree in the stately Walnut Room is a time-honored tradition for generations of Chicagoans. (See Chapter 19.)

Cheering the Cubbies

Wrigley Field is not to be missed. In fact, Chicagoans regularly play hooky to hang out in the bleachers on a perfect summer's afternoon. Eat a hot dog. Exercise your lungs during the singing of "Take Me Out to the Ballgame." Take a kid with you. I'm sure you'll leave agreeing with me that Wrigley Field is the most charming ballpark in America. (See Chapter 16 for more on Wrigley Field.)

Getting the Blues

This most American of music forms is venerated by Chicagoans, who keep the blues alive nightly in the city's clubs. Chicago-style blues is what most people think of when you mention live blues played in a nightclub setting. You can still find tiny bandstands in a smoky bar where musicians jam away on electric guitars, amplified harp (or harmonica to those of you who are still uninitiated to the blues), piano, bass, and drums. You can find a remarkable range of clubs to choose from, from down-to-earth Buddy Guy's Legends in the south Loop to Kingston Mines in Lincoln Park, where musicians perform continuously on two stages. (See Chapter 24 for more on the blues.)

Hearing Music Under the Stars

Ah, summertime. In Chicago, summer is the season for spreading blankets and picnicking on the lawns at the Ravinia Festival, located in suburban Highland Park. Ravinia is one of the nation's best-known — and just plain best — summer music festivals. It runs throughout the summer. Ravinia is the unofficial summer home of the Chicago Symphony Orchestra and also features pop performers, such as Tony Bennett, Lyle Lovett, and many more. On summer eves, you can see many people running to catch the Metra train, carrying a picnic hamper. Grab your own refreshments and join them. (See Chapter 23 for more on Ravinia Festival.)

Taking in a Show

Chicagoans love their homegrown theater companies, including the Goodman (which has a spectacular new home in the Loop) and the innovative Steppenwolf Theater. You can also choose from shows in the revitalized North Loop Theater District with its Broadway-style theaters. The city's resident Shakespeare troupe is also well loved, and the theatre is located in a new home on Navy Pier. (See Chapter 22 for the Chicago theater scene.)

Riding the El

The El is noisy, dirty, and it blocks sunlight from the streets it runs above, but it is a quintessential part of Chicago. Even if you have nowhere in particular to go, hop on the El (Chicago's elevated train) and ride around the Loop. The brown line heading south takes you on an up-close-and-personal view of Chicago's financial center. (See Chapter 11 for more on the El.)

Discovering Wonders at Chicago's Museums

Generations of Chicagoans recall permanent exhibits at Chicago museums with nostalgia. For me, it was Colleen Moore's Fairy Castle at the Museum of Science and Industry — the most fantastic dollhouse you'll ever see. For my brother, it was more likely the Santa Fe Model Railway at the same museum. Whatever your fancy, you can find it somewhere among Adler Planetarium & Astronomy Museum, Field Museum of Natural History, Art Institute, Museum of Science and Industry, John G. Shedd Aquarium, or Museum of Contemporary Art. (See Chapter 16 for more on Chicago's museums.) Chicago's museum campus is home to a trio of museums — Field Museum, Adler Planetarium & Astronomy Museum, and the John G. Shedd Aquarium — on a landscaped 57-acre area with terraced gardens and broad walkways. In my humble opinion, the museum campus is the most impressive collection of museums in the most beautiful setting anywhere in the country — so don't miss out!

Chapter 26

Top Ten Things to Do in Bad Weather

. . . .

In This Chapter

▶ Making the best of bad weather

▶ Hanging out indoors

▶ Keeping your spirits high when the wind blows

. . . .

*L*et's face it. Chicago's weather can throw you a curveball at just about any moment. From sunny and warm to windy and cold, you can easily find yourself wanting to take shelter from the city's occasionally inclement weather. If the weather gets in the way of enjoying Chicago, try one of these indoor activities.

Taking Tea

For about $20, you can be served in one of Chicago's finest hotels and linger for hours over steaming pots of tea, finger sandwiches, scones, and pastries. Civilized, relaxing, and, best of all, sheltered from the storm, tea is a great way to while away the day. Try the **Drake Hotel, Ritz-Carlton,** or **Four Seasons** (see Chapter 8 for more on hotels).

Hitting a Michigan Avenue Mall

Chicago has a unique innovation: the downtown, high-rise mall. (See Chapter 19 for more on shopping.) The **900 North Michigan** mall, **Water Tower** mall, **Chicago Place,** and **Shops at North Bridge** can keep you warm and dry and entertained for hours.

Immersing Yourself in the Art Institute

Head straight for the **Art Institute of Chicago's** renowned collection of Impressionist art, which includes one of the world's largest collections of Monet. A little Impressionistic romance is just the thing on a rainy or snowy day. (See Chapter 16 for more on museums.)

Luxuriating at a Spa

Indulge yourself in a massage, facial, or manicure at one of Chicago's many spas. Ask your concierge for a spa near you, or check out my favorite, **Mario Tricoci Salon and Day Spa,** 900 N. Michigan Avenue (☎ 312-915-0960).

Reading at a Cafe

Go to **Borders Books & Music** on Michigan Avenue across from Water Tower Place, pick up a book (a *For Dummies* book, of course!), and head for a comfy cafe. A local favorite is **Seattle's Best Coffee** at Chicago and Wabash Avenues, just three blocks from Borders. Grab a steaming latte and settle in on a couch in front of the fireplace.

Working Out in a Health Club

Ask your concierge about your hotel's health club facilities. If your hotel doesn't have its own club, the hotel often has an agreement with a nearby club that you can visit for a minimum fee.

Seeing the Stars at the Planetarium

Even in cloudy weather, you can see the stars at **Adler Planetarium & Astronomy Museum's** (☎ 312-922-STAR; Internet: www. adlerplanetarium.org) sky shows. Choose from a tour of the solar system, or of the Hubble Telescope's view of the visible universe. You can also take a voyage to the edge of a black hole. Shows change frequently, so call ahead for the latest. (See Chapter 16 for more on museums.)

Catching Up on a Movie

Time it right, and you may even get the matinee rate at one of Chicago's many theaters (see Chapter 17 for some listings). To find out what's on, call MovieFone at (☎ 312-444-FILM). One of my personal favorites is the **Music Box Theatre**, 3733 N. Southport Avenue (☎ 773-871-6604; Internet: www.musicboxtheatre.com). The ornate theater opened in 1929 and has an ornate hodge-podge Spanish-Italianate décor built to suggest that you are watching a movie in an outdoor plaza somewhere in Italy. The theater, which shows mostly small, independent movies, still has its own organist who plays before shows. Wherever you go, buy some candy and popcorn, and you won't mind that rain and blowing wind so much after all.

During the holidays, the Music Box Theatre sponsors a holiday movie marathon and sing-a-long. In between showings of movies such as *White Christmas* and *Holiday Inn,* the organist and Santa lead the audience in singing carols. Bring your jingle bells and Santa hat and get into the spirit.

Watching the Weather from the Oceanarium

John G. Shedd Aquarium is home to a three-million-gallon saltwater oceanarium. A wall of windows reveals the lake outside, creating the illusion of miles of sea. You'll find Beluga whales, dolphins, otters, and seals, none of whom could care less that it's raining or snowing outside. (See Chapter 16 for more on the aquarium.)

Going Out for Dinner

When the weather gets bad in wintertime, Chicagoans don't hole up at home. You'll find them overcoming cabin fever by dining at one of many fabulous restaurants. Go out, lounge at the bar, eat a leisurely meal, and dream of the day that you can run off your meal on the lakefront. For Chicagoans, hope springs eternal that it'll be spring soon. (See Chapter 14 for restaurants.)

Chapter 27

Top Ten Things to Do with Kids

In This Chapter

▶ Entertaining kids in the city

▶ Hanging out indoors

▶ Eating ice cream

Chicago is a kid-friendly city. You can find plenty to keep them entertained. In the process, you just may find yourself having a pretty good time, too.

Exploring North Bridge Activities

ESPN Zone, located at 10 W. Ohio Street (☎ **312-475-0263**), is a sports-themed entertainment and dining complex containing the Studio Grill, designed with replicas of studio sets from the network's shows; the Screening Room, a sports pub with a 16-foot screen and TV monitors; radio sets carrying broadcasts of games; and the Sports Arena, a gaming area with interactive and competitive attractions. Nearby, **DisneyQuest,** at 55 E. Ohio Street at Rush Street (☎ **312-222-1300**), is a five-story, indoor interactive theme park using virtual reality technology.

Delighting in Animals

Lincoln Park Pritzker Children's Zoo & Farm-in-the-Zoo is located at 2200 N. Cannon Drive (☎ **312-742-2000**) and allows kids to touch many of the animals, which are handled by zookeepers. A glass-walled zoo nursery is a popular feature for kids, who can watch baby animals tended to by zoo workers.

Nurturing Future Baseball Fans

Peanuts, licorice whips, hot dogs, cotton candy . . . oh, and baseball! Check out **Comiskey Park** or **Wrigley Field** (see Chapter 16 for more on Wrigley; Chapter 17 for information on Comiskey). Certain days feature promotions with giveaways for kids (past giveaways include Sammy the Bear — named after home-run star Sammy Sosa — a perennial Beanie Baby favorite at Wrigley Field).

Getting Interactive at a Museum

One of the city's most popular cultural attractions is designed just for kids. **Chicago Children's Museum,** located on Navy Pier, has areas for preschoolers as well as for older children. A schooner allows kids to climb from the gangplank up to the crow's nest. In the inventing lab, kids can build their own airplane. WaterWays allows kids to construct dams and fountains while finding out about using water resources wisely. (For more on the museum, see Chapter 16.)

Cruising Michigan Avenue

The **Disney Store, American Girl, FAO Schwartz, Sony,** and **Niketown** are a few of the kid-friendly shops on the Magnificent Mile. American Girl also has a theater and a cafe: Book well in advance. (For more information, see Chapter 19.)

Riding the Roller Coaster

If your kids have thrill-seeking personalities, head for **Six Flags Great America,** located on I-94 at Route 132, about 45 minutes' driving time north of Chicago in Gurnee, Illinois (☎ **847-249-4636;** Internet: www.sixflags.com; open daily from April to October, from10 a.m. to 8 or 10 p.m.). Ten roller coasters are guaranteed to shake up even the most daring daredevil. In 2000, the park unveiled the Giant Drop, a 227-foot tower from which riders drop at 60 miles an hour. Admission is $36 for adults and $18 for kids over two and under 48 inches tall.

Getting Your Hands Dirty

The Kraft Education Center at the **Art Institute of Chicago,** 111 South Michigan Avenue (☎ **312-443-3600;** Internet: www.artic.edu), is an excellent hands-on art area for kids. The center is open during regular museum hours and family programs are free with museum admission. Special exhibitions are designed for kids with accompanying hands-on programs. Kids might be taught by a visiting children's book illustrator, for example, and learn how to make their own books. Other classes might include drawing with pastels or making your own weather vane. (See Chapter 16 for more on the museum.)

Oohing and Aahing at the Dinos

With the acquisition of Sue, the T-Rex, the **Field Museum of Natural History** has increased its cache as a beloved destination for kids. (See Chapter 16 for more on the museum.) Dinosaur Hall is a permanent exhibit filled with real and replica dinosaur skeletons.

Watching the Presses Roll

Chicago Sun-Times (401 N. Wabash) allows a peek at printing technology. On a weekday, you can cut through a long hallway running the length of the main floor from the Wabash entrance to the east door and watch the presses through picture windows. Kids can follow the editions racing through the rollers.

Indulging in a Sundae

Worth the trip is **Margie's Candies,** 1960 N. Western Avenue at Armitage Avenue (☎ 773-384-1035), a classic ice cream parlor that makes its own hot fudge, real butterscotch, and caramel. The place is frozen in time (from the looks of it, time froze in the 1940s). Sundaes are served in giant dishes shaped like conch shells.

Appendix

Quick Concierge

AAA

General, ☎ 312-298-9612; emergency road service, ☎ 800-222-4357.

Ambulance

Call ☎ 911.

American Express

Several locations, including across from the Art Institute, at 122 S. Michigan (☎ 312-435-2595); across from Crate & Barrel, at 625 N. Michigan (☎ 312-435-2570); and in Lincoln Park, at 2338 N. Clark (☎ 773-477-4000).

Area Codes

The **312** area code covers the Loop and all neighborhoods south of North Avenue. The rest of the city has a **773** area code. Suburban area codes are **847** (northern), **708** (west and southwest), and **630** (far west).

ATMs

ATMs are widely available. The Cirrus (☎ 800-424-7787; Internet: www.mastercard.com/atm) and Plus (☎ 800-843-7587; Internet: www.visa.com; click on "ATM locator") networks are the most popular. Check the back of your ATM card to see which networks your bank belongs to; then use the 800 number to locate ATMs in Chicago.

Baby-sitters

Check with the concierge at your hotel, who is likely to have worked with sitters in the past. One such service is **American Registry for Nurses & Sitters Inc.** (☎ 800-240-1820 or 773-248-8100), a state-licensed service that can match you with a sitter. It's best to make a reservation 24 hours in advance.

Business Hours

Stores traditionally stay open later on Thursday night, until 8 p.m. or so. Department stores stay open until about 7 p.m. all other nights except Sundays, when they open around 11 a.m. and close around 6 p.m. Smaller stores close by 5 p.m. or 6 p.m. Most businesses operate on a 9 a.m. to 5 p.m. schedule. Banks are open starting at 9 a.m. to about 6 p.m. and Saturday from 9 a.m. to noon.

Cameras and Photo Developing

Wolf Camera has a convenient downtown location at the corner of Chicago and Rush streets (☎ 312-943-5531). You can get instant reprints and enlargements as well as one-hour film processing.

Convention Centers

McCormick Place, located at 23rd Street and Lake Shore Drive (☎ 312-791-7000; Internet: www.mpea.com), is Chicago's major convention hall.

Credit Cards

Toll-free emergency numbers include: American Express ☎ 800-528-4800; VISA ☎ 800-847-2911; and Mastercard ☎ 800-307-7309.

Doctors

Hotel concierge and staff often keep lists of doctors (and dentists). If it's an emergency, call for the hotel physician or go to the nearest hospital emergency room. Downtown, **Northwestern Memorial Hospital** has an excellent emergency room located at 250 E. Erie St. near Fairbanks Court (☎ 312-926-5188).

Emergencies

For police, fire, and ambulance, call (☎ **911**).

Hospitals

Northwestern Memorial Hospital is located right off of North Michigan Avenue at 251 E. Huron St. (☎ 312-908-2000).

Hotlines

Two crisis hotlines are **Ravenswood Hospital** (☎ 773-278-5015) or the **Institute of Psychia-try** at (☎ 312-908-8100). The drug abuse line in Chicago is (☎ 773-278-5015).

Information

See the "Getting More Information" section toward the end of this Appendix.

Internet Access and Cyber Cafes

Open an account at a free e-mail provider, such as Hotmail (Internet: www.hotmail.com) or Yahoo! Mail (Internet: www.mail.yahoo.com), and all you'll need to check your mail is a Web connection. You can easily get on the Web at Net cafes and copy shops. In Chicago, Kinko's has many stores located downtown. For locations, call ☎ 800-2KINKOS, or visit www.kinkos.com. For net cafes, visit the Net Café Guide at www.netcafeguide.com for locations of hundreds of Internet cafes around the globe.

Liquor Laws

The minimum legal age to buy and consume alcoholic beverages in Illinois is 21. Most bars have a 2 a.m. license that also allows them to stay open until 3 a.m. Sunday (Saturday night). Others have a 4 a.m. license but may remain open until 5 a.m. on Sunday.

Mail

Chicago's main post office is at 433 W. Harrison (☎ 312-654-3895) and has free parking. Other convenient branches are located in the Sears Tower, John Hancock Center Observatory, the Federal Center Plaza at 211 S. Clark St., the John R.

Thompson Center at 100 W. Randolph, and at 227 E. Ontario, two blocks east of Michigan Avenue.

Maps

Rand McNally has a retail store at 444 N. Michigan Ave. (☎ 312-321-1751), just north of the Wrigley Building. A Chicago map costs about $4; a smaller, laminated version is about $6.

Newspapers/Magazines

The two major daily newspapers are the Chicago Tribune (☎ 312-222-3232; Internet: www.chicagotribune.com) and Chicago Sun-Times (☎ 312-321-3000; Internet: www.suntimes.com). Chicago Reader (☎ 312-828-0350; Internet: www.chicagoreader.com) is a free weekly that has extensive entertainment listings. Chicago Magazine is the city's glossy monthly (☎ 800-999-0879; Internet: www.chicagomag.com).

Pharmacies

Walgreen's, 757 N. Michigan Ave. (at Chicago Ave.) is open 24 hours.

Police

Dial **911** for emergencies and **311** for non-emergencies.

Radio Stations

WBEZ (91.5 FM) is the local National Public Radio station. WXRT (93.1 FM) is a progressive rock station that deserves a listen. WGN (720 AM) and WLS (890 AM) are long-time talk radio stations with solid sports coverage. WBBM (780 AM) has nonstop news, traffic, and weather.

Religious Services

Out-of-towners seeking to attend Sunday services may contact Chicago's Episcopalian Diocese at 65 E. Huron, Chicago, IL 60611, ☎ 312-751-4200; Internet: www.epischicago.org; Catholics can call ☎ 1-800-masstimes (1-800-627-7846);

Internet: www.masstimes.org. Shabbat services throughout Chicago are listed online at www.jewishchicago.com; click on "Synagogue Guide." Your hotel can also provide you with the location of nearby churches and the times of their services.

Restrooms

Public restrooms do not exist on Chicago's streets. You'll need to visit a large hotel or fast-food restaurant. Department stores, railway stations, and museums are other safe bets.

Safety

At night, stick to well-lit streets along busy areas such as the Magnificent Mile, Gold Coast, River North, and Lincoln Park. Stay out of parks and dark residential streets. It's always smarter to travel in a group. Use caution when walking in the Loop's interior after dark, when the business district is empty, and in outlying neighborhoods. As for transportation, take a taxi late at night, rather than wait for a bus or the El on a deserted platform. If it's after rush hour, I suggest you do the same.

Smoking

Chicago restaurants are more smoker-friendly than those in New York and Los Angeles. Most restaurants still have smoking sections. Most hotels have smoking and nonsmoking rooms.

Taxes

Chicago has an 8.75% sales tax. Restaurants in the central part of the city are taxed an additional 1%, for a whopping total of 9.75%. Hotel room tax is 3%.

Taxis

You can easily catch a taxi in the Loop, Magnificent Mile, Gold Coast, River North, and Lincoln Park. If you are in outlying areas, you may need to call. Cab companies include **Flash Cab** (☎ 773-561-1444), **Yellow Cab** (☎ 312-TAXI-CAB), and **Checker Cab** (☎ 312-CHECKER).

Time Zone

Chicago is on Central Standard Time.

Tipping

Standard tips include 15% for restaurants, 10% for cabs, and $1 per bag for bellhops and airport porters.

Transit Info

The Chicago Transit Authority (CTA) operates the train and bus systems in the city. (☎ 312-836-7000 for information from 5 a.m. to 1 a.m.; Internet: www.transitchicago.com). PACE buses (☎ 312-836-7000) cover the suburbs. The Metra commuter railroad (☎ 312-322-6777, Mon–Fri 8 a.m.–5 p.m.; at other times call the Regional Transit Authority at ☎ 312-836-7000; Internet: www.metrarail.com) has 12 train lines serving the six-county area around Chicago.

Weather Updates

For the National Weather Service's current conditions and forecast, call ☎ 312-976-1212 (for a fee) or check the weather on the Web at www.weather.com. Most television stations (NBC 5, CBS 2, and ABC 7) show the current temperatures in the bottom right corner of the screen during morning news shows.

Toll-Free Numbers and Web Sites

Major North American carriers

Air Canada
☎ 888-247-2262
www.aircanada.ca

America West Airlines
☎ 800-235-9292
www.americawest.com

American Airlines
☎ 800-433-7300
www.aa.com

Canadian Airlines International
☎ 800-426-7000
www.cdnair.ca

Continental Airlines
☎ 800-523-3273
www.continental.com

Delta Air Lines
☎ 800-221-1212
www.delta.com

Frontier Airlines
☎ 800-432-1359
www.frontierairlines.com

Northwest Airlines
☎ 800-225-2525
www.nwa.com

Southwest Airlines
☎ 800-435-9792
www.iflyswa.com

Trans World Airlines (TWA)
☎ 800-221-2000
www.twa.com

United Airlines
☎ 800-241-6522
www.ual.com

USAirways
☎ 800-428-4322
www.usairways.com

Car rental agencies

Alamo
☎ 800-327-9633
www.goalamo.com

Avis
☎ 800-831-2874
☎ 800-TRY-AVIS in Canada
www.avis.com

Budget
☎ 800-527-0700
www.budgetrentacar.com

Dollar
☎ 800-800-4000
www.dollar.com

Enterprise
☎ 800-325-8007
www.enterprise.com

Hertz
☎ 800-654-3131
www.hertz.com

National
☎ 800-CAR-RENT
www.nationalcar.com

Rent-A-Wreck
☎ 800-535-1391
rent-a-wreck.com

Thrifty
☎ 800-847-4389
www.thrifty.com

Major hotel and motel chains

Best Western International
☎ 800-528-1234
www.bestwestern.com

Clarion Hotel
☎ 800-CLARION
www.hotelchoice.com

Comfort Inn
☎ 800-228-5150
www.comfortinn.com

Courtyard by Marriott
☎ 800-321-2211
www.courtyard.com

Crown Plaza Hotel
☎ 800-227-6963
www.CrownePlaza.com

Days Inn
☎ 800-325-2525
www.daysinn.com

Doubletree Hotel
☎ 800-222-TREE
www.doubletreehotels.com

Econo Lodge
☎ 800-55-ECONO
www.hotelchoice.com

Fairfield Inn by Marriott
☎ 800-228-2800
www.fairfieldinn.com

Hampton Inn
☎ 800-HAMPTON
www.hampton-inn.com

Hilton Hotel
☎ 800-HILTONS
www.hilton.com

Holiday Inn
☎ 800-HOLIDAY
www.holiday-inn.com

Howard Johnson
☎ 800-654-2000
www.hojo.com

Hyatt Hotels & Resorts
☎ 800-228-9000
www.hyatt.com

Marriott Hotel
☎ 800-228-9290
www.marriott.com

Quality Inn
☎ 800-228-5151
www.hotelchoice.com

Radisson Hotels International
☎ 800-333-3333
www.radisson.com

Ramada Inn
☎ 800-2-RAMADA
www.ramada.com

Residence Inn by Marriott
☎ 800-331-3131
www.residenceinn.com

Ritz-Carlton
☎ 800-241-3333
www.ritzcarlton.com

Sheraton Hotels & Resorts
☎ 800-325-3535
www.sheraton.com

Super 8 Motel
☎ 800-800-8000
www.super8motels.com

Travelodge
☎ 800-255-3050
www.travelodge.com

Westin Hotels & Resorts
☎ 800-937-8461
Internet: www.westin.com

Wyndham Hotels & Resorts
☎ 800-996-3426
www.wyndham.com

Getting More Information

Everything you need to know, you can find right here in this book. But if you really want to be thorough, before you book your ticket or plan a driving route, you can arm yourself with stacks of free information. You'll be able to assemble a file of maps, brochures, calendars of events, and schedules for sports, theater, concerts, and other happenings in the Windy City. When you visit the Web sites listed in this section, you can take a virtual tour as a dry run for your real-life visit.

Visiting tourist offices

Chicago has two major sources of tourism information. Both can be of service to the individual traveler, but information from the Chicago Convention and Tourism Bureau is more likely to relate to dues paying members.

✔ **Chicago Office of Tourism:** The staff will mail you a free package of information that includes maps and details of upcoming events and attractions. The agency also operates visitor centers at 77 E. Randolph Street (in the north lobby of the Chicago Cultural Center) and at 163 E. Pearson Street (in the pumping station of Chicago's landmark Water Tower). Chicago Cultural Center, 78 E. Washington St., Chicago, IL 60602. ☎ 312-744-2400; Internet: www.ci.chi.il.us/Tourism.

✔ **Chicago Convention and Tourism Bureau:** The bureau distributes lodging, dining, and sightseeing information, and the free "Chicago Official Visitors Guide." 2301 S. Lake Shore Dr., McCormick Place on the Lake, Chicago, IL 60616-1490. ☎ 800-2CONNECT or 312-567-8500; Internet: www.chicago.il.org.

Surfing the Web

Type the keyword "Chicago" into any search engine and you may find yourself buried under an avalanche of information. I've helped you sort it all out by listing a few of the most useful sites. They're packed with information, and some include detailed maps that pinpoint major sites and even provide sound effects.

✔ **www.ci.chi.il.us/Tourism:** Chicago from A to Z — art and architecture to zoo. The Chicago Office of Tourism site offers a calendar and a roundup of festivals, listings of the current month's activities, and schedules for the noontime "Under the Picasso" entertainment at Daley Plaza. An interactive clickable map of downtown features photos, addresses, historical information, and trivia about attractions and landmarks.

✔ **www.chicago.il.org:** Links connect with hotels, restaurants, attractions, and other members of the Chicago Convention and Tourism Bureau.

✔ **www.frommers.com:** Frommer's Web site has a Chicago section.

✔ **www.chicagoreader.com:** *Chicago Reader,* Chicago's leading free newspaper, offers all you need to know about theater and entertainment, with reviews, listings, and lively classified pages.

✔ **www.chicago.digitalcity.com:** This information-packed site includes a sizable section about gay and lesbian living that has a comprehensive list of bars and clubs.

✔ **www.enjoyillinois.com:** Illinois Bureau of Tourism will send you a packet of information about the city, the 'burbs, and beyond.

✔ **www.metromix.com:** Chicago Tribune's entertainment Web site is an excellent source for restaurants, bars, theater, music, and cultural activities.

Hitting the books

Your local bookstores likely have the following titles in stock or they can order them. Or you can buy them online from Amazon.com, borders.com, or barnesandnoble.com.

✔ **Frommer's Chicago:** *Frommer's Chicago* features gorgeous color photos of the sights and experiences that await you. The book covers all the traditional tourist favorites but also lets you in on local finds, neighborhood hangouts, and little-known gems.

✔ **Frommer's Memorable Walks in Chicago:** Walking is the best way to get to know a city intimately, exploring its neighborhoods and taking time to savor its details and hidden treasures — so follow Frommer's for an up-close-and-personal look at Chicago. There are eleven fabulous walking tours, designed to take in the city's most intriguing neighborhoods.

✔ **Frommer's Portable Chicago:** This guide offers all the detailed information and insider advice found in the larger *Frommer's Chicago* — but in a concise, pocket-size format. It's perfect for the short-term traveler who insists on value and doesn't want to wade through or carry a full-size guidebook.

✔ **The Unofficial Guide to Chicago:** You'll get concise introductions to all of Chicago's fascinating neighborhoods, plus advice on how to avoid crowds, lines, traffic, and other hassles. The book features a zone system and maps that make it easy to get around, plus a hotel chart that narrows the choices quickly and easily.

✔ **Frommer's Irreverent Guide to Chicago:** Chi-town has never seemed as vibrantly alive as it does in the pages of *Frommer's Irreverent Guide to Chicago,* a book that tells the story of the real Chicago, from an insider's standpoint.

Making Dollars and Sense of It

Expense	Amount
Airfare	
Car Rental	
Lodging	
Parking	
Breakfast	
Lunch	
Dinner	
Babysitting	
Attractions	
Transportation	
Souvenirs	
Tips	
Grand Total	

Notes

Fare Game: Choosing an Airline

Travel Agency:_____ Phone:_____

Agent's Name:_____ Quoted Fare:_____

Departure Schedule & Flight Information

Airline:_____ Airport:_____

Flight #:_____ Date:_____ Time:_____ a.m./p.m.

Arrives in:_____ Time:_____ a.m./p.m.

Connecting Flight (if any)

Amount of time between flights:_____ hours/mins

Airline:_____ Airport:_____

Flight #:_____ Date:_____ Time:_____ a.m./p.m.

Arrives in:_____ Time:_____ a.m./p.m.

Return Trip Schedule & Flight Information

Airline:_____ Airport:_____

Flight #:_____ Date:_____ Time:_____ a.m./p.m.

Arrives in:_____ Time:_____ a.m./p.m.

Connecting Flight (if any)

Amount of time between flights:_____ hours/mins

Airline:_____ Airport:_____

Flight #:_____ Date:_____ Time:_____ a.m./p.m.

Arrives in:_____ Time:_____ a.m./p.m.

Notes

Sweet Dreams: Choosing Your Hotel

Enter the hotels where you'd prefer to stay based on location and price. Then use the worksheet below to plan your itinerary.

Hotel	Location	Price per night

Menus & Venues

Enter the restaurants where you'd most like to dine. Then use the worksheet below to plan your itinerary.

Name	Address/Phone	Cuisine/Price

Places to Go, People to See, Things to Do

Enter the attractions you would most like to see. Then use the worksheet below to plan your itinerary.

Attractions	Amount of time you expect to spend there	Best day and time to go

Going "My" Way

Itinerary #1

☐ _____
☐ _____
☐ _____
☐ _____

Itinerary #2

☐ _____
☐ _____
☐ _____
☐ _____

Itinerary #3

☐ _____
☐ _____
☐ _____
☐ _____

Itinerary #4

☐ _____
☐ _____
☐ _____
☐ _____

Itinerary #5

☐ _____
☐ _____
☐ _____
☐ _____

Itinerary #6

☐ _____
☐ _____
☐ _____
☐ _____

Itinerary #7

☐ _____
☐ _____
☐ _____
☐ _____

Itinerary #8

☐ _____
☐ _____
☐ _____
☐ _____

Itinerary #9

☐ _____
☐ _____
☐ _____
☐ _____

Itinerary #10

☐ _____
☐ _____
☐ _____
☐ _____

Notes

Index

• A •

AARP (American Association of
    Retired Persons), 40
accessibility of attractions, 41
accommodations. *See also*
    Accommodations Index
  bed and breakfasts, 62–63
  best room, getting, 66
  budgeting for, 33
  categories of, 2
  choosing, 57, 58–59
  cost of, 26
  discounts, 66–67
  Gold Coast, 60
  kid-friendly, 36, 63, 70
  kitchens in, 32
  last-minute reservations, 68
  Loop, the, 60–61
  Magnificent Mile, 59–60
  maps, 72–73, 77
  minibars in, 33
  neighborhoods, 90–91
  prices, 2–3, 58, 69–70, 91–92
  rack rates, 65, 69–70
  Streeterville, 61
  taxes and fees, 67
  travelers with disabilities, 63
  types of, 62
  Web sites, 278–279
Active Endeavors, 202
activities. *See* attractions
Adler Planetarium & Astronomy
    Museum, 13, 163, 164, 168, 268
Agnes B., 202
airfares, 31, 51–52
airlines, 278
airports, 47, 52–53, 105–109
Allstate Arena, 245, 256

Ambassador East Hotel, 251
American Express, 275
American Girl Place, 35, 202, 272
Amtrak, 55, 109
amusement park, 272
Andersonville, 112, 152
Andy's Jazz Club, 255
Ann Taylor, 202
Anthropologie, 202
Antiquarians Building, The, 212
antique row, 212
Aragon, 256
architecture
  Baha'i House of Worship
      (Wilmette), 226
  boat tours, 165, 168
  Fourth Presbyterian Church,
      179–180
  Hotel Inter-Continental, 214
  Marquette Building, 180
  Oak Park, 170, 223
  overview of, 13
  Robie House, 229
  Rockefeller Memorial Chapel, 229
  tours, 81, 179, 196
  Tribune Tower, 214
  Water Tower, 180, 215
  Wicker Park neighborhood, 180–181
area codes, 275
Armitage Antique Gallery, 212
Around the Coyote, 23
arriving in Chicago
  by bus, 109
  Midway Airport, 108–109
  O'Hare International Airport,
      106–107
  overview of, 105
  by train, 109
Art 2001 Chicago, 21

Art Institute of Chicago, 13, 163
  description of, 165, 268
  jazz at, 182
  Kraft Education Center, 272
Artful Dodger, 248
Athletic Club, 190
ATMs, 30–31, 119, 275
attractions. *See also* architecture;
    itineraries
  accessibility of, 41
  best, 11–13, 263–266
  "Big Five," 163
  for book lovers, 187–188
  costs of, 27
  for fishermen, 183
  free, 33, 118, 164, 173
  for kids, 188–189, 271–273
  map, 166–167
  for movie lovers, 181–182
  for museum buffs, 184–187
  by neighborhood, 177
  for romantics, 182
  for sports fans, 183–184
  for teens, 190–191
  by type, 177
Auditorium Theatre, 236
Aveda, 202
Azalea and Camellia Flower Shows, 19

• *B* •

B. Collins Ltd., 210
Baby Doll Polka Club, 257
baby sitting services, 37, 275
Baha'i House of Worship
    (Wilmette), 226
Banana Republic, 202
Bank One, 119
Barenboim, Daniel, 12, 243
Barneys New York, 207
baseball, 11, 20, 183, 184, 271–272
basketball, 183, 184
Baum, L. Frank, 217
beach, 215
Bed & Breakfast/Chicago, Inc., 63

bed and breakfasts, 62–63
Berlin, 259
Big Chicks, 259
Bike Chicago, 190
Bloomingdale's, 200
Blue Chicago, 254
B.L.U.E.S., 254
blues music, 11, 254, 265
boat tours, 165, 168, 194–195,
    263–264
book lovers, attractions for, 187–188,
    229, 268
booking room at last minute, 68
Borders Books & Music, 202, 268
Brehon's, 248
Briar Street Theatre, 237
Brookfield Zoo, 189–190
Brooks, Lonnie, 215
Brooks, Wayne Baker, 215
Brooks Brothers, 202
Buckingham Fountain, 171
Bucktown, 111, 124, 152, 210–211
Buddy Guy's Legends, 11, 215,
    254, 265
budgeting tips, 31–33
building renaissance, 9–10, 69
Burberry's Ltd., 203
burgers, 159
Burnham, Daniel, 13
Burroughs, Edgar Rice, 223
buses, 115–116, 117
business hours, 248, 275
Byrne, Jane, 100

• *C* •

cabs, 108, 109, 118, 277
calendar of events, 19–24
cameras and photo developing, 275
car
  driving, 54–55
  parking, 54, 174
  renting, 32, 42, 95–97, 108, 278
  traveling with children by, 39
Caray, Harry, 142

"Caroling to the Animals," 216
Carson Pirie Scott, 200
Cartier, 203
cash from ATMs, 30–31, 119, 275
Celtic Crossing, 248
Centerstage Chicago, 99
Cermak, Anton, 100
Chalet Wine & Cheese Shop, 203
chartering boat, 183
Chicago Air & Water Show, 22
Chicago Architecture Foundation, 13
  boat tours, 165, 168
  tours, 99, 196
Chicago Auto Show, 20
Chicago Bears, 183
Chicago Blackhawks, 183
Chicago Blues Festival, 21
Chicago Board of Trade, 168–169
Chicago Boat, Sports, and RV
  Show, 19
Chicago Bulls, 99, 183
Chicago Children's Museum, 174,
  214, 220, 272
Chicago Convention & Tourism
  Bureau, 69, 113, 280
Chicago Cubs, 11, 183, 264
Chicago Cubs Convention, 19
Chicago Cultural Center, 28, 169,
  181, 243
Chicago Dance Coalition, 241
Chicago Duck Tours, 189, 194
Chicago Gospel Festival, 21
Chicago Historical Society, 182,
  184–185
Chicago International Film
  Festival, 23
Chicago Jazz Festival, 22
Chicago magazine, 98, 99, 218,
  234, 241
Chicago Marathon, 23
Chicago Music Alliance, 241, 243
Chicago Neighborhood Tours, 196
Chicago Office of Tourism, 112, 280
Chicago Opera Theater, 244
Chicago Place (mall), 206, 267

Chicago Reader, 98–99, 234, 241
Chicago River, 109, 263–264
Chicago Shakespeare Theater, 12,
  233, 237
Chicago Sportfishing
  Association, 183
Chicago Sun-Times, 98, 217, 234,
  241, 273
Chicago Symphony Orchestra, 12,
  241, 242, 243, 244, 265
Chicago Theatre, 236, 240
Chicago Tribune, 98, 197, 234, 241
Chicago Tribune Company, 99
Chicago White Sox, 183
children
  accommodations for, 36, 63, 70
  attractions for, 35–36, 188–189, 203,
    271–273
  baby sitter, hiring for, 37, 275
  flying with, 38–39
  itinerary for, 219–220
  restaurants for, 36–37
  road trips with, 39
  room charges for, 32
  safety of, 37
  teenagers, attractions for, 190–191
  theater and, 239
  trip planning and, 37
Chinatown, 111, 127
Chinese New Year Parade, 20
Christmas Around the World/
  Holidays of Light Festival, 23
Christmas Carol, A, 24
Christmas season, 17, 264
Cinco de Mayo Festival, 20
Circus, 257
City Escapes tour, 49
CityPass, 27, 32
Civic Opera House, 243
climbing wall, 190
Clique, 257
Closet, 259
clothing, 100–101, 128, 238
Club 720, 257
Club 950, 257

Club Inta's, 257
coffee shops, 159–160, 268
Colleen Moore's Fairy Castle, 266
Collision Damage Waiver (CDW)
    insurance, 97
Columbus Day Parade, 23
comedy clubs, 258
Comiskey Park, 20, 184, 271–272
consolidators, 52
convention center, 275
convention dates, 69
Cool Chicago Links, 99
Coq d'Or, 251
cost of trip
    attractions, 27
    entertainment, 28
    estimating, 25, 31–33
    examples of, 28
    gratuities, 29
    incidentals, 29
    lodging, 26
    parking, 54
    restaurants, 27
    shopping, 27
    taxes and fees, 29, 67, 127, 277
    transportation, 26
Coughlin, "Bathhouse" John, 100
Crate & Barrel, 203
credit cards, 31, 119–120, 275
Crobar, 257
Crystal Gardens, 220
CTA (Chicago Transit Authority)
    buses, 115–116
    description of, 277
    El, 107, 116–117
    maps, 32
    from Midway, 108
    from O'Hare, 107
    parking, 54
    senior fares, 40
    visitor passes, 32–33, 116
    Web site, 99
Cubby Bear, 248
Cullen's Bar and Grill, 248

Cultural Center and Mercantile
    Exchange, 27
cultural renaissance, 10
cyber cafes, 276
Cynthia Rowley, 210

• *D* •

Daily Herald, 98, 234, 241
Daley, Richard M., 10
Dance Chicago, 241, 242
dance performances, 244–245
Dawes, Charles Gates, 225–226
Delilah's, 250
department stores, 199–200
Diesel, 203
dietary needs and airlines, 54
dining. *See* Restaurant Index;
    restaurants
disabilities, travelers with, 41–42, 63
discounts
    accommodations, 66–67
    budgeting tips, 31–33
    CityPass, 27, 32
    CTA visitor passes, 32–33, 116
    free admissions, 33, 118, 164, 173
    Hot Tix, 28, 98, 112, 235
    senior travelers, 40–41
    travel agents and, 65
Disney Store, 272
DisneyQuest, 271
Ditka, Mike, 143
Division Street, 110
Do-It-Yourself Messiah, 24
doctors, 275
Double Door, 217, 255
Drake Hotel, 33, 251, 267
dress code, 101, 128, 238
drinking age, legal, 247
driving, 54–55
DuSable Museum of African-
    American History, 185

• E •

Eddie Bauer, 203, 210
El (elevated train), 107, 116–117, 265
Elbo Room, 256
Elderhostel, Inc., 41
Elements, 207
emergencies, medical, 95, 275, 276
Empty Bottle, 217, 255
Endo-Exo Apothecary, 210
entertainment costs, 28
Equator Club, 257
Ernest Hemingway Museum, 223
escorted tours, 49–50
ESPN Zone, 271
Evanston, 225–226, 227
Evanston Historical Society, 225–226
events schedule, 19–24

• F •

Fado, 248, 250
fall, 15, 17
families. *See* children
FAO Schwarz, 35, 203, 272
Farm-in-the-Zoo, 220, 271
Father Time Antiques, 212
Federal Reserve Bank of Chicago, 27
Ferris wheel, 220
festivals. *See* calendar of events
Field Museum of Natural History,
    163, 168
  description of, 169–170
  Dinosaur Hall, 273
  spending night in, 189
  T-Rex fossil, "Sue," 12–13
57th Street Books, 229
Filene's Basement, 203, 209
Findables, 210
Fireside Bowl, 255
fireworks, 22, 24
fishermen, activities for, 183
Flatiron Building, 181
Fleet Feet Sports, 211
flight insurance, 94

flying. *See also* airports
  carry-on luggage, 101–102
  with children, 38–39
  preparing for, 53
  seats, choosing, 53–54
football, 183, 184
Ford Center for the Performing Arts-
    Oriental Theater, 236, 237, 240
Forever Plaid (play), 234
Four Seasons Hotel, 10, 267
Fourth Presbyterian Church,
    179–180, 218–219
Frank Lloyd Wright Home and
    Studio, 170, 223
free admission, 33, 118, 164, 173
Fugitive, The (movie), 71

• G •

Gallery 37 Store, 209–210
Gamekeepers, 248
gangster tours, 197
gardens, 22, 220
Garfield Park Conservatory, 19, 20
Gaslight Club, 107
Gay and Lesbian Pride Parade, 21
gay and lesbian travelers
  nightlife, 259
  tips, 42–43
Georg Jensen, 203
German restaurants, 126
ghost and haunted house tours, 197
Glow Nightclub, 257
Gold Coast
  accommodations, 90
  description of, 60, 111
  restaurants, 152
Gold Coast Tickets, 245
golf, 90, 191
Goodman, Steve, 250
Goodman Theater, 10, 12, 233,
    236, 240
Grant Park, 171, 242, 243
Grant Park Music Festival, 21

Grant Park Symphony and
  Chorus, 243
gratuities, 29, 127, 238
Great Fire of 1871, 13, 180
Great Lakes, 109
Greek restaurants, 126
Greektown, 126
Green Dolphin Street, 240, 255
Green Mill, 255

● *H* ●

Halsted Street, 110, 125
Hammacher Schlemmer, 214
Handle With Care, 211
Harmony, 256
Harold Washington Library
  Center, 187
health clubs, 268
Hello Chicago, 203
Hemingway, Ernest, 221, 223
Hemingway Birthplace, 223
Henry Crown Space Center, 173
Heritage Bed & Breakfast Registry of
  Chicago, 62
Hermes of Paris, 207
Historical Society of Oak Park and
  River Forest, 223
hockey, 183, 184
Holiday Club, 250
holidays. *See* calendar of events
Holy Trinity Russian Orthodox
  Cathedral, 181
hot dogs, 158
Hot Tix, 28, 98, 112, 235
Hotel Burnham, 10
Hotel Inter-Continental, 33, 214
hotels. *See* accommodations;
  Accommodations Index
hotlines, 276
House of Blues, 254
Hubbard Street Dance Chicago,
  242, 245

Hyde Park. *See also* Museum of
  Science and Industry
attractions, 228–229
description of, 112
getting to, 227–228
map, 228
restaurants, 229

● *I* ●

Illinois Center Golf Course and
  Driving Range, 90, 191
Illinois Marketplace at Navy Pier, 112
illness during trip, 94–95
IMAX theater, 174
Improv Olympics, 258
Independence Day Celebration, 22
International Antique Center,
  The, 212
International Cluster of Dog
  Shows, 20
Internet access, 276
Irish bars, 248, 250
Italian ice, 158
Italian restaurants, 125–126
itineraries
  five day, 216–218
  for kids, 219–220
  for shopaholics, 218–219
  three day, 213–215
Ivanhoe Theater, 237

● *J* ●

Jake's Pub, 250
jazz music, 182, 254–255
Jazz Showcase, 255
jewelry shops, 209
Jil Sander, 207
Jilly's, 251
Joffrey Ballet, 12, 242, 244–245
John G. Shedd Aquarium, 13, 163,
  168, 175–176, 269
John Hancock Center Observatory,
  25, 171–172, 215

• K •

Kate Spade, 207
kids. *See* children
Kingston Mines, 254, 265
Kitty O'Shea's, 250
Kohl Children's Museum
  (Wilmette), 226

• L •

Lake Michigan, 109, 263–264
lake perch fishing, 183
lakefront, 172, 213–214, 263
Lakefront Millennium Park, 10, 244
Lakeview neighborhood, 43, 247
L'Appetito, 203
Lava Lounge, 250
League of Chicago Theaters, 235
legal drinking age, 247
Lemmings, 250
Leno, Jay, 124
Leonard, Roy, 81
liability insurance, 97
Lighthouse Park (Evanston), 226
Lincoln Park, 36, 111, 163, 172, 216
Lincoln Park Conservatory, 19,
  20, 216
Lincoln Park neighborhood
  accommodations, 91
  nightlife, 252–253
  restaurants, 124, 152
  shopping, 210
  theater, 236–237
Lincoln Park Zoo, 36, 118, 173, 216,
  220, 271
Linens 'n' Things, 203
liquor laws, 247, 276
Little Italy, 152
Little Saigon, 127
lodging. *See* accommodations;
  Accommodations Index
Long Grove, 224–225
Lookingglass Theatre Company,
  236, 237

Loop, the
  accommodations, 60–61, 90–91
  attractions, 177
  description of, 109, 110
  nightlife, 249
  restaurants, 124, 125–126, 152
  shopping, 208–210
  theater, 236
Lord & Taylor, 200
Lori's Designer Shoes, 210
lost-luggage insurance, 93, 94
Lyric Opera, 12, 242, 244, 245

• M •

Madison Street, 110
Magnificent Mile
  accommodations, 59–60, 91
  description of, 109–110, 111
  holidays, weekends, and, 218
  kid-friendly shopping, 35
  malls, 204–207
  restaurants, 124, 153
  shopping, 201–207
Magnificent Mile Lights Festival,
  23–24
mail, 276
Mallers Building, 209
Manhole, 259
maps, 276
Margie's Candies, 273
Mario Tricoci Salon & Day Spa,
  219, 268
Marquette Building, 180
Marshall Field's, 13, 199, 200, 264
Marshall's, 203
Material Possessions, 204
Matilda's, 251
Mature Outlook, 40
McCormick Place, 275
Medic Alert Identification Tag, 94
medical insurance, 93–95
Merchandise Mart, 217
Metra, 117
Metro, 256

Michigan Avenue. *See also*
Magnificent Mile
accommodations, 10
attractions, 177
description of, 111
shopping, 35, 264, 267
Midway Airport, 47, 52–53, 105,
108–109
Mig & Tig, 211
Millennium Park, 10, 244
money, 30–31, 119–120, 275
Morton Arboretum, 191
MOSAIC (My Own Little Shop on
Armitage), 210
"Mount Chicago," climbing, 190
movie lovers, sights for, 181–182,
248, 269
Museum Campus, 168, 266
Museum of Broadcast
Communications, 33, 169,
185–186
Museum of Contemporary Art, 10,
13, 186, 214
Museum of Science and Industry,
163, 173
attractions, 13, 37, 228, 266
museums
Adler Planetarium & Astronomy
Museum, 13, 163, 164, 168, 268
Chicago Children's Museum, 174,
214, 220, 272
Chicago Historical Society, 182,
184–185
DuSable Museum of African-
American History, 185
Ernest Hemingway Museum, 223
Field Museum of Natural History,
12–13, 163, 168, 169–170,
189, 273
free admission at, 164
Kohl Children's Museum
(Wilmette), 226
Museum Campus, 168, 266

Museum of Broadcast
Communications, 33, 169,
185–186
Museum of Contemporary Art, 10,
13, 186, 214
Museum of Science and Industry,
13, 37, 163, 173, 227, 228, 266
Oriental Institute Museum, 28, 33,
181, 186, 229
overview of, 266
Peggy Notebaert Nature Museum,
13, 188
Polish Museum of America, 181
Terra Museum of American Art,
187, 215
music. *See also* performing arts
blues, 11, 254, 265
Buddy Guy's Legends, 11, 215,
254, 265
carillon concerts, 229
festivals, 19–24
Fourth Presbyterian Church,
218–219
Grant Park, 242, 243
jazz, 182, 254–255
Ravinia Festival, 21, 241, 242, 265
rock, 255–256
"Under the Picasso" concerts,
28, 170
venues, 256
Music Box Theatre, 248, 269

• *N* •

Navy Pier
description of, 36, 174
Ferris wheel, 220
Illinois Marketplace, 112
Shakespeare Repertory, 12, 233, 237
trolley shuttle, 196
view from, 10
Near North neighborhood, 59, 91,
111. *See also* Lincoln Park
neighborhood

Near West neighborhood, 111
neighborhoods. *See also specific*
    neighborhoods, such as Lincoln
    Park neighborhood
  accommodations by, 90–91
  attractions by, 177
  descriptions of, 110–112
  restaurants in, 124, 152–153
  tours of, 196
Neiman Marcus, 200
New City, 98, 99, 234, 241
New Leaf, A, 211
New Year's Eve, 24
Newberry Library, 188
newspapers, 98, 276
nightlife. *See also* music; performing
    arts; theater
  bars, 248–253
  best of, 12
  Buddy Guy's Legends, 11, 215,
    254, 265
  business hours, 248
  club scene, 257–258
  comedy clubs, 258
  Double Door, 217, 255
  Empty Bottle, 217, 255
  56 West, 240
  gay and lesbian scene, 259
  Green Dolphin Street, 240, 255
  Loop, the, 249
  overview of, 247
Niketown, 35, 204, 272
900 North Michigan Avenue (mall),
    205, 267
Nordstrom's, 200
North Beach (bar), 251
North Michigan Avenue. *See*
    Magnificent Mile
North Shore, 226–227
North Shore (magazine), 98, 99, 234
North Side neighborhood, 124, 153
North Wells Street (Old Town), 211
Northwestern Memorial Hospital, 95,
    275, 276
Northwestern University, 225

• *O* •

Oak Park
  attractions, 177
  map, 222
  restaurants, 224
  touring, 223
  traveling to, 221, 223
Oak Street Beach, 215
Oak Street shopping, 207
Oceanarium, 175–176, 269
off-season, 67
O'Hare International Airport
  arriving at, 106–107
  description of, 47, 52–53, 105
  traveling into city from, 107
Old Navy, 209
Old St. Patrick's World's Largest
    Block Party, 22
Old Town
  restaurants, 153
  shopping, 211
Old Town Art Fair, 21
Old Town School of Folk Music, 12
Olde Chicago Ltd. Antiques, 212
Omnimax Theater, 173
opera, 12, 242, 244, 245
Oprah Winfrey Show, 174–175
Oriental Institute Museum, 28, 33,
    181, 186, 229
Oriental Theater, 10, 12, 236, 237, 240
orientation of city, 109–110
orientation tours, 193–194
Original Levi's Store, 204
Oz Park, 217

• *P* •

package tours
  budget and, 31
  escorted, 49–50
  pros and cons of, 50–51
  travelers with disabilities, 42

packing
  for children, 38
  for road trips, 39
  suitcase, choosing, 101–102
  for weather, 100–101
Paderewsky, Ignacy Jan, 181
Pagoda Red, 210
Palace Theater, 10, 12, 233, 236
Paper Source, 211
parades, 20, 21, 22, 23
Park Hyatt, 10
parking
  CTA, 54
  Navy Pier, 174
parks, 177
  Evanston, 226
  Grant Park, 171, 242, 243
  Lakefront Millennium Park, 10, 244
  Lincoln Park, 36, 111, 163, 172, 216
  Oz Park, 217
Peggy Notebaert Nature Museum,
    13, 188
Peninsula Hotel, 10
performing arts. *See also* music;
    theater
  annual cycle, 241
  Chicago Symphony Orchestra, 12,
    241, 242, 243, 244, 265
  Civic Opera House, 243
  cultural seasons, 242
  dance, 244–245
  Grant Park Symphony and
    Chorus, 243
  Joffrey Ballet, 12, 242, 244–245
  listings, 241
  opera, 244
  tickets, obtaining, 98, 245
  transportation to, 245
personal accident insurance, 97
personal effects insurance, 97
Petrillo Music Shell, 245
pharmacies, 276
Phoebe 45, 211
piano bars, 251

Picasso sculpture, 215
Pilsen neighborhood, 20, 196
Pink, 212
pizza, 123
planning trip
  attractions, cost of, 27
  budgeting tips, 31–33
  children and, 37
  entertainment costs, 28
  estimating cost, 25, 28
  hidden expenses, 29
  lodging costs, 26
  restaurant costs, 27
  shopping costs, 27
  transportation costs, 26
  travel agents, 48
Polish Museum of America, 181
politics, 100
Polo Ralph Lauren, 204
Pops for Champagne, 255
P.O.S.H., 212
Pottery Barn, 204
Prada, 207
Primitive Art Works, 211, 217
Printers Row Book Fair, 21
Pump Room, 251
Puppet Parlor's, 36

• *R* •

rack rates, 65, 69–70
radio stations, 276
Rainbo Club, 251
Rand McNally Map and Travel Store,
    209, 276
Randolph Street Market District,
    124, 153
Ravinia Festival, 21, 241, 242, 265
Red Dog, 258
religious services, 276–277
rental car
  additional charges, 96–97
  at airport, 108
  pros and cons of, 32, 95

rates, 96
refueling package, 97
travelers with disabilities, 42
Web sites, 96, 97, 278
renting. *See also* rental car
bike, 190
skates, 191
reservations
restaurants, 97–98, 129
room, last minute, 68
resources, 281. *See also* Web sites
restaurants. *See also* Restaurant
      Index
best, 13
burgers, 159
carnivore favorites, 157–158
Chinese, 127
coffee shops, 159–160, 268
counter, sitting at, 129
cuisine, 153–154
dress code, 128
ethnic, 127–128
favorites, 124–125
German, 126
Greek, 126
hot dogs, 158
Hyde Park, 229
Italian, 125–126
kid-friendly, 36–37
Long Grove, 225
maps, 134–135, 138–139, 145
neighborhoods, 124, 152–153
Oak Park, 224
prices, 2–3, 27, 32, 131–132, 154–155
reservations, 97–98, 129
sandwiches, 158–159
smoking in, 128, 277
tea, taking, 267
theater districts, 239–240
tipping in, 127
Wilmette, 227
restrooms, 277
reverse commuting, 54–55

Richard M. Weisz Antiques, 212
Ritz-Carlton, 10, 267
River East neighborhood, 59, 91
River North neighborhood
accommodations, 91
description of, 59, 111
restaurants, 124, 153
shopping, 211
Riviera Theater, 256
road trips with children, 39
Robie House, 229
rock music, 255–256
Rockefeller Memorial Chapel, 229
Rohe, Mies Van Der, 13, 213–214
romantics, activities for, 182
Roscoe's, 259
Rosemont Theatre, 237
Royal George Theatre Center,
      236, 237
rush hours, 54–55

• S •

safety
at ATMs, 31, 119
children and, 37
overview of, 2, 277
from pickpockets and purse-
      snatchers, 120
transportation, 95, 107
walking, 118
Saks Fifth Avenue, 200, 206
salmon fishing, 183
Salvatore Ferragamo, 204
sandwiches, 158–159
Sawbridge Studios, 211
Sawyer, Eugene, 100
Schuba's Tavern, 256
Schwimmer, David, 236
sculpture, 87, 215
Seadog, 189
Sears Tower, 175

seasons
  fall, 17
  overview, 15–16
  spring, 16
  summer, 16–17
  winter, 17–18
Seattle's Best Coffee, 268
Second City, 12, 258
second-run movie theaters, 182
Seminary Co-Op Bookstore, 229
senior travelers, 40–41
Shabby Chic, 204
Shakespeare Repertory, 12, 233, 237
She One, 212
Shear Madness (play), 234
Sheffield Garden Walk, 22
Sheridan Road (Evanston), 227
shopping
  Bucktown/Wicker Park, 210–211
  cost of, 27
  department stores, 199–200
  itinerary, 218–219
  kid-friendly, 272
  Lincoln Park, 210
  Long Grove, 224–225
  Magnificent Mile, 201–207
  Marshall Field's, 264
  Michigan Avenue, 264, 267
  Oak Street, 207, 209
  Old Town, 211
  River North neighborhood, 211
  Southport Avenue, 212
  State Street/The Loop, 208–210
  store hours, 199
  West Lakeview, 212
Shops at North Bridge, The, 10,
    206–207, 267
Shubert Theatre, 236, 240
Siannis, "Billy Goat," 125
Sidetrack, 259
sightseeing, do-it-yourself, 117. *See
    also* attractions; tours
Signature Room at the 95th, The, 25

Six Flags Great America, 272
Skate on State, 191
Smart Bar, 258
smoking, 128, 277
Soldier Field, 184
Solti, Georg, 243, 244
Sony Gallery of Consumer
    Electronics, 204, 272
Southport Avenue, 212
souvenirs, 33
SportMart store, 219
sports fans, activities for, 183–184
spring, 15, 16
Spring Flower Shows, 20
St. Patrick's Day Parade, 20
State Street
  address numbering and, 110
  description of, 60, 61
  shopping, 10, 208–209
  trolley shuttle to Navy Pier
    from, 196
steakhouses, 123
Steppenwolf Theater, 12, 236, 237,
    238, 240
stolen money, 119–120
Strawberry Festival, 225
Streeterville. *See also* Navy Pier
  accommodations, 91
  description of, 61, 111
  Museum of Contemporary Art, 10,
    13, 186, 214
  restaurants, 153
Su-Hu, 217
Sugar Magnolia, 207
suitcase, choosing, 101–102
Sulka, 207
Sullivan, Louis, 200
summer, 16–17
Sydel & Sydel Ltd., 209
Symphony Center, 243, 245

• T •

Tabula Tua, 210
talk shows, 14, 174–175
Taste of Chicago, 21
taxes, 29, 67, 127, 277
taxis, 108, 109, 118, 277
tea, taking, 267
teenagers, attractions for, 190–191
temperature, average, 18
Terra Museum of American Art,
    187, 215
theater. *See also* performing arts
  arriving late, 239
  children and, 239
  dining and, 239–240
  dress for, 238
  etiquette, 238
  Ford Center for the Performing
    Arts-Oriental Theater, 236,
    237, 240
  Forever Plaid, 234
  Goodman Theater, 10, 12, 233,
    236, 240
  Hot Tix, 28, 98, 112, 235
  Lincoln Park, 236–237
  listings and reviews, 234
  Loop, the, 236
  overview of, 265
  Palace Theater, 10, 12, 233, 236
  Shakespeare Repertory, 12, 233, 237
  Shear Madness, 234
  tickets, obtaining, 234–236
  tipping, 238
  Tony and Tina's Wedding, 234
  transportation to, 240
  Web sites, 234, 235
theft of money, 119–120
Third Coast, 12
Thompson Center, 113
tickets, obtaining
  performing arts, 98, 245
  theater, 234–236

Tiffany & Co., 204
Timberland, 204
time zone, 36, 277
tipping, 29, 127, 238
T.J. Maxx, 209
Tony and Tina's Wedding (play), 234
tourist information, 69, 112–113,
    280–281
tours. *See also* package tours
  architecture, 165, 168, 179, 196
  boat, 165, 168, 194–195, 263–264
  Chicago Duck Tours, 189, 194
  Chicago Tribune, 197
  Evanston Historical Society,
    225–226
  neighborhoods, 196
  Oak Park, 223
  orientation, 193–194
  specialty, 197
  Wicker Park, 181
Toys 'R' Us, 209
traffic, 54–55
train travel, 55, 109
transportation
  accessibility of, 41
  Amtrak, 55, 109
  buses, 115–116, 117
  cabs, 108, 109, 118, 277
  costs of, 26
  CTA (Chicago Transit Authority),
    32–33, 40, 277
  El, 107, 116–117, 265
  Metra, 117
  to Navy Pier, 196
  to performing arts venues, 245
  public, using, vs. renting car, 95
  to theater, 240
travel agents, 48, 65
travel insurance, 93–94
traveler's checks, 30
travelers with disabilities, 41–42, 63
Tribune Tower, 214
trip cancellation insurance, 93

• U •

Ultimo, 207
"Under the Picasso" entertainment, 28, 170
Union Station, 109
Union Tysen Entertainment Ticket Service, 245
United Center, 184
Unity Temple, 223
University of Chicago, 227, 228
Untouchable Tours, 197
Urban Outfitters, 204

• V •

Velvet Lounge, 254
Venetian Night Boat Parade, 22
Vic Theater, 256
Victory Gardens Theater, 236, 237
views, best, 10
visitor information, 69, 112–113, 280–281
Vrodolyak, Edward, 100

• W •

Wacky Pirate Cruise, 36
walking, 118
Water Tower, 180, 215
Water Tower Place (mall), 205–206, 267
Water Tower Pumping Station, 112, 215
WBEZ-FM, 11, 220
weather, 15, 16, 18, 100–101
weather updates, 277
Web sites
  accommodations, 278–279
  airfares, 52
  airlines, 278
  car rental, 96, 97, 278

news and information, 98–99
theater, 234, 235
visitor information, 280–281
weekend packages, 66, 67
West Lakeview neighborhood, 212
WGN radio, 99
WGN-TV, 11
Whimsy, 212
Wicker Park neighborhood, 111, 124, 152, 180–181, 210–211
Wild Hare and Singing Armadillo Frog Sanctuary, 258
Wilmette, 226–227
winter, 15–16, 17–18
WinterBreak Chicago, 18
Wolford, 207
World Music Festival Chicago, 23
Wright, Frank Lloyd, 13, 170, 200, 221, 229
Wrigley Field, 11, 20, 176, 264, 271–272
Wrigleyville, 112, 252–253
Wrigleyville Antique Mall, 212

• Z •

Zanies Comedy Club, 258
Zebra Lounge, 251
Zoo Lights Festival, 24
zoos
  Brookfield Zoo, 189–190
  Farm-in-the-Zoo, 220, 271
  Lincoln Park Zoo, 36, 118, 173, 216, 271

• *Accommodations Index* •

Belden Stratford Hotel, 70
Best Western River North Hotel, 88
Chicago Hilton and Towers, 71
Chicago Marriott Downtown, 71
City Suites Hotel, 62, 67, 89
Claridge, 74–75
Courtyard by Marriott, 63
Courtyard by Marriott Chicago
    Downtown, 75
Crowne Plaza Chicago, The/The
    Silversmith, 75
DoubleTree Guest Suites, 74, 76
Drake, The, 33, 62, 74, 76, 251, 267
Embassy Suites, 67, 74, 76, 78
Fairfield Inn, 74
Fairmont Hotel, 62, 74, 78
Four Seasons Hotel, 10, 62, 78–79,
    205, 267
Hampton Inn & Suites Hotel, 79
Hilton Garden Inn, 89
Homewood Suites, 89
Hotel Allegro, 62, 67, 80
Hotel Burnham, 10, 62, 80
Hotel Inter-Continental Chicago, 33,
    62, 63, 74, 80–81, 214
Hotel Monaco, 67, 81–82
House of Blues Hotel, a Lowes
    Hotel, 82
Hyatt on Printers Row, 82
Hyatt Regency Chicago, 83
Le Meridien Hotel, 74
Lenox Suites Hotel, 89
Motel 6, 62, 83
O'Hare Hilton Hotel, 107
Omni Ambassador East Hotel, 83–84
Park Brompton Hotel, 67, 89
Park Hyatt, 10, 84
Peninsula Hotel, 10, 74
Quality Inn Chicago Downtown, 74
Radisson Hotel & Suites, 89
Raphael, 62, 84–85

Regal Knickerbocker Hotel, 90
Renaissance Chicago Hotel, 85
Ritz-Carlton Chicago, 10, 85–86, 267
Sheraton Chicago Hotel & Suites, 86
Surf Hotel, 67, 90
Sutton Place Hotel, 86
Swissotel, 90
Talbott Hotel, 87
Tremont, 62, 87
Westin Hotel, 87–88
Whitehall Hotel, 62, 74, 88

• *Restaurant Index* •

Al's Italian Beef, 158
Ambria, 70, 132
Andiamo, 107
Ann Sather, 127, 132
Arun's, 124, 133
Atwood Café, 123, 133, 218
Avenue Ale House (Oak Park), 224
Ben Pao, 127
Berghoff, The, 126
Beyond Words Café, 187
Bice Ristorante, 126, 133
Big Shoulder Café, 182
Billy Goat Tavern, 37, 124, 125, 159
Bistro 110, 136
Bistro Zinc, 136
Blackhawk Lodge, 136
Blind Faith Café (Evanston), 226
Blue Point Oyster Bar, 124
Bockwinkel's, 206
Bubba Gump Shrimp Co., 174
Byron's, 158
Café Absinthe, 137
Café Brauer, 216–217
Café Iberico, 137
Cape Cod Room, 76, 79
Centro, 126, 137
Charlie Trotter's, 137, 140
Chez Joel, 140
Chicago Brauhaus, 126
Coco Pazzo, 126
Corner Bakery, 159, 171, 205, 218

Cru, 13, 219
Cyrano's Bistro & Wine Bar, 140
Ed Debevic's, 36–37
Eli's The Place for Steak, 123
Emilio's Tapas Bar & Restaurant, 150
Emperor's Choice, 127
Everest, 124
56 West, 240
Flat Top Grill, 140–141
Foodlife, 159, 205, 220
Frontera Grill, 13, 124, 141
Galileo's, 164
Gene & Georgetti, 123
Gibson's Steakhouse, 13, 123, 141
Gino's East, 13, 123, 141–142
Gold Coast Dogs, 125, 158
Green Dolphin Street, 240, 255
Hard Rock Café, 36, 220
Harry Caray's, 37, 142, 219
Harvest on Huron, 142
Heaven on Seven, 37, 143
Hecky's Barbecue, 125, 150
Home Bakery, 128
Hubbard Street Grill, 143
Iron Mike's Grille, 13, 123, 143, 219
Italian Village, 126
Jane's, 144
Joe's Seafood, Prime Steak and Stone Crab, 144
Kamehachi, 13, 144, 146
La Perla, 150
L'Appetito, 218
Le Bouchon, 146
Lou Mitchell's, 27, 129, 146
Mallers Building Coffee Shop & Deli, 209
Marché, 124
Margie's Candies, 273
Mario's Italian Lemonade, 125, 158
Mashed Potato Club, 126
Mellow Yellow (Hyde Park), 229
Meritage Wine Bar & Cafe, 146, 217
Meyer's Delicatessen, 126
Mia Francesca, 147
Mity Nice Grill, 205
Mossant, 123, 147

Mr. Beef on Orleans, 124, 157–158
Mrs. Levy's Delicatessen, 158–159
Nine, 147–148
Pane Calde, 126
Pegasus, 126
Phil Smidt's, 150
Potbelly Sandwich Works, 158
Pump Room, 128, 148
Rainforest Café, 36
Red Light, 124
RIVA, 174
R.J. Grunt's, 217
Robinson's No. 1 Ribs, 125, 150
Rock-N-Roll McDonald's, 159, 219
Rosebud Café, 125
Ruth's Chris Steak House, 123
Saloon, The, 148, 214
Salpicon, 13
Santorini, 126
Scafuri Bakery, 125
Shaw's Crab House and Blue Crab Lounge, 149
Smith & Wollensky, 123
Starbuck's, 159
Sushi Wabi, 149
Svea Restaurant, 127
Swedish Bakery, 128
Tango Sur, 149
Three Happiness, 111, 127
Tom and Wendee's Homemade Italian Ice, 158
Topolobampo, 141
Trattoria No. 10, 150
Tucci Bennuch, 205
Tuscany on Taylor, 13, 150–151
Twin Anchors, 13, 125, 151
Typhoon, 205
Uncommon Grounds, 160
Village Tavern (Long Grove), 225
Vivo, 124, 151
Walker Bros. Original Pancake House, 227
White Fence Farm, 150
Wishbone, 151–152, 175
Zinfandel, 152

Notes

Notes

Notes

Notes

Notes

Notes

FOR DUMMIES
BOOK REGISTRATION

Register This Book and Win!

We want to hear from you!

Visit **dummies.com** to register this book and tell us how you liked it!

- Get entered in our monthly prize giveaway.

- Give us feedback about this book — tell us what you like best, what you like least, or maybe what you'd like to ask the author and us to change!

- Let us know any other *For Dummies* topics that interest you.

Your feedback helps us determine what books to publish, tells us what coverage to add as we revise our books, and lets us know whether we're meeting your needs as a *For Dummies* reader. You're our most valuable resource, and what you have to say is important to us!

Not on the Web yet? It's easy to get started with *Dummies 101: The Internet For Windows 98* or *The Internet For Dummies* at local retailers everywhere.

Or let us know what you think by sending us a letter at the following address:

For Dummies Book Registration
Dummies Press
10475 Crosspoint Blvd.
Indianapolis, IN 46256

BESTSELLING BOOK SERIES